THE LAST
OUTLAWS

THE LAST OUTLAWS

THE LIVES AND LEGENDS OF

BUTCH CASSIDY *and* THE SUNDANCE KID

THOM HATCH

New American Library

New American Library
Published by New American Library, a division of
Penguin Group (USA) Inc., 375 Hudson Street,
New York, New York 10014, USA
Penguin Group (Canada), 90 Eglinton Avenue East, Suite 700, Toronto,
Ontario M4P 2Y3, Canada (a division of Pearson Penguin Canada Inc.)
Penguin Books Ltd., 80 Strand, London WC2R 0RL, England
Penguin Ireland, 25 St. Stephen's Green, Dublin 2,
Ireland (a division of Penguin Books Ltd.)
Penguin Group (Australia), 250 Camberwell Road, Camberwell, Victoria 3124,
Australia (a division of Pearson Australia Group Pty. Ltd.)
Penguin Books India Pvt. Ltd., 11 Community Centre, Panchsheel Park,
New Delhi - 110 017, India
Penguin Group (NZ), 67 Apollo Drive, Rosedale, Auckland 0632,
New Zealand (a division of Pearson New Zealand Ltd.)
Penguin Books (South Africa) (Pty.) Ltd., 24 Sturdee Avenue,
Rosebank, Johannesburg 2196, South Africa

Penguin Books Ltd., Registered Offices:
80 Strand, London WC2R 0RL, England

First published by New American Library,
a division of Penguin Group (USA) Inc.

Copyright © Thom Hatch, 2013
Maps by Chris Erichsen

REGISTERED TRADEMARK—MARCA REGISTRADA

ISBN 978-1-62490-678-7

Set in Bell MT
Designed by Spring Hoteling

Printed in the United States of America

PUBLISHER'S NOTE
While the author has made every effort to provide accurate telephone numbers, Internet
addresses, and other contact information at the time of publication, neither the publisher nor
the author assumes any responsibility for errors, or for changes that occur after publication.
Further, publisher does not have any control over and does not assume any responsibility for
author or third-party Web sites or their content.

To my lovely and talented wife, Lynn,
and brilliant and beautiful daughter, Cimarron

CONTENTS

ACKNOWLEDGMENTS

Countless influences affect a writer while working on a book, but one stands out for me. While researching and writing about these outlaw cowboys, I could not help but think about living here in Colorado cattle country, and how ranchers are still running cow-calf operations without much change since the days of Butch and Sundance. And when thinking about cattle being raised around here, I thought often about one man—rancher John A. "Jay" Yoder.

When Jay was growing up in Kansas, he loved to read Zane Grey novels and dreamed of someday becoming a cattle rancher. In 1955, his dreams came true when he and his wife, Betty, a schoolteacher, settled on their spread in Colorado and began turning grass into beef for a living while rearing two boys.

In past years, every once in a while Jay would invite me to escape my office and spend the day "cowboying" with him on his ranch. We would put in a full day branding or doctoring cows with the crew, or mending fence, or breaking ice from water tanks, or going to auction, or hauling hay or cake out to pastures full of gazing cattle.

What made each of those days memorable, however, was not necessarily the cowboy work learning experience I would receive but the companionship of Jay Yoder, who would freely share with me his sage insight about life's principles, values, and morals. His compassion, generosity, and love of family, God, and the lifestyle of the Western range became a great inspiration to me. If there ever was a man suited to proudly bear the title of "American rancher" and be a steward of the land, it was Jay Yoder.

To my enduring sadness, Jay passed away on August 1, 2011, at the age of eighty-six.

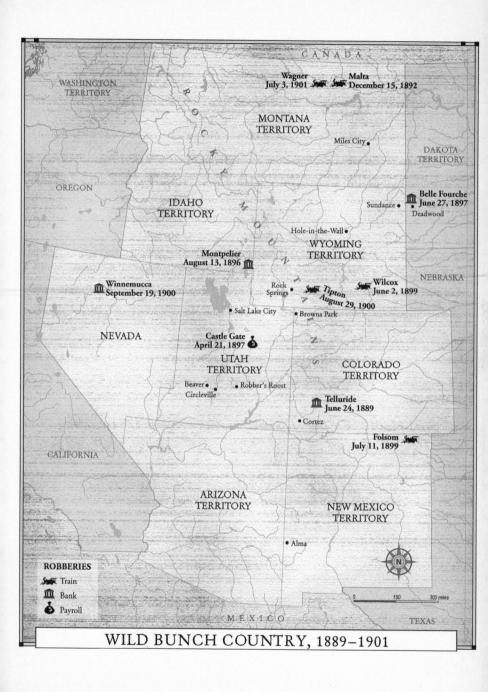

CANADA

WASHINGTON
TERRITORY

OREGON

Wagner
July 3, 1901   **Malta**
December 15, 1892

MONTANA
TERRITORY

Miles City •

DAKOTA
TERRITORY

IDAHO
TERRITORY

Sundance •   **Belle Fourche**
June 27, 1897
Deadwood

Hole-in-the-Wall •

WYOMING
TERRITORY

Montpelier
August 13, 1896

NEBRASKA

Winnemucca
September 19, 1900

Rock
Springs   **Tipton**
August 29, 1900

Wilcox
June 2, 1899

• Salt Lake City   • Browns Park

NEVADA

Castle Gate
April 21, 1897

UTAH
TERRITORY

COLORADO
TERRITORY

Beaver •   • Robber's Roost
Circleville

Telluride
June 24, 1889
• Cortez

Folsom
July 11, 1899

CALIFORNIA

ARIZONA
TERRITORY

NEW MEXICO
TERRITORY

• Alma

ROBBERIES

Train
Bank
Payroll

0   150   300 miles

N

MEXICO

TEXAS

WILD BUNCH COUNTRY, 1889–1901

BUTCH AND SUNDANCE IN SOUTH AMERICA, 1901–1908

THE LAST OUTLAWS

PROLOGUE

November 4, 1908, promised to be a clear, sunny day high up on a barren pass where a creek-bed trail had been carved around the base of Huaca Huanusca (Dead Cow Hill), fifty miles north of the frontier mining town of Tupiza, Bolivia. This was a desolate place where weather-shaped cliffs soared above, a dozen shades of brown mixed with fields of brilliant green cactus among spindly, scraggly brush, and dusty winds whipped tumbleweed into motion. In this remote stretch of primitive trail, two men with their faces covered by bandannas and their rifles tightly clutched in their hands waited anxiously behind a large rock.

On the trail behind this pair of gunmen came plodding along three men leading two pack mules that were heavily laden with saddlebags. To the uninitiated eye, the presence of this small caravan would not attract any attention. But the two men knew better.

Days earlier, they had checked into a hotel in Tupiza and maintained a twenty-four-hour vigil on the office of the Aramayo, Francke, & Cia Silver Mine. Eventually, they learned that an 80,000-*bolivianos* payroll—about half a million American dollars—was about to be shipped from Tupiza to the tin mine operation located at Quechisla.

On November 3, Carlos Pero, his son Mariano, and another man departed the Aramayo office leading two pack mules, and headed out of town in the direction of the mine. The two outlaws followed at a safe distance, aware that it would take three days of travel to the mine, crossing over oftentimes treacherous terrain with excellent sites where they could set up an ambush. There was no need to hurry.

Their patience had paid off. The outlaws had chosen an ideal holdup site in this hauntingly beautiful Andean landscape where the trail wound treacherously along the edge of a rust-colored canyon. Every sound on that high mountain pass was magnified, and the two men could distinctly hear the dull clomp of hooves striking dirt approaching from the distance. They exchanged a meaningful glance. It was time to spring the trap.

When the pack train came into sight around a bend on the cactus-studded hill, the two robbers, who wore dark red, thin-wale corduroy suits with narrow, soft-brimmed hats pulled low so that only their eyes were visible, stepped out from behind the rock to reveal themselves and brandish their weapons.

The pack train was taken by surprise, and the three men froze.

The heavyset man did the talking while the thin one covered Señor Pero and his companions from a distance. His voice was soft and polite, with one distinct trait—he spoke with a North American accent.

"I'd appreciate it if you would get down off those mules," he directed in a calm voice, "and back away, please."

The other man then came forward, reached into a saddlebag, and pulled out a package wrapped in homespun cloth. He carefully peeked inside. "It's here," he said, a slight grin lifting one corner of his mouth.

The big gunman nodded and spoke softly. "Now, you gentlemen should head on down that trail and not look back. I would hate to have to clean my gun today."

Carlos Pero and his companions could not believe their ears. It would have been quite simple for these robbers to eliminate any chance of capture by killing them out there on that lonesome stretch of trail. Instead, they were free to go, without even handing over their personal possessions.

The three mining employees did not hesitate. Pero grabbed the rope attached to the mule, and the men scampered away down the trail.

In time, they arrived at the village of Guadalupe. Almost immediately, military patrols and bands of angry armed miners were combing every road, ravine, train station, mine, ranch, or settlement in southern Bolivia.

These two foreigners could run, but it was doubtful that they could hide for long, especially in a place where they could not blend in with the populace. And the identities of the two outlaws soon became more than just a matter of speculation.

There were only two *Americanos* in that part of the country who would commit a robbery in that polite and gentlemanly way and avoid bloodshed—Butch Cassidy and the Sundance Kid.

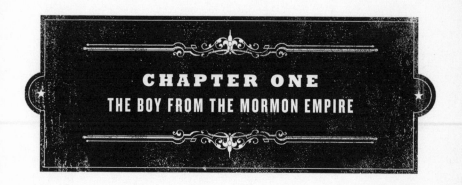

CHAPTER ONE
THE BOY FROM THE MORMON EMPIRE

Ye Saints who dwell on Europe's shore,
Prepare yourselves for many more
To leave behind your native land
For sure God's judgments are at hand. . . .

For some must push and some must pull,
As we go marching up the hill.
So merrily on our way we go,
Until we reach the valley-o.

—"The Handcart Song"

The year 1866 found the people and government of the United States wrestling with myriad vexing legacies of the Civil War. This bitter clash had disfigured and scarred the face of American society. Reconstruction had begun in the South, accompanied by racial conflicts when Congress passed the Civil Rights Act of 1866 over President Andrew Johnson's veto, to secure all the rights of citizenship intended by the Thirteenth Amendment for former slaves. As a gesture of healing, the bodies of 2,011 unidentified Civil War soldiers from both sides of the conflict were buried in a mass grave at Arlington National Cemetery, across the Potomac from Washington, D.C., under a granite sarcophagus that called the entombed a "noble army of martyrs." Tennessee became the first Southern state to be readmitted to the Union following the war—and before long the Ku Klux Klan was established there in the town of Pulaski.

Cholera killed more than fifty thousand Americans during 1866. New York City was hit hard by the epidemic, which encouraged the creation of the Municipal Board of Health, the first of its kind in this country. Construction of the Central Pacific and Union Pacific railroads, slowed due to wartime, began to pick up speed. Neither road had laid more than forty miles of track by the start of the year, but the pace increased to one mile per day due to improved building methods. Alfred Nobel invented dynamite, which was originally sold as "Nobel's Blasting Powder," a safe alternative to gunpowder or nitroglycerin. The Cincinnati Base Ball Club, that sport's first professional team, was established. The world's first roller-skating rink opened in Newport, Rhode Island.

Texas ranchers could now drive cattle north for the first time on the Chisholm Trail, named after the half-Cherokee scout Jesse Chisholm. The trail connected Texas herds with markets along the railroad in Kansas for shipment to the East. Sioux warriors massacred Captain William Fetterman and eighty U.S. Army soldiers on the Bozeman Trail in Montana during what became known as "Red Cloud's War," the only time in history when Native Americans forced the government to accept treaty demands. The Winchester Repeating Arms Company of New Haven, Connecticut, introduced the .44-caliber Model 1866 rifle, the first weapon manufactured by that firm. The American Society for the Prevention of Cruelty to Animals (ASPCA) was founded in New York City with intentions of stopping the abuse of horses, the animal that provided virtually all the power for urban transit and agricultural production in most of the world. Congress approved the minting of a nickel five-cent coin, made of copper and nickel with no more than 25 percent nickel, eliminating its predecessor, the half dime.[1]

Out west, the rush of pioneers, which had continued even during the Civil War, was given a powerful new impetus. The vast region was still sparsely settled under territorial governments when the Army of Virginia laid down its arms. Former soldiers and common citizens, now released from the strain of war, crowded to the frontier by the thousands. These homesteaders were joined by hordes of immigrants from Europe, adding to the rapid growth of agricultural, industrial, mining, lumber, and other enterprises west of the Mississippi River.

Utah and the Mormon Empire, located far away from the main theaters of the Civil War, had not suffered the same hardship, loss, or divisiveness as had those people back east. There had been several isolated encounters with Native American warriors when regular troops went back east to fight in the war—and a massacre of Shoshones in their camp at Bear River by the U.S. Army—but otherwise the territory had escaped the war unscathed.[2]

One significant event in 1866, however, stood out in the pages of Utah history. It was only fitting that in the same year that the James gang held up their first bank and the Reno gang committed the country's first robbery of a moving train that Robert Leroy Parker—who as Butch Cassidy would become one of the most celebrated outlaws in the Old West—was born in Beaver, Utah.[3]

Bob, as he would be called as a youngster, was the first member of the Parker family to be born in America. His people had their roots a long distance away from Utah's purple sage, craggy-mouthed canyons and murmuring melodies of wind and water. The story of the Parkers stands as a testament to the pioneer spirit that typified the westward expansion.

The Parker clan who established the family in Utah Territory had their origins in Lancashire, England, where in 1836, Robert Leroy Parker, Butch Cassidy's grandfather and namesake, was visited by American missionaries from the Church of Latter-day Saints—the Mormons—as they evangelized throughout Europe. Robert, an expert weaver in a textile mill, became a fervent convert and dedicated his life to his newfound faith.

His bride-to-be, Ann Hartley, who worked in the same mill, was less than enthusiastic about the Mormons. Her hesitancy to embrace Mormonism was due to disapproval from her parents of this new and controversial sect. But Ann was eventually convinced—or avowed publicly anyway—that Mormonism represented the true church, and she was duly baptized. The act cleared the way for the two twenty-three-year-olds to be married on May 25, 1843.[4]

The Church of Jesus Christ of Latter-day Saints had its beginnings in western New York State in the 1820s. Joseph Smith Jr., a resident of Fayette, was dictating the Book of Mormon, which he professed was a translation of words found on a set of golden plates that had been buried near his home. He had been shown the location of the plates by an angel named Moroni, who told Smith that he had been chosen as a religious leader. His translation work was completed in 1829, and the Book of Mormon was published the next year.

By that time, Smith and six others had organized the first Church of Christ, and he was viewed as a prophet. The Church rapidly grew in number as Smith's family, friends, and neighbors, who comprised his first congregation, undertook missionary activities in earnest. The following year, Smith and his followers came under persecution for their new faith, primarily for practices that included polygamy. The prophet temporarily moved his church to Kirtland in northern Ohio while planning to establish a spiritual community in Missouri. Envisioning and mapping in his mind a utopian city near Independence, which he called the "city of Zion," Smith and his congregation set about trying to purchase land for their settlement.

Almost immediately after the establishment of the new sect, missionaries were dispatched to Europe to spread the teachings of Mormonism to the masses. They were rewarded with profound success: This new religion based on an angel and a set of golden tablets swept through the continent like a prairie wildfire.

Most of the European converts, like Robert Leroy Parker, came from the working classes. These common people were intimately familiar with the teachings of the Bible, and had become disillusioned with traditional doctrines. They had already been seeking a new denomination, and welcomed a church that had apostles, prophets, and New Testament spiritual gifts.[5]

Mormon "saints," as the individuals were known, believed that the religion established by Jesus Christ had fallen into spiritual decay, and that their church was a literal restoration of primitive Christianity. It was their belief that the Lord's teachings had been altered and His ordinances changed. From its mystical beginnings, the doctrines of the Mormon Church differed from those on which Protestant and Catholic Christianity were based. Mormons also believed that existing denominations followed incorrect doctrines and were in fact an abomination in the sight of God. Traditional Christians viewed the articles of faith of the Mormon Church as politically and culturally subversive, which led to immediate discord between the faiths.[6]

Meanwhile, Robert and Ann Parker devoutly followed this new, controversial church at their home in Lancashire. The couple would become parents to six children—with Maximillian, the eldest and the future father of Butch Cassidy, born in 1844. "Maxi," as he was known, was followed by another boy, Arthur, and three girls, Martha Alice, Margaret, and Emily. Margaret and Emily, however, would die in infancy. In the early 1850s, Robert, who was said to be a natural leader, was appointed conference president of the new Mormon church in Preston, where another girl, Ada, was born.

Eleven-year-old Maxi was apprenticed at the mill where his father worked, but hated the drudgery. One day Maxi ran away from his workplace, much to the ire of the proprietors and the shame of his family. Robert severely disciplined his son, but Maxi vowed that he would never return to the mill, no matter how terrible his punishment. Maxi would pass on to his son, the future Butch Cassidy, his own rebellious nature.[7]

Back in the United States, life was anything but idyllic for members of the Church of Latter-day Saints. They were being discriminated against, often violently, for their beliefs that were out of step with mainstream religions. Joseph Smith was imprisoned for six months in Missouri, where the people objected to Mormon abolitionist beliefs. When he was released, Smith and his followers built a city as the new church headquarters north of Quincy, Illinois, that they called "Nauvoo," after a Hebrew word meaning "beautiful." The community prospered and grew, but relations between residents of nearby towns and the Mormons deteriorated. Finally, Smith was charged with treason for shutting down a newspaper he considered libelous toward Mormonism. He surrendered to authorities in Carthage, and while in custody, on June 27, 1844, he and his brother, Hyrum, were murdered by an angry mob that stormed the jail.

Brigham Young succeeded Smith as leader of the Church. Joseph Smith had confided to Young before his death that he believed that the future of the Mormons waited in the unsettled American West. Young acted upon this vision, and commenced making plans to take his people to the fertile valley of the Great Salt Lake in Utah.

Their destination, this place called Utah, was said to have been inhabited from about 10,000 B.C. by desert nomads, according to artifacts discovered by archaeologists. Around A.D. 300 another culture known as the Anasazi—the ancient ones—flourished as sedentary and agricultural people, but by circa 1300 there was a rapid decline in the population of this culture, and the remaining people became nomadic. A Spanish exploration party sent by Francisco Vásquez de Coronado arrived in Utah during the sixteenth century. But it was not until 1776 that Europeans documented their presence in the territory while searching for a route from Santa Fe to Monterey, California, that would eventually become known as the Spanish Trail.

By this time, however, the Spanish and Mexicans were not the only people passing through Utah. Fur trappers from the Hudson's Bay Company traveled as far as present-day Mountain Green (near Ogden) in 1825, and others, including legendary mountain man Jedediah S. Smith, were said to have visited a few years earlier. Eventually, a number of private trading posts were established, marking the first Anglo settlements in Utah. In the early 1840s, several wagon trains crossed the territory on their way to California or Oregon. Soon after that, notable explorers, such as Joseph Walker and John C. Frémont, headed government expeditions into the present borders of Utah. Frémont named the "Great Basin," and published what could be called a guidebook that would become invaluable to the Mormons.[8]

In July 1847—in the era of Manifest Destiny—Brigham Young followed the vision of Mormon founder Joseph Smith. He led a wagon train of Saints into the Salt Lake Valley, the "Great Basin," and claimed that western land for the Church of Latter-day Saints. At that time, the territory was technically under Mexican rule, but became part of the United States the following year under the Treaty of Guadalupe Hidalgo, which ended the Mexican War. Young quickly transformed what was regarded as a wasteland by utilizing a clever system of irrigation that yielded fields of bountiful crops. He laid out Great Salt Lake City from the mental plan developed in 1833 by Joseph Smith for his "city of Zion."

The Mormon pioneers struggled at first, but were saved by the gold rush of 1849, when they could sell supplies at inflated prices to the passing prospectors. That year, Young established a Mormon theocracy, and named the area the State of Deseret. He petitioned for statehood, which was rejected, but Congress did give Utah territorial status. In 1851, Young was appointed governor.

Following the establishment of Great Salt Lake City, the surrounding territory was settled by an aggressive colonization approach sponsored by the Church. By 1852 more than a hundred thousand Saints, who had pushed and pulled handcarts across mountain and plains, had settled in towns across the Great Basin—and more were on the way. In fact, within just a few short years after the first people arrived, only San Francisco was a larger city west of Missouri than Salt Lake City.

In 1856, Young called for skilled tradesmen to leave the old country and help establish Mormon settlements across the Atlantic Ocean in this "promised land" located in the Western United States. He invoked the Thirteenth General Epistle of October 29, 1855, which read: "Let all things be done in order, and let the Saints who can, gather up for Zion and come while the way is open before them. . . . Let them come of foot, with handcarts or wheelbarrows; let them gird upon their loins and walk through, and nothing shall hinder or stay them."[9]

In Lancashire, Robert Leroy Parker believed that his skill as an expert weaver would be in high demand at these new settlements in America. In addition, young Maxi would have the opportunity to pursue a life more suited for him than working in the mill. Robert heeded Brigham Young's plea for Saints to settle Zion. He sold everything he owned—his cottage, cow, and every stick of furniture—to raise the money for his family to immigrate to America. Robert was able to raise just enough money to cover their passage by ship. Ann judiciously packed only clothing and necessities, but could not bear to part with her silverware or two paintings rendered by Robert. These items were carefully placed in the bottom of the trunk.

On March 22, 1856, Robert, Ann, and their four children—aged eleven years to eight months—boarded the ship *Enoch Train* and arrived at Boston, Massachusetts, five weeks later. The family traveled by train from New York City to the end of the Rock Island Line to join the McArthur Company at Iowa City on May 12. The company formed over the next month, learning that they would be walking while pushing and pulling two-wheeled handcarts loaded with their possessions more than thirteen hundred miles to their destination. The reason for handcarts rather than livestock was Brigham Young's belief that the carts would be quicker and easier, not to mention more practical, to use due to the unfamiliarity of these city dwellers with driving teams of oxen or horses. There simply would not be time to teach them how to handle working animals. In addition, the walk would solidify their faith and purpose, and build character.

On June 9, 1856, the Ellsworth Company, the first Mormon handcart train, departed Iowa City with 274 people. Two days later, Robert Leroy Parker and his family were members of a party numbering 221 that comprised the McArthur Company, named for the leader, Daniel McArthur. There would be no turning back now—they were on the trail to Zion and the Mormon promised land.[10]

Never in the history of the American West has there been a more unlikely group of pioneers than those English men, women, and children from mill towns far across the ocean. They had for the most part never slept in a tent or on the ground, or cooked over a campfire, or walked as far over rough terrain burdened by anything like a cart, or learned even the most rudimentary skills of frontier living. The handcarts would weigh between four and five hundred pounds, with most travelers ignoring the rule of seventeen pounds of baggage for each adult and ten for each child. Yet they traveled on faith and hope, with the belief that this marathon walk across mountains and plains would lead them to a paradise and new life in a place named Zion.[11]

Young Maxi Parker, who had just turned twelve, assisted his father in the effort of moving their handcart across the difficult terrain toward Zion. Baby Ada rode on the cart, while the older children walked and looked after the younger children. The family sang and joked with other members, helping to keep up the spirits of the company on their arduous march through the wilderness. At night, although worn-out from the miles they had traversed, they danced to the music of the Birmingham Band, which had accompanied them to America aboard the ship. Sundays were reserved for devotion, with services both morning and night. By and large, their hearts were light, and they regarded the trip not as a test of their endurance or a challenge physically or mentally, but as a celebration of their faith.

The journey of a Mormon handcart company across the Great Plains would not be complete without at least one tale of a harrowing experience, and what happened to the Parker family certainly qualifies in every respect.

On the afternoon of July 1, during a sudden rainstorm, six-year-old Arthur Parker became separated from the expedition in hostile Indian country. Ann was beside herself as everyone searched and prayed for the missing boy, who had seemingly disappeared without a trace. The hunt continued throughout the night and into the next day, but still no sign of Arthur. The company could not be delayed any longer, and finally, reluctantly, Elder McArthur made the heart-wrenching decision that they must push onward.

Robert urged Ann and the family to move on with the company, while he would backtrack in an attempt to find the missing boy. With Maxi pushing the family handcart, the company headed out—at a slower-than-normal pace to allow Robert time to catch up. At nightfall, the caravan camped. There had been no word from Robert.

Poor Ann Parker grieved for her lost son, not sleeping, and crying and praying all night for his safe return. July 3 and 4 came and went, and still no sign of Robert or Arthur. By then, Ann was certain that both had been killed by Indians or wild animals and she would never see them again. She prayed harder than ever, and placed any hope she had left in the hands of her Lord.

On July 5, the company halted early to camp after a particularly difficult day of traveling. It was late afternoon when Ann visited a rise in the terrain to scan their back trail, as she had done for five days whenever they had stopped. Before long, lo and behold, her eyes focused on some unrecognizable object moving in the distance. Closer and closer it came, until . . . she was dumbfounded—could it be?

Yes, Robert Parker had returned after five days—accompanied by Arthur, who was weary but in good health.

Robert related the particulars of his search to his joyous family and the rejoicing members of the company who crowded around the Parker campfire. On his second night away from the handcart company, Robert had happened upon a trading post, where he learned that a young boy had been found by a couple who lived not too far away. Robert hurried to this cabin, and was reunited with Arthur. The boy told his father that on his first night lost he had been surrounded by vicious "big dogs," which Robert knew would have been wolves, but the animals never approached him. Arthur had then been found by the man and his wife, who had taken him to their cabin.

Robert Parker was exhausted after tramping through the wilderness for five days. The morning following his return it was arranged for him to ride in a supply wagon in order to rest up as the relieved company continued onward toward Zion.[12]

On September 26, after a journey of three and a half months of walking and pushing and pulling the handcart, the Parker family arrived in the valley. They remained in Great Salt Lake City until fall, and then moved on to the town of American Fork, twenty-five miles south of that city, where Robert taught school.[13]

Robert, however, was soon called upon to use his skills to help establish a woolen mill at Beaver, a town that had been founded in 1856 as one of a string of Mormon settlements extending the length of Utah—all planned as a day's ride apart. This town in west-central Utah lay to the west of the Tushar Mountains, which boasted peaks rising to more than twelve thousand feet. It would be in the town of Beaver that young Maximillian Parker would meet Ann Campbell Gillies, his future bride.

The Gillies family's journey to Utah had far exceeded in physical endurance and survival skills the experience of the Parkers. Annie Gillies's father, also named Robert, had been converted to the Mormon

Church in England at about the same time as the elder Parkers. On May 25, 1856, this Scottish family—father, Robert; mother, Jane; and their children, two boys, Moroni (age ten) and Daniel (age seven), and two girls, Annie (age nine) and Christina (age three)—answered Brigham Young's call for immigrants to America and departed Liverpool aboard the ship *Horizon*. They arrived in New York City six weeks later, and then traveled to Iowa City by way of Albany, Buffalo, and Chicago. The family signed on with the William B. Hodgett Company, which would be traversing the plains to Utah with the Edward Martin Handcart Company.[14]

The expedition of the Gillies family was every bit as arduous as that of the Parker family, with walking and pushing handcarts, except that these companies had picked the wrong time of the year for their trek. By November, winter had arrived and the caravan became trapped by storms and subzero temperatures in Wyoming's upper Sweetwater Valley, near South Pass. Food was scarce, and each person was rationed less than a half pound of flour per day. By the time a rescue party had reached them, nearly 150 people out of the 576 in the train had perished.

The Gillies family, however, made it through alive and well and reached the Great Salt Lake Valley on November 30. Robert and Jane Gillies initially settled their family north of Salt Lake City at Woods Cross. They later were called to Beaver, Utah, where Robert could better ply his trade as a skilled carpenter and cabinetmaker.[15]

Meanwhile, the Parkers had arrived in Beaver too late in the year to build a cabin. Consequently, they lived in a primitive dugout that first winter, with water trickling down the walls to turn the floor into mud, making for a miserable, cold, and damp existence. That next summer, however, Robert and Maxi constructed a cabin that would be added on to during ensuing years to accommodate the expanding family. Robert Jr. was born in 1858, but died as an infant, and Ellen and Caroline were born in 1859 and 1860, respectively.

In 1862, when Maxi—who now went by the nickname "Max"—was eighteen years old, he served the Church by making two excursions to

St. Louis to guide immigrating Saints to Utah. In the big city, he worked at a job while waiting for his charges to assemble, and brought home presents for the family, including cooking kettles and other household items that were unavailable in the West. Supposedly Max, who loved to dance, bought himself a pair of fancy dancing shoes on one of these trips.[16]

Perhaps it was at a dance or possibly during the plays and programs put on as entertainment for young people back in Utah that Max caught the eye of Annie Gillies, and vice versa. Both were social and gregarious—Max playing the role of comedian and Ann known for her superb singing voice. Evidently Max and Annie at some point became a couple, whether publicly or privately cannot be determined. Regardless of particulars, when Robert and Annie Parker were called to move to a new cotton mill in Washington, Utah, their eldest son, Max, remained behind in Beaver. And there was only one reason—he simply could not leave Ann Gillies.

On July 12, 1865, Maximillian Parker and Ann Campbell Gillies were married—on Ann's nineteenth birthday.[17]

Max and Annie settled on a ranch located on North Creek, a few miles from the town of Beaver. Max supported the family by carrying the mail on horseback from Beaver along the Sevier River to Sanford Bench. His route took him through the Circle Valley, a rough, primitive country that was sparsely populated. The ride presented a constant threat to his safety—he occasionally was obliged to dodge arrows fired by Ute warriors—but he was skillful enough to evade this enemy. Fortunately, Max could depend on the few honest Mormon homesteaders to come to his aid, if necessary. Although there was always a possibility of being attacked by a war party, Max was enamored by the beauty and promise of the Circle Valley, and regarded it as a potential place to settle someday—when the Native American threat had subsided.

Brigham Young had instituted a policy of feeding the local Native Americans rather than fighting them. He encouraged the Mormons to make friends and share resources with these tribes, such as the Shoshone. This policy worked to a certain extent, but as more and more settlers arrived, Native Americans were forced away from traditional prime hunting and gathering places and resorted to stealing livestock. Mormon settlers soon developed resentment about having to feed and put up with the Native Americans, and the tribes developed their own resentment about having been displaced. Several skirmishes ensued, but for the most part the Mormons coexisted with their Native American neighbors.[18]

On April 13, 1866—Friday the thirteenth—Robert Leroy Parker, who would one day become known as Butch Cassidy, was born to Max and Annie Parker. He was named for his grandfather, who had brought the family name to America. His parents would call him Leroy, but everyone else knew him as Bob. He would be followed over the years by twelve brothers and sisters—Dan, Arthur, Jen, Bill, Knell, Eb, Blanch, Lula, Mark, Nina, Leona, and Rawlins.[19]

In the spring of 1879, when Bob was thirteen years old, Max fulfilled his mail-carrying dream and moved the family south onto 160 acres in the Circle Valley. His land was located about three miles south of Circleville—which at that point in time was only a few buildings and a schoolhouse—at the mouth of Circleville Canyon, near the southern edge of Circle Valley. The parched earth in that place was badly in need of irrigation, and only a handful of settlers had mustered enough courage to try to make a go of raising crops and cattle there.

The family, at that time with six children, and their meager possessions were packed into a tiny two-room cabin built by the former owner at the base of a small slope. That first summer Max, with young Bob's help, was able to clear away enough brush to plant a crop of wheat. But before long the relentless wind had torn his seeds from the ground. His second planting suffered the same fate. There was nothing this farmer could do to combat the elements, especially those blasts of dry wind that roared from the west over the northern edge of what became known as Hurricane Cliffs. A farmer could do nothing, that was, except try again. The third planting was a charm. Just before summer ended, the winds diminished and Max's crop took hold and began to grow.[20]

After the wheat was in the ground, Max left his family in Circle Valley and sought out a variety of jobs, mainly with mining companies. Utah's mining business was a boom-and-bust proposition, with towns springing up from nowhere when digging began and dying when the mines played out.

Max eventually secured a job with the Silver Reef Mine, which paid higher-than-average wages. He was hired to cut and haul wood in the Pine Valley Mountains northeast of St. George, nearly one hundred miles from Circle Valley. Silver Reef, a new non-Mormon town built for the miners, became known as a raucous and dangerous place, with frequent brawls and murders. Max survived his stay in Silver Reef by being known as a Mormon—the gentiles respected the ways of the Saints and rarely molested them. The Parker family remained at the Circle Valley ranch, and Max managed to visit them only on the occasional Sunday.[21]

Much of the work around the Circle Valley ranch fell on the shoulders of thirteen-year-old Bob Parker, who welcomed the challenge. Bob was always tall for his age, and had inherited his father's work ethic. Any chore that required his attention was handled as best as the boy was able. He could never hope to replace the skills of his father, but the ranch did not suffer terribly by the purposeful efforts of Bob.

While growing up, young Bob had a special affinity and affection for animals, both wild and domestic. He seemed to understand the habits and traits of farm animals or wildlife far better than the average person. Bob made a pet of a magpie that his sister claimed he had taught to talk and would say, "Hello," to people. He was always tending to livestock, such as Sarah, the family cow, who was mischievously named after a lady from town. Bob would occasionally play rodeo by riding calves with his brothers and neighbors, or he would hook up the goat to a homemade cart and have a rousing chariot race. He also raised a menagerie of indigenous wildlife, including rabbits, pigeons, and chipmunks—and he named each one.

Bob understood his role as the eldest child with a father away from home, and went out of his way to entertain the younger children—his siblings and the children of relatives or neighbors. Whether it was riding calves or taking them for wild and woolly rides in the goat-drawn cart, Bob was a magnet for kids, because he was always involved in something fun and outlandish. He would boost the little ones up onto his horse, often putting so many up there that they would teeter precariously, and then lead them around for a spirited ride. On one occasion he built a raft, and had every kid who would fit climb aboard while he propelled the craft around a nearby pond for a wet and watery adventure. Another time, he had all the children gather up as many grasshoppers as they could catch. He then skillfully attached strings to the back legs of the insects, distributed one to each child, and held grasshopper races, pretending that each hopper was a prize racehorse.[22]

All evidence indicates that the Parkers were a strict but loving family who tried to raise their children properly. To this end, Ann believed that the Mormon religion should be paramount in their lives. After all, that was the reason that her father and Max's father had brought their families from England to that faraway place.

Ann was a faithful churchgoer and strictly adhered to Mormon rules and restrictions. Max, on the other hand, gradually became known as what was commonly referred to as a "jack-Mormon," a term used for those who were inactive. Perhaps this falling-out with the Church had something to do with Max's youthful resentment over his own father's zealousness for the faith, to the point that his father would make Max polish the shoes of missionaries who visited their home. Max had also developed the habit of smoking, which was prohibited by the Mormons. He attended church rarely, and instead of following Church tradition that the man of the household had the responsibility to lead prayers and Church teachings, he left that task to his wife.

Ann would hold family devotions and read from the Bible and the Book of Mormon. During these occasions, she would also teach literature and other subjects to supplement the education the older children received from the school in Beaver. Bob learned to read and write from both his mother and his sporadic schoolhouse education.

Max, when he was home, would enthusiastically participate in what were known as "home evenings," when the entire family would gather together after chores were done to sing and tell stories in an attempt to provide entertainment at the isolated ranch. Bob would often play his harmonica while all the children sang songs led by their parents.[23]

There can be little doubt that Max's defection from the Church influenced his oldest son. Young Bob soon followed his father's example and neglected his Mormon responsibilities. Although the Parker children were never forced to attend church, they usually obeyed their mother and would willingly go each week. Bob, however, had quit going to his mother's weekly religious meetings, and when it came to going to church, his sister states: "Bob wasn't a willing attender. If he could find some chore—any chore—that needed his attention, he stayed home to take care of it. Any excuse was convenient." He also was known to sneak a smoke of tobacco when he thought he was safe from being found out. Max caught his son hiding his stash under the granary floor one day, but chose to ignore this transgression, perhaps due to his own tobacco habit.[24]

Bob loved and respected his hardworking father, but according to his sister Lula, he absolutely adored his mother. Lula writes: "When he [Bob] was in a frolicsome mood, he waltzed her [his mother] around the room, then picked her up bodily and set her on the table. 'Come on, kids,' he announced. 'Bring the crown. Ma's the queen.'" His mother would happily protest and cherish every moment of special attention showered on her by her oldest son.[25]

As Bob grew older, he graduated from working with small animals to taking care of full-grown horses. Long hours were spent at the corral grooming, doctoring, and studying every nuance and movement made by the animal that intrigued him so much. He eventually developed a special bond with these four-legged beasts of burden, and was able to easily break and train just about any horse—even the most wild-eyed and untamed stallion that would not allow others to approach him. It was as if there were a private line of communication and an inherent bond of trust between the youngster and the beast. Bob could compel the most rambunctious bronc to obey his soothing voice and patient manner. He seemed to know the precise words and gestures that the horse needed to hear to trust the human.

In fact, Bob's fascination with horses could be likened to a modern-day teenage boy's love affair with the automobile. He wanted to know how every part worked, and how each part affected the other parts, and what steps and care it would take to keep these parts in perfect shape and great running condition. There was not a horse around that Bob could not ride. Horses would become his first love, his passion, and remain so throughout his life.

The Parker family never had much money, and the children contributed to the family's earnings whenever possible. Bob, whose aptitude with horses was widely known, would hire out to neighboring ranches as a cowboy when he was not needed at home. In at least one instance, when Bob took a job far enough away that he was obliged to live away from home, his removal from parental supervision would turn ugly.

One day while working for rancher Patrick Ryan at Hay Springs, near Milford, Bob took time off to ride into town to purchase a new pair of badly needed overalls. This errand would appear to be innocent enough, but when Bob arrived in town he found that the store was closed. This presented him with a quandary. He was irked that he had ridden all that distance on the hot, dusty road for nothing—until he was struck with the idea that his credit would be good.

With that in mind, Bob forced his way into the building, and rummaged through the shelves until he found his size jeans. One account claims he also helped himself to a piece of pie. In the West, it was accepted that a man's word was his bond. Bob wrote out an IOU in good faith, promising to pay for the overalls on his next trip to town. He rode back to the ranch wearing his new work clothes without mentioning his actions to anyone.

Apparently the storekeeper was not impressed by Bob's promissory note. The man notified the town marshal, and Bob was taken into custody.

The matter was eventually sorted out to the satisfaction of the storekeeper, but not until Bob Parker had been thoroughly humiliated and had brought shame upon his family name, which in Mormon country was taken seriously. There can be no question that this incident would have given Bob a bitter taste of justice, and reason to question the legal system and its treatment of him.[26]

According to Parley P. Christensen, the sheriff of Juab County for thirty years, Bob was involved in another criminal occurrence around this same time. Although no record of this incident exists, the sheriff claimed that Bob was arrested for stealing a saddle, possibly in Garfield County. In this case, Bob claimed that he had been mistreated while in custody. But there has been no mention of any consequences, such as jail time, if a crime indeed had been committed. The episode could have been a misunderstanding, and may have been forgotten at the time when the "borrowed" saddle had been returned. Or it may not have happened at all. People have a way of remembering questionable events in the lives of famous people long after they have become famous.[27]

It can only be speculated whether Max's alienation from the Mormon Church might have had some effect on the stern attitude of both the Milford shopkeeper and the authorities involved in the stolen jeans and alleged saddle theft. Utah was a Mormon Empire, and outsiders or those who did not abide by the faith could suffer unspoken consequences.

When the Silver Reef Mine played out, Max took a job in the San Francisco Mountains at the town of Frisco. The Utah Southern Railroad had come to Frisco and the Squaw Creek Mine, compliments of New York financier Jay Cooke, the man responsible for the Panic of 1873. Max once again chopped and hauled wood for railroad ties, but there was one happy factor—this move to Frisco brought him within shouting distance of Pat Ryan's ranch at Hay Springs. Max could at least visit with his son, and hope to be a positive influence on the boy, who by now had a bad taste in his mouth for authority.[28]

To supplement the family income, Ann Parker was able to find work helping with the dairy chores at the Marshall Ranch, a sprawling spread surrounded by mountains some twelve miles south of Circleville near the northern edge of the present-day Dixie National Forest. Jim Marshall, the owner, also offered a job to thirteen-year-old Bob and two younger brothers. Ann was relieved that her oldest son would now be working at the Marshall Ranch, which meant he could live at home.

The income from Ann and Bob, plus Max's pay, permitted the family to buy several head of cattle. As luck would have it, the winter of 1879 was one of the worst on record in southern Utah, and the small herd of cattle perished, other than two cows named Hutch and Sal.[29]

Max decided that he must expand his homestead in order to succeed. The family was becoming larger, now with four boys and three girls. Mormons were encouraged to have large families. Granted, rural families were traditionally large in order to have hands for chores, but Church doctrine proclaimed that it was a woman's highest glory to bear as many children as possible. And a man's reward in heaven would be partially determined by how many children would accompany him there. The size of the family could be assisted by having more than one wife to bear children. Evidently Max did not subscribe to the teachings and example of Brigham Young when it came to polygamy. Brigham had twenty-seven wives; Max was satisfied with just one.[30]

In order to raise additional crops and cattle for his family, Max bought a neighboring parcel of land—or so he thought. His claim was challenged by the former owner, a fellow Mormon. Ordinarily the matter would have ended up in court, but the area was lacking authorities to adjudicate civil law. With that being the case, the ownership of the property in question was placed in the hands of the local Mormon bishop. Predictably—at least to Max's way of thinking—the other man in the dispute, a dues-paying Mormon, won the judgment over Max, the jack-Mormon. To be fair, the bishop may have simply been following an edict set forth by Brigham Young that stated that a man should not own more land than he could personally cultivate.

Nevertheless, Max was furious, and believed that the Mormon Church had been prejudiced against him and had punished him for his less-than-attentive attitude toward Church responsibilities.[31]

Back at the Marshall spread, Jim Marshall eventually allowed Ann and her three sons to live in a small cabin on his property, a move that was grudgingly accepted by Max but did not sit well with him. The rancher was impressed that the diligent and productive young teen Bob Parker could do the work of a full-grown man. Bob would work alongside the other cowboys, and handle his chores as efficiently as any of them.

Before long, however, Bob would make the acquaintance of a cowboy at the Marshall spread who would have a profound effect on such an impressionable youngster—and this man would change the life of Bob Parker forever.

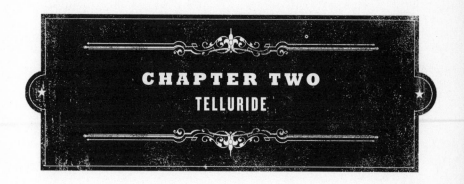

CHAPTER TWO
TELLURIDE

I've been working on the railroad
All the live-long day.
I've been working on the railroad
Just to pass the time away.

Can't you hear the whistle blowing
Rise up so early in the morn
Can't you hear the captain shouting
Dinah, blow your horn

—"I've Been Working on the Railroad"

By the 1850s, the railroad stretched from the East Coast to the Mississippi River, with short lines connecting neighboring cities. There was no standard gauge or width of the tracks, which limited where each train could travel. This lack of any standard was a major inconvenience and caused costly delays in moving both passengers and goods. A greater inconvenience, however, was the fact that commerce by rail ended at Omaha, Nebraska. To reach into the West, goods had to be shipped by stagecoach, pack train, or steamship where waterways were available—a practice that Congress recognized as a hindrance to the country's economic infrastructure. But America has always risen to the challenge of finding a solution to perplexing situations, especially when trade and finance are involved.

The Transcontinental Railroad, known as the Overland Route, began as an idea published in the 1832 book *The Emigrant*. This notion of railroad tracks spanning the continent intrigued many men over the years, but it was not until after the discovery of gold at Sutter's Mill in California that Congress was compelled in 1853 to fund a survey to determine potential routes—with future Confederate president Jefferson Davis in charge of the expedition. Eventually, a combination of the zeal of Theodore Dehone Judah, known as "Crazy Judah," and the skill of a young engineer named Grenville Dodge resulted in President Abraham Lincoln signing the Pacific Railway Act on July 1, 1862.

Huge loans and government grants were awarded to two private companies to handle the construction of this enormous project. The

Central Pacific Railroad would begin laying track eastward out of Sacramento, and the Union Pacific Railroad would begin work heading west out of Omaha.

By the early 1860s, nearly fifty thousand young Chinese immigrants had flooded to California, but had been run off gold mining claims and sought any kind of work. The railroad was eager to hire these hard workers. Chinese laborers would be required to chisel, plow, and blast their way through the Sierra Nevada Mountains, struggling against blizzards and deep snow as well as the dangers of working with risky gunpowder. These immigrants would be assisted by Paiute and Shoshone workers when they laid track across the flat Nevada desert.

Irish workers dominated the ranks of the Union Pacific, using shovels and pickaxes to dig and level rail beds across the Great Plains. It was backbreaking work in both directions, rife with danger from accidents, hostile Native Americans, and the merciless elements. Another hazard to the health and safety of the workers was the temporary towns that would spring up as the crew arrived at a new spot. Bars and gambling halls were not places for the fainthearted, and shootings were frequent and often deadly.

Newspapers chronicled this race across the Western United States as both companies viewed their mission with a competitive eye and forged ahead full speed from the starting gun. Even so, it took seven years of grueling physical labor for the two crews to come within sight of each other.

On May 10, 1869, at a place in Utah called Promontory Summit, the president of the Central Pacific Railroad, Leland Stanford, pounded one final golden spike into position. At that moment, a telegraph operator who was present for the ceremony tapped out a message to crowds of people waiting across the country. "Almost ready now. Hats off," he sent through the lines. "Prayer is being offered . . . Done!"

The Central Pacific had laid 690 miles of track from Sacramento to Promontory Summit. The Union Pacific countered with 1,086 miles of track from Omaha to Promontory Summit.

The nation now had a railroad that spanned the continent. The laying of the tracks, crossing plains and mountains, would stand as one of the greatest human technological achievements in the history of the United States—right up there with the voyage of Columbus in 1492 and the moon landing of Neil Armstrong in 1969.

Railroad owners and investors quickly got busy building towns near their lines on land granted them by the United States government, which led to the development of countless communities in the West. What was once a foreboding wilderness was now open for business and settlement. People weary of the ills of the East seeking a fresh start or desiring to establish a new business could board a train that would deposit them and their belongings on the prairies, or in the mountains, or all the way to the ocean on the West Coast.

At first there was one problem with this new system of rails. Most towns set their clocks independently, according to solar time. This difference in time from town to town created confusion when regular train service commenced. As a result, in 1883, the railroads had towns adopt a national system of time zones. Broad sections of the country now showed the same time, which made life easier for passengers and businesses that shipped goods. These time zones remain in use to this day.

The transcontinental railroad made it cheaper, faster, and more practical to ship goods, and in fact revolutionized business and industry by creating national markets. Railroads enabled one type of industry in the West in particular to prosper—the cattle business.[1]

Easy access to the railroad had brought the so-called "cattle barons" into the vast public lands of Utah. They turned loose enormous herds of animals that would freely roam the range and fatten up on pasture grass until driven to the tracks for shipment. Small homesteaders also flocked to these public lands, consuming resources and interfering with cattle operations. This invasion of cattle country caused resentment among the powerful cattle barons and resulted in conflict over land use, especially water, often involving violence.

The primary concern of the owners with these great cattle herds that grazed for hundreds of square miles of open range was a lack of supervision. Even a big outfit simply could not hire enough cowboys to patrol and guard the entire range. Consequently, unbranded strays, known as "mavericks," could be rounded up by homesteaders—or anyone else, for that matter—and then burned with a brand and claimed as their own.

Technically, rounding up cattle known to belong to someone else was defined as rustling and could be punishable by death—occasionally on-the-spot swift justice at the end of a rope without benefit of a trial. But who could prove that an unbranded stray was the property of the cattle baron and not the settler whose brand was emblazoned on its hide? After all, the cattle barons owned thousands upon thousands of cows. They could not keep track of them all; nor would they miss a few head here and there. True, a few missing head normally would not invite reprisals. Unfortunately, greed entered into the equation. It was just too easy to round up these strays and drive them home. As a result, the numbers of appropriated cattle grew until the men who were taking them had crossed the line and become outlaws known as rustlers.

And that was precisely what was happening at Jim Marshall's ranch twelve miles south of Circleville, where Ann Parker and her boys were working for their second season. When Marshall was away on a trip to town or had ridden to another part of his spread, several of his cowboys were bringing mavericks back to the ranch and branding them right there in the home corral. The leader of this band of wrangler-rustlers was a young but experienced cowpuncher who called himself Mike Cassidy.

Cassidy was a drifter who likely was no stranger to rustling and other unlawful endeavors. He apparently had been on his own from an early age, and had by necessity developed survival skills that hardened him. No one knew where he had come from, where he was reared, or what his ambitions might have been. But it was clear that although he was a capable ranch hand, he was not above taking advantage of opportunistic situations, if one presented itself, such as claiming stray cattle.

Mike Cassidy was also a friendly sort—another trait of those who lived by their wits, whether sincere or not—and he struck up an immediate friendship with Bob Parker, who was several years younger. In fact, it was as if Cassidy had selected Bob as his protégé by showering his young friend with attention and favors.

Bob openly admired Mike Cassidy, whom he viewed as a romantic figure who could wander the range at will, making do for himself, and was eager to learn everything this man wished to teach him—from cowboy chores to shooting a six-gun. To that end, Cassidy presented Bob with the gifts of a saddle and a handgun. Bob would spend many hours under the tutelage of Mike Cassidy learning how to handle and shoot that six-gun.[2]

Bob Parker was enthralled by stories related by the earthy Mike Cassidy about rough-and-tumble cattle towns, rollicking saloons, painted dance hall girls, and money won and lost at games of chance. Bob had never ventured outside of Mormon country, where towns, other than isolated mining boom towns, were orderly and law-abiding. Saloons, brothels, and other dens of iniquity were strictly forbidden. Cassidy knew the ways of the world and freely shared his experiences with a spellbound Bob Parker.

Ann Parker noticed the branding of mavericks in the corral, a task in which her son had participated, as well as her son's relationship with Mike Cassidy, a man she intuitively recognized as a negative influence. She was greatly troubled by this turn of events in the life of her impressionable oldest son. Ann was aware, however, that if she tried to lecture Bob about the enticing evils of which Cassidy preached or asked him to stay away from the man, it would serve only to alienate him. She did let Bob know—as only a mother can do with that spiritual connection—that she was not blind to what was happening around the Marshall Ranch or to his association with Mike Cassidy.

Ann could only hope that Bob's early education in the Mormon faith would help him maintain his ethics, morals, and principles, and allow him to prevail over the temptations of the secular world. No doubt the good Saint Ann Parker spent much time on her knees praying that her son's heart would be touched by spiritual influences—and for guidance for herself in her quest to try to keep him out of trouble.[3]

In the spring of 1884, Ann decided to move back home, hoping that Bob would follow her. He was eighteen now, a grown man, and the family could use on their own ranch the skills and experience he had learned from working around the area. Max remained away from home much of the time working various jobs, and tended to the ranch as best he could with the help of Ann and the rest of the children. She knew that Bob loved his family, and in the end, she reckoned, he would choose to follow the example set by his hardworking, dedicated father. Bob was the oldest son, and he should be embracing family tradition and taking more responsibility around his Circle Valley home.[4]

One sunny, warm day in June, Bob Parker came home. Ann was baking bread in the kitchen when her oldest son tramped inside. His demeanor was more solemn than usual. There was no boisterous greeting or the flippant tossing of his hat as he was apt to do. Ann noticed immediately that something was amiss. She served him a slice of her bread with a generous topping of homemade butter and bilberry preserves. Ann could tell that Bob wanted to talk, but was hesitant to do so with the younger children around. His siblings had clung to him, hugging his legs or punching his arms, from the moment he had entered the door. With Max away, Bob was once again the man of the house, and the big brother who instilled comfort and security in the children.

Later that evening, Bob spoke his mind. "Ma, I'm leaving bright and early in the morning," he said to his mother. "There's not much here for me. No future. Pay in Utah is low—you know that. Maybe twenty or thirty dollars a month with board—and the board's not much to brag about in most places. There's no excitement around here. I'm not a kid anymore. Gotta be thinking about my future . . . I look at the struggle you and Dad have had, and it don't look very good to me. Always somebody to cheat you out of what you've got coming—like the time you lost the homestead . . . If it ain't some righteous Saint getting the best of you, then it's the weather that's agin you, freezing the stock or the crops. I can't do it. I've got to get into something that brings me hard, solid gold in my hand. Thought maybe I could get a job in Telluride in the mines."[5]

Ann was crestfallen. It was evident Bob had made up his mind, and he was mule stubborn once he made a decision. Bob would be leaving for Colorado in the morning. She knew that nothing she could say could dissuade him, but tried anyway by pointing out that he was only eighteen years old and he could not very well travel all that way alone.

Bob had prepared for any objection she might have presented. He reminded her that most of his friends were off on their own, and some of them were even married and raising families. Besides, he assured her, he would not be alone on his trip to Colorado.

Ann's heart skipped a beat. Was he going to rendezvous with that outlaw Mike Cassidy?

"No, I won't be alone," Bob continued. "Eli Elder is going, too."

Ann was relieved that it was one of Bob's local friends and not Cassidy who would be accompanying him. She made one last plea. "Please wait until your father comes home," she implored. "He'll probably be back tomorrow night." Max had always been a loving father, never laying a hand on any of his children in anger, and had offered sage advice and guidance to Bob that had been obediently followed.

There was the possibility that Max had already talked Bob out of leaving home some months earlier. According to sister Lula, Bob had privately approached his father about tagging along with Mike Cassidy when the wrangler-outlaw decided to leave the territory. Max had counseled Bob that his place was there in Circle Valley, that he was too good a person to be partnering with that shady character. Apparently Bob had accepted his father's advice at that time.[6]

Mike Cassidy had drifted on to another range alone, perhaps knowing that it was dangerous for him to remain for too long in any one place. Rumor had him headed south, possibly going to Mexico, carrying with him the reputation of an unscrupulous man who was

familiar with a cinch ring or a running iron to modify brands on stolen cattle.[7]

Ann's request to wait for his father, however, did not sway Bob
this time. "Can't," he said. "I should've been gone today, but I wanted
to say good-bye to you and the kids. I better turn in. Got a long ride
ahead of me, and I'll need sleep."[8]

At dawn, Bob Parker swung up into the saddle of his mare, Babe,
and held the lead rope to his Thoroughbred colt, Cornish. He took one
last long look around, and then gently nudged Babe, who started off
at a walk. His route took him past the five poplar trees west of the
house that he had helped his mother plant—on the beginning of a ride
that would eventually lead to infamy.

Ann heard the baby crying inside the house and slowly, sadly,
turned away from Bob to tend to her family. She could not help but
wonder whether she would ever lay eyes on her firstborn again.[9]

Max Parker arrived home that night and was shocked and disappointed to learn that Bob had departed for Colorado. This behavior
was not typical of his oldest son. There must have been a reason he
left so abruptly, without even waiting to say good-bye to his father.
Max decided to get to the bottom of it immediately. He rode into town
the following morning and, much to his dismay, found out why Bob
had ridden off without much notice.

According to Bob's sister Lula, Max was told that two of Mike
Cassidy's friends and accomplices—cowpunchers named Charley and
Fred—had branded cattle that were recognized as being owned by
other ranchers. When asked to show a bill of sale for these animals, the
two men had produced a document signed by one Robert Leroy Parker.

Max was beside himself, and confronted the constable, James
Wiley, who had in fact drawn up the bill-of-sale papers. Wiley had
been regarded as a friend, and Max wanted to know how Bob's name
could be cleared.

Somehow the two unscrupulous men—likely enabled by Constable
Wiley—had persuaded Bob to sign the paper to make it appear that
the young man had been the owner of the cattle in question. This bill

of sale would clear Charley and Fred of any wrongdoing and point the finger of suspicion directly at Bob Parker. Evidently this arrangement had been predetermined, perhaps as a payoff or a favor. Charley and Fred were said to have been family men, Mormons in good standing, and they could not afford to be incarcerated or tainted by scandal. Bob, on the other hand, had no such attachments.

Constable Wiley suggested that Max just let Bob take the blame, have him disappear for a few years, and when he returned everything would be forgotten. After all, the cattle had been returned to their rightful owners. No harm had been done.

This advice stuck in Max's craw. He knew Bob could never return and be a trusted or respected member of the community after being caught up in this criminal enterprise. He wondered whether there would be any way for the truth to come out to clear Bob's name. Wiley reminded Max that it would be Bob's word against those two up-standing citizens', which would make it impossible for Bob to prevail through a bishop's trial. Once again, Max must have fumed, the Church would be the one adjudicating justice. Max did, however, ad-monish Wiley for his treachery, saying that he would never pull such an underhanded stunt on Wiley's son.

Max Parker's first inclination was to ride after Bob and bring him back to try to right this terrible wrong. When he came to his senses, however, he realized that such an effort would be futile. He might never be able to find him, and the ranch needed his attention. He could not leave his job or his chores for however long it would take to locate Bob out on the trail.[10]

Could it have been that Bob had taken the rap for two men who had much to lose—that, right or wrong, he had been protecting his friends, Mike Cassidy's friends, by his actions?

Robert Leroy Parker, the man who would become the notorious outlaw Butch Cassidy, would be known as someone who was fiercely loyal throughout his life to his friends and his employers. But perhaps there are other stories that are a more relevant and believable depic-tion of why Bob had been hell-bent to leave Utah on that June day. It

could be that Bob's primary purpose in heading for Telluride had to
do with other underhanded schemes that would send him riding the
outlaw trail.

The story about the bogus bill of sale was documented by his sister Lula, but other reasons for Bob's hasty departure from the Circle
Valley have been presented over the years. Bob may have indeed fully
intended to find a job in the mines at Telluride, Colorado, but his real
purpose for traveling to that town has been a matter of speculation.

The first story involved a known rustler by the name of Cap
Brown, who made his headquarters within the desolate country known
as Robbers Roost. The Roost was a savage, parched wilderness of
steep-walled canyons and hidden draws in the high desert of eastern
Utah, sandwiched between the Colorado River, the Green River, and
the Dirty Devil River. This area of rough, inhospitable terrain afforded hundreds of square miles of places to hide without detection,
and was easily defended, if necessary.[11]

The Roost had been occupied by transient rustlers for some
time, but Cap Brown's outfit was the most successful to date. He would
raid ranches and rope strays throughout southern Utah, and then
sell the animals to mining communities in Colorado. His business began as a one-man operation, but eventually expanded as he recruited
local cowboys who were anxious to supplement their wages. It was
likely that Mike Cassidy had worked for Cap Brown, and may have
brought along with him at one time or another a young man by the
name of Bob Parker. Indeed, Bob would years later establish an impen-
etrable hideout within this rugged maze of canyons known as Robbers
Roost.[12]

In the spring of 1884, at the same time Bob was leaving home,
old-timers who hung around Robbers Roost swore that Bob Parker
had been hired by Cap Brown. The two men had planned to drive
about twenty head of horses through the Utah badlands over to
Colorado, and finally to the town of Telluride. Bob's scheduled rendezvous with Brown may have been why he departed home without
being able to remain long enough to say good-bye to his father.[13]

Another theory that has gained credibility over the years blamed the departure on Bob's stealing some horses from neighbor Jim Kittleman. The Kittleman story has been embellished over time to include Bob's capture by two lawmen, whom he later gave the slip— and his briefly returning to them after stealing their horses and finding their canteens tied to the saddles and not wanting to leave them high and dry in the parched canyonlands.[14]

No record of this "arrest" has surfaced, but it has been noted that Jim Kittleman did lose some horses to rustlers around that time period, and he suspected, given Bob's disappearance, that Bob had been the culprit. Sister Lula, however, wrote that "Bob would as soon have stolen from his own father as Jim Kittleman." She cited Bob's loyalty toward friends and relatives as the reason that Bob could not have taken advantage of his neighbor, whom he had always regarded as a personal friend. Bob did in fact ride near the Kittleman spread that day, but supposedly only to meet Eli Elder, who would be accompanying him to Telluride.[15]

Whether he had stolen Jim Kittleman's horses, or was working in cahoots with Cap Brown, or had fled from the illegal bill of sale, one way or another, Bob Parker was on his way to Telluride, Colorado, a town where he would define his future career.

Telluride had been built at the east end of a six-mile-long, high-walled, flat-bottomed gorge called San Miguel Park, a valley where the San Miguel River was formed by streams that tumbled down from Blue Lake and Ajax Peak. Mining claims had first been filed there in the mid-1870s, with the most promising lodes located at least eleven thousand feet above sea level. The name of the town had been changed from the confusing Columbia to Telluride in the late 1870s to reflect a name derived from the ore of tellurium, a half-metallic element found in combination with gold that prospectors had mistakenly identified—the ore was actually pyrite, fool's gold. But there was indeed real gold and silver in them there hills, and gold fever had brought prospectors and miners with picks and pans from all over the world to dig into the earth to remove it. Placer-mining companies were working huge claims—sending gravel sliding down wooden chutes to the San Miguel River to separate the precious metal from the dirt and rock.[16]

Bob would have heard tales about the wild social life in Telluride from the talk around Circle Valley by those curious fortune seekers who had ventured to that town. Brigham Young had urged his Saints to remain in Utah and mine for iron, lead, and coal rather than leave for the gamble of striking it rich in Colorado. When times became tough, however, a number of people ignored Young's advice and journeyed to the mines in the Colorado mountains. Those who had worked there and sampled the amoral pleasures claimed that the name Telluride had been derived from the phrase "to hell you ride."[17]

Although Bob Parker thought he might have known what to expect in Telluride, he was not prepared that spring for the pseudo-glitz and glamour that greeted him when he rode into town. One Utah cowboy described it best when he said he was astounded by the "saloons, gambling dives, dance halls, and board sidewalks, where thousands of strange, crazy people pulled amazing scads of money out of their pockets and tried to gamble it off or throw it away on drinks and dance hall girls as fast as they could, and who tricked, robbed, shot, and stabbed each other to an amazing extent."[18]

Bob, the sheltered Mormon, would not have shied away from the fantastic sights of this rip-roaring mining town that made his eyes pop out of their sockets. Right there within reach of his eager senses was the primary reason he had departed Utah and the Circle Valley. Here awaited the wicked excitement and adrenaline-pumping adventure that he had craved, and he intended to sample every available vice as soon as possible.

Bob made an arrangement with a rancher to pasture Babe and Cornish west of town, and then found a job packing ore down the mountain from the mines to the mill by mule train. The fact that he had sought employment immediately does not lend itself to the theory that he had driven rustled horses to Telluride, for which he would have been well paid. A young man visiting the big city for the first time with coins jingling in his pocket would have pursued pleasure rather than work. And Bob had found hard work, to be sure, but it paid well. Whether his wages were well spent was another matter. At night, Bob could be found carousing with his newfound friends in the saloons. To be fair, he did occasionally send money home, but most of the time he squandered his pay on the pretty girls and libations of Telluride.[19]

Trouble, or misunderstandings, seemed to follow Bob Parker, and Telluride was no exception. Bob may have spent the winter months when mining slowed down in Wyoming or Nebraska, but by the spring of 1885 he had returned to Telluride and became embroiled in a controversy.[20]

He had sold his horse, Babe, and now turned to breaking and training his colt, Cornish. Bob had pastured the colt with the same rancher for the past two years. Cornish was three years old when Bob began gentling the colt and breaking him to the lead rope and then the saddle, a fact not overlooked by the rancher who owned the pasture. This man had evidently watched Cornish closely while Bob had been away, and recognized the colt's potential. He had taken a fancy to the horse, and asked Bob to sell Cornish to him. Bob refused; he also knew good horseflesh, but more than that, Cornish was a link to his family home.

The next time Bob arrived to work with his colt, he was arrested. The rancher had sworn out a warrant on the charge of horse theft. Neighbors and friends of the rancher would attest to Cornish's being in the sole possession of the rancher on his property for quite some time, and Bob had been nowhere to be found. Bob could not point to a brand or any paperwork, which made it difficult for him to prove ownership.

It would stand to reason that there was probably another issue besides the refusal to sell the horse that came between this rancher and Bob, perhaps an unpaid bill for feed and pasturing that was in dispute. Nevertheless, Bob was taken to Montrose and tossed into jail. He was not without friends himself, however, who knew who truly owned Cornish. They wired Max Parker in Circleville to inform him about this potential injustice unfolding in Colorado.[21]

Max hurried to Montrose, and found Bob reclining in his jail cell reading a magazine—with the cell door unlocked and hanging wide-open. Max was astounded, and said, "This is the first time I ever heard of a prisoner being imprisoned behind an open cell door." Bob explained that the authorities knew he would not try to escape.[22]

Bob Parker was forced to stand trial over the accusations of the rancher. Max's appearance made a world of difference in impacting the justice system in Montrose. He was a respected property owner, a man with integrity and credibility when testifying in front of a judge and jury. Other character witnesses for Bob also had their say. He had made many friends in Telluride, and would always make friends wherever he went, which would greatly assist him in the future as he evaded the law.

The judgment was rendered, and Bob was acquitted of any wrongdoing. He could not have stolen his own horse. No record exists to document whether money changed hands between the Parkers and the rancher for boarding Cornish, but the rancher's claim to ownership of the animal had ended without merit.

After the trial, Max tried to persuade Bob to return home to Circleville with him. There can be no doubt that Bob was tempted by the plea, especially when his father related how his siblings were growing up so quickly. In the end, Bob recalled that trapped feeling he had experienced in Utah, and reluctantly declined to leave Colorado. He did pacify his father by telling him that when he had saved up enough money he would be home. With churning emotions, Bob handed his father some cash to give to his mother. Max replied, "Your mother will appreciate the money, but it's no substitute for you."[23]

It has always been a difficult task for researchers to trace those Old West characters, no matter how notable, who crisscrossed the line separating respectable work and banditry, and to determine precisely where they might have spent time, and Bob Parker was a typical example. Bob departed Telluride after the Cornish affair, and his whereabouts cannot be documented. He likely drifted up to Wyoming, possibly moving on to Miles City, Montana, where he may have worked as a ranch hand.[24]

Sometime during Bob's absence, Max and Arthur Parker traveled to Telluride with intentions of opening a livery stable and cashing in on the mining boom. The elevation was too high for Max, however, and he soon returned to Circleville. Arthur remained in Telluride, and made a name for himself as a jockey riding local favorites. During one Fourth of July celebration, Arthur was entered in the featured race of the day. Unfortunately, the horse he was riding lost its footing and Arthur was thrown, breaking his leg. A doctor was immediately summoned, but Arthur never regained consciousness. He died within a few days, likely from a blood clot. By the time this news arrived in Circleville, a stricken Ann and Max Parker and their children realized they could not reach Telluride in time for Arthur's funeral. They would mourn the loss of Arthur in Utah.[25]

In 1887, Bob wandered back to Telluride. The town had continued to grow and prosper in his absence, even constructing a new two-story courthouse made of red brick that matched the color of the surrounding valley walls. Nothing can be found about how Bob Parker made a living at this time, although it can be speculated that he went back to his old job hauling ore from the mines while waiting for a better opportunity to present itself. That opportunity appeared one evening in a saloon, when Bob happened upon another Utah boy about his own age with Mormon roots and they struck up a conversation.[26]

This stranger, who was to become a lifelong friend, introduced himself as Matt Warner, although his real name was Willard Erastus Christiansen. Warner had hastily departed Utah after a fight with another young man over the affections of a girl. He feared that he might have killed his rival and was now wanted for murder. Matt Warner had given up horse stealing as a profession, and was now in the horse racing business. He owned a horse named Betty that had been outdistancing every other horse in the area that was willing to race.[27]

Horse racing on straight tracks that were usually a quarter or half mile in distance was a popular sport of the day, and enjoyed attendance in the hundreds, with thousands of dollars wagered on each match. In one instance, the town of Saguache, Colorado, was so proud of and confident in their local favorite, Red Buck, that they wagered more than $12,000 on one race against a pony of unknown pedigree from New Mexico. Red Buck was soundly defeated, and the town of Saguache nearly went bankrupt.[28]

Matt Warner evidently liked what he saw in this fellow Utahan, and asked Bob Parker to partner with him in his racing endeavor. Bob gladly accepted. At about five-foot-ten, with a lean physique and the reputation as an expert horseman, he would serve as the new jockey for Betty.[29]

Another partner of Matt Warner was a man named Tom McCarty. Facts are few and sketchy about McCarty's early days, but he was known as a veteran rustler and common outlaw who came from a well-to-do family—his father was said to have been a doctor. At age eighteen, he had married Tennie Christiansen, Matt Warner's older sister, but apparently she had passed away at some point. His downfall from the penthouse to the outhouse could be blamed on gambling, which had obliged him to ride on the wrong side of the law in order to finance that obsession.

One day Matt, Bob, and Tom matched Betty against a one-eyed Ute tribe pony called White Face. The winner of this race would be entitled to ownership of the defeated horse. But when Betty, with Bob Parker in the saddle, beat White Face, the Utes protested losing their prize horse and a load of blankets that also had been wagered. One of the warriors went as far as to try to take the blankets from the wagon and make off with them. Hot-tempered Tom McCarty carried a quirt, and brought it into play to severely thrash this young man. The companions of the lashing victim were reaching for their weapons to retaliate when the three white men pulled out their Winchester rifles. The Utes were held at bay while Matt, Tom, and Bob slowly backed away and safely made their escape.

The trio of victorious horse racers holed up in Tom McCarty's cabin near Cortez, Colorado, which they reached just before daylight after riding all night. Hot on their trail were the aggrieved Utes, who, instead of attacking, tried to make a deal to retrieve their lost pony. They would forget about the lashing of their friend and not push the issue any further if the white men would only return White Face to them. Bob, Matt, and Tom attempted to reason with the men, explaining that the horse had been the prize for their winning the race. They were not about to part with this valuable animal. The answer did not sit well with White Face's former owners.

Suddenly one of the Ute men leveled his Winchester at Tom McCarty, who drew his six-shooter. Fire and smoke burst from the barrel of the short gun. The Ute warrior was blown off his horse onto the ground—the shots killing him instantly. The dead man's shocked companions silently loaded the body onto a horse and grudgingly rode away. Apparently nothing more came of this killing, except how it had affected one of the witnesses.[30]

Bob's sister Lula wrote about the shooting: "This went against Bob's grain. Killing wasn't part of the game for him, and he was sick inside."[31]

It could be interpreted that Lula was simply trying to portray her brother as something other than a stereotypical cold-blooded outlaw who would settle his disagreements with a gun. But credence can be found for her words. Butch Cassidy was known never to have killed a man until the day he died, by his own admission and a fact of history as far as researchers can determine, and he used his weapons only for intimidation or protection. The killing of the warrior was probably the first human being Bob Parker had seen shot to death. Unlike many gunfighters and outlaws who received a charge of adrenaline from the act of bloodshed, he had been repulsed by the act. Perhaps the White Face episode, happening at such an impressionable age, had affected him more than could be imagined, and it was then that he had vowed to himself never to kill anyone in cold blood unless absolutely necessary.

It can also be assumed that the thought ran through his mind that his place was not here, where men were killed over a horse race, but back home in Utah, sweating over honest work with livestock and crops. The rustling and other petty crimes in which he had participated apparently were of little consequence to his conscience, but the killing of this Ute warrior was another story altogether. Bob must have had the capacity to either erase it from his mind or come to terms with it, however. He turned his back on home once again, and remained with partners Matt Warner and Tom McCarty.

The three men went on a binge with their accumulated racetrack earnings, and partied until all their money had been wasted on women, whiskey, fashionable clothing, fine dining, and gambling. Suddenly they were broke and without prospects. Everyone in the territory had heard about Betty, and knew better than to challenge her to a race. For all intents and purposes, they had no source of revenue.

Bob and Matt hired on as cowhands at the Spectator Ranch, owned by Harry B. Adsit, located about forty miles west of Telluride. Adsit ran up to five thousand head of cattle, along with a herd of horses, and sold the beef to feed the miners and the horses as working stock to mining companies. Tom McCarty had had his fill of being a cowhand, and returned to his Cortez cabin to contemplate his future.[32]

Before long, however, the idea of cowboying became disagreeable to free spirits Bob and Matt. Whether they just wanted to escape the daily monotony of range work or had other plans in mind cannot be determined. In late winter 1889, they informed Harry Adsit that they were returning home to Utah, and asked for their final wages. Adsit had been so impressed by the wrangler skills demonstrated by the two men that he gave each a recently broke horse as a bonus. Bob Parker left the ranch leading a dappled brown colt.

The two men did not return to Utah, however, and instead headed for Tom McCarty's cabin in Cortez. Matt Warner wrote: "At McCarty's cabin we didn't have a thing to do but talk about our next move." McCarty added: "Having been quiet for so long a time, my restlessness annoyed me. Times being now rather dull and becoming acquainted with men that had no more money than myself, we thought it time to make a raid of some sort."[33]

There was only one logical raid for them to pull off to replenish their empty wallets, at least in their minds—robbing a bank.

On March 30, 1889, there was a raid—or rather an extortion plot—on a Denver bank when a well-dressed gentleman confronted the president of the First National Bank with a vial containing a clear liquid that he claimed was nitroglycerin. Fearing that the building would be blown sky-high, the president handed over $21,000, part of which was a thousand-dollar bill. An accomplice to the man with the nitro was waiting at the doorway, and they made their escape. This crime has been alternately attributed to Tom McCarty and Matt Warner, or Warner and Bob Parker. Both McCarty and Warner in their memoirs denied participation, which, if true, would make it unlikely that Bob was involved.[34]

The first major recorded crime in which Bob Parker was identified as a participant occurred on June 24, 1889, in Telluride. The story was reported in the *Rocky Mountain News*:

> The robbery of the San Miguel Valley Bank of Telluride on Monday by four daring cowboys of the Stockton outfit on the Mancos is one of the boldest affairs of the kind ever known. The four rode over to the bank, and leaving their horses in charge of one of the number, two remained on the sidewalk and the fourth entered the bank and presented a check to the clerk.
>
> As the latter was bending over the desk examining the check this party grabbed him around the neck, pulling his face down on the desk, at the same time admonishing the surprised official to keep quiet on pain of instant death. He then called to his partners on the sidewalk, saying 'Come on, boys, it's all

right.' The boys came in and cleaned up all available cash amounting to $20,750, while their comrade held the trembling clerk over the desk by the neck. When their work was complete the clerk was released and fell in a heap on the floor. Surveying the quaking mass of humanity the robber said he had a notion to shoot him anyway for being such a coward, and then joining his comrades they mounted their horses and rode leisurely away. When they had ridden a couple of blocks they spurred their horses into a gallop, gave a yell, discharged their revolvers and dashed away."[35]

The newspaper story of the robbery has been reprinted here instead of debating the various accounts of eyewitnesses, or that of Tom McCarty or Matt Warner, which document only minor discrepancies in the particulars. There has been no dispute that Matt Warner, Tom McCarty, and Bob Parker participated in this brazen holdup. The identity of the fourth man, if indeed there was a fourth man, has never been revealed, and without evidence it can serve no purpose to name names. It has been believed, however, that Tom remained outside with the horses, while Bob Parker and Matt entered the bank. Matt put his gun under the teller's nose, while Bob filled a sack full of money. Bob also visited the vault and reappeared with what Matt described as "bales of greenbacks and a lotta gold."[36]

The bank robbers raced out of town, and later on the road passed either one or two riders—probably rancher Harry Adsit—who could identify Matt Warner and Bob Parker. They did not stop to pass the time of day, as might be expected, but dug their spurs into their horses' flanks and galloped off.

Warner wrote: "Just that little accident made all the difference in the world to us the rest of our lives. It gave 'em a clue so they could trace us for thousands of miles and for years. Right at that point we broke with our half-outlaw past, became real outlaws, burned our bridges behind us, and had no way to live except by robbing and stealing."[37]

Bob Parker—along with his two partners in crime—was now riding hell-for-leather, heading for Utah and Robbers Roost with a sheriff's posse of armed and angry Telluride citizens hot on their trail.

CHAPTER THREE
THE BOY FROM PENNSYLVANIA

I've got a mule, her name is Sal
Fifteen miles on the Erie Canal
She's a good old worker and a good old pal
Fifteen miles on the Erie Canal

We've hauled some barges in our day
Filled with lumber, coal, and hay
And we know every inch of the way
From Albany to Buffalo

—"Low Bridge"

Harry Longabaugh, the man who became the Sundance Kid, known as the "fastest gun in the West," carved a niche in criminal history as the partner of Butch Cassidy and coleader of the notorious Wild Bunch. But his Baptist upbringing and early hard work ethic gave no indication that he would ever choose to ride the outlaw trail.

Harry was the youngest of five children born to Josiah and Annie Longabaugh, likely in the spring of 1867 in either Mont Clare or Phoenixville, Pennsylvania, two towns that lay on opposite banks of the Schuylkill River about ten miles north of Philadelphia.

The Longabaugh family had its origins in America when Conrad Langenbach emigrated from Germany as an indentured servant to John Hunter aboard the brig *Morning Star*, which docked in the Philadelphia harbor on Christmas Eve, 1772. Conrad was free of his debt to Hunter after five years of working for him in Coventry Township, Chester County, Pennsylvania. He then served his country, along with his brother Balsar, for about two months during the Revolutionary War with the Northampton County Militia. This unit was said to have endured the winter under the command of George Washington at Valley Forge. When he was mustered out of the service, Conrad Langenbach settled in New Hanover, Montgomery County, Pennsylvania, and changed his name to a more Anglo-friendly-sounding "Longabaugh."[1]

In 1781, Conrad married Catharina, who would bear him seven children, the last being Jonas Isaac, who was born in 1789. Jonas would marry Christina Hillbert in 1821, and be blessed with five children, the oldest being Josiah, born on June 4, 1822, in Montgomery County, Pennsylvania. Jonas was a man with property, who counted among his extensive holdings a house on Railroad Street in Phoenixville, as well as two lots and a farm in Chester County.

Josiah, the man who would become the father of the Sundance Kid, married Anne G. "Annie" Place, the daughter of Henry and Rachel (Tustin) Place, on August 11, 1855, in Phoenixville, Pennsylvania. Annie's father was a prominent citizen in that city who served as a member of the Central Union Association, and was a deacon and founding father of the local Baptist church. He also had political connections, and could boast as a personal acquaintance Governor Francis R. Shunk. Josiah and Annie would have five children—Elwood, Samanna, Emma, Harvey, and finally Harry, who was born in the spring of 1867 when the family was living in half a duplex at 122 Jacobs Street on the Schuylkill Canal in Mont Clare.[2]

At the time of Harry's birth, Josiah was working on canal boats with his brother, Michael Longabaugh. Michael was a well-to-do man with a large home in Mont Clare purchased with profits from both his canal boat service and small store. He would ship merchandise from his own store, as well as carry loads of coal and other products to cities as distant as Erie, New York, Boston, and Scranton.

It would stand to reason that with an influential father-in-law and successful brother, Josiah would have found success at some profitable endeavor, but that was not the case. It would not be fair to classify Harry's father as a total ne'er-do-well, but he never held a steady job for long, never owned property, and the family was constantly suffering through hard times. His fortunes as a soldier were no better than civilian life. Mustered into service during the Civil War on November 5, 1863, he served in Company H, 175th Regiment, which had been formed with men from Montgomery County. His time in uniform was quite brief, however, and he was discharged and later granted a pension for "general debility"—in other words, Josiah was plagued by hemorrhoids.[3]

The two Pennsylvania towns where Harry Longabaugh was

reared—Mont Clare and Phoenixville—were populated by blue-collar workers, mainly immigrants of Italian, Irish, and German descent. The village of Mont Clare, formerly known as Quincyville, was located in Upper Providence Township, on the inside bend of the Schuylkill River, which forms the western and southern sides of the village, at the site of the former Jacobs' ford. Mont Clare was a boatman's community, and work centered on the Schuylkill Canal.

Across the river from Mont Clare lay Phoenixville—originally called Manavon—which was an industrial community. The Phoenixville labor market of the nineteenth century was dominated by the powerful local Phoenixville Iron Company. The company board of directors served as officers of the "Iron Bank," and provided the money necessary to open an employees-only general store and housing, a town park, and even donated free family housing to workers who enlisted in the Union Army. By 1881, the Phoenixville Iron Company was using sixty thousand tons of ore annually in its blast furnaces to produce thirty thousand tons of pig iron, and employed fifteen hundred men.

In addition to the great iron and steel mills, Phoenixville was home to a match factory, boiler works, a silk mill, underwear and hosiery factories, and the famous and highly collectible Etruscan majolica pottery. The town owed its diverse growth to its nearby waterways—the broad Schuylkill River was bisected by fast-moving French Creek, which was harnessed for water power.

The Phoenixville ironworks was responsible for manufacturing the Ordnance Rifle, or "Griffen Gun," named after its designer, John Griffen, which gained the reputation of being the best arm of its kind in the service. The gun was adopted by the Federal Ordnance Department in early 1861, and during the Civil War was deployed in the light artillery more than any other weapon. The design of this artillery piece made entirely of wrought iron was recognized by the absence of any discontinuities in the surface of the gun. The Ordnance Rifle was prized for its long-range accuracy—a ten-pound elongated shell could be accurately propelled by a one-pound charge of gunpowder for a distance of about two thousand yards. Artillerymen preferred this wrought-iron piece because it rarely exploded upon firing, as opposed to a cast-iron cannon, which would, and it was one hundred pounds lighter than the ten-pound Parrott rifle, which made it highly mobile. The Phoenixville ironworks produced over one thousand three-inch Ordnance Rifles during the Civil War at a cost of about $350 each. This weapon was highly prized, and always targeted for capture by the Confederate Army.[*]

One can only wonder why Josiah Longabaugh did not prosper along with the town. Perhaps he had a rebellious attitude about being owned by the company store, a trait he may have passed on to son Harry.

Young Harry Longabaugh's life was anything but stable growing up. The family moved from one rental house to another—in either Mont Clare or Phoenixville—while his father changed jobs frequently, working usually as a day laborer, or carpenter, or farmhand. The one constant, however, was religion. Harry's mother in particular made certain that the family filled a pew at the First Baptist Church in Phoenixville every Sunday. Annie also made an effort to hold the family together with frequent home gatherings and devotionals. Harry and his siblings memorized verses from the Holy Bible, and were taught how to live a moral, ethical, and principled life based on the scriptures.

To help support the family, Harry and his brother Harvey from an early age would hire on with their uncle Michael's canal boat service, and drive the mules along the shoreline or pole the boats down the canal. In fact, it would be fair to state that throughout his childhood Harry Longabaugh would have been immersed in the canal culture. He not only resided and worked on those waterways, but would have counted among his closest friends those boys and girls who lived the canal way of life and would share stories about their travels and experiences.

Canal boat children were an essential part of a crew on a family-owned boat. During the spring, summer, and fall, these children would be working on the boat instead of attending school. They would receive whatever education they could absorb during winter, perhaps three or four months at most when the boats were tied up, but work always came first. By contrast, most working-class children would be employed year-round in the factories and mills, and would not attend school at all.

Both boys and girls worked as mule drivers until they were twelve or thirteen years old. At that time, most girls were taken off the towpath, and would be taught the domestic arts by their mothers. These canal girls would often be married by age fourteen. Boys would usually drive the mules or pole the boats until they were eligible to captain their own craft or left the business entirely. On most canals, a boy could become a boat captain at age sixteen if he was married. Some of the children who worked on canal boats were orphans or hired as servants from poor families, which often led to abusive treatment.

The work performed by Harry Longabaugh and the other canal children consisted of long hours and laborious tasks. Children under five or six years of age would spend most of the day playing on deck—the little ones tethered by a rope to prevent them from falling overboard. But children over six would work as mule drivers and lead the animals along the towpath from four a.m., when the canal opened, until ten p.m., when the locks on the canal were closed.

The mule was the most common draft animal used on canals. Livestock were used because powered vessels proved to be harmful to the infrastructure. The wake produced by steamboats would tend to erode the fragile canal banks, and were therefore banned from most waterways. As a result, the captains would utilize towropes and towpaths along the shore that enabled mules to pull the boats to their destination. Speed limits of no more than four miles per hour were strictly enforced to prevent damage to the canal banks.

The preferred animal, the mule, was a sterile hybrid produced by mating a male donkey with a female horse. Mules had many advantages over other beasts of burden, especially over draft horses. They ate and drank less than horses, and could accomplish the work of a horse while consuming one-third less food, which usually consisted of hay and grain mixed with molasses. Mules also were known to be more disease-resistant and more sure-footed. And, as opposed to horses, which would wear out quickly, mules could work at slower, steadier speeds of about two to three miles per hour, as well as cover greater distances and work longer hours.

Mules combined the endurance and intelligence of a donkey with the size and strength of a horse. One mule by itself could pull up to sixty-five tons of freight on water. The animals would begin work at around age three or four, work for perhaps twenty or more years, and live until they were as old as thirty-five. Canal mules would perform their duties from four a.m. to ten p.m.—an eighteen-hour day. These animals, however, were often stubborn and cantankerous, which actually was a self-preservation instinct. A mule would sit down and not budge until completely rested if pushed beyond endurance; otherwise they would work without complaint. Canal companies would breed and raise mules to sell to boat captains, while others were purchased from local farmers and livestock dealers.

Harry Longabaugh and the youngsters who worked as mule drivers would have to rise every morning at three thirty a.m. to feed, brush, and harness the mules in order to have them ready to work when the canal opened at four a.m. If a child was the only driver in the family, he or she would be required to walk the entire day, which would usually be a distance of about twenty-five miles. The only downtime would come when the boat passed through a lock. At the end of the day, the children were responsible for caring for the mule team before they could go to bed for the night. This consisted of removing harnesses, feeding, watering, brushing, and finally stabling the mules. And then the process would begin again in the morning, except for Sundays, which were reserved as days of worship.

In 1880, when he was thirteen, Harry Longabaugh traded one manner of hard labor for another. He left the canals and was sent off to work as a hired servant for the Wilmer Ralston family in neighboring West Vincent Township, about ten miles away from home. The Ralston family farmed more than one hundred acres and ran an extensive horse breeding and raising operation. Harry would usually rejoin his family on Sundays to attend the First Baptist Church in Phoenixville. His brother Harvey was also sent away to work, but, oddly enough, two older children, Elwood and Emma, remained living at home, while the oldest girl, Samanna, was already married and living with her husband.[5]

When he was not working with horses or tilling the soil at the Ralstons' farm, Harry whiled away his free time reading books. On January 31, 1881, he purchased a one-dollar library card from the Young Men's Literary Union. And if a youngster of less than modest means paid that much for the privilege of borrowing books, there was a good chance he was a voracious reader.

At that point in literary history, young people were reading books about animals, travelogues, coming-of-age novels, science fiction, and realistic novels depicting nature. The most influential anti-cruelty-to-animals novel of its time, *Black Beauty* by Anna Sewell, was making a huge impact on society. Harry would have thrilled to the tales of gold mines, Western life, and Native Americans written by Bret Harte, especially the poem "Plain Language from Truthful James," which brought the author national fame, and the short story "The Luck of Roaring Camp." He probably also read *Roughing It* and *The Adventures of Tom Sawyer* by Mark Twain, and *The Underground City* and *Around the World in 80 Days* by Jules Verne.

Later in life, Harry revealed that his favorite book was *Robbery Under Arms* by Rolf Boldrewood (a pseudonym for Thomas Alexander Browne), a classic Australian novel. The theme contains repeated regrets for narrator Dick Marston's crimes, and highlights how seemingly minor offenses can lead to an inescapable criminal life. The story centers on the lovable villains, who are adventurers and thieves but nevertheless with high moral standards of honor and loyalty, and are trapped by circumstances of their own making.[6]

Given the adventurous nature of Harry Longabaugh, it was highly likely that he preferred to stick his nose into the heart-thumping excitement and spine-tingling danger of sensationalized dime novels, which were plentiful at the time. Frank Tousey published what was called the "big six": *Work and Win, Secret Service, Pluck and Luck, Wild West Weekly, Fame and Fortune,* and *The Liberty Boys of '76,* all of which ran thousands of weekly issues apiece. Another major publisher was Street and Smith, which offered *Tip Top Weekly, Brave and Bold Weekly,* and the *New Nick Carter Weekly.*

But there was a good chance that Harry Longabaugh was completely captivated by Western pulps and weeklies that featured stories with generous doses of wildness and gentility, and often portrayed their protagonists as heroic bad men. Harry would have devoured Edward Wheeler's series about that Robin Hood of the Black Hills, "Deadwood Dick," which numbered more than one hundred novels. With stirring titles such as *Deadwood Dick's Doom; or, Calamity Jane's Last Adventure,* these books featured tales of secret maps to gold mines, kidnapped heroines, missing daughters, falsely accused men, and always a nail-biting climax. Other authors like Ned Buntline romanticized real-life outlaws such as Jesse James and Billy the Kid and bolstered the careers of Buffalo Bill Cody and Wyatt Earp with embellished exploits.

Young Harry would have fantasized and role-played as he read, dreaming of riding off to this mysterious Western range of endless adventure and hairbreadth escapes—never imagining that someday he would become as famous as any of those hard-riding, gun-slinging Western outlaws and lawmen.[7]

After two years of working at the Ralston farm, Harry Longabaugh moved back in with his parents, who were living in Phoenixville at 354 Church Street. He was fourteen now, and returned to his studies at the Gay Street School, three blocks from his house. His education up to that point could be called inconstant, to say the least. He had probably received much of his schooling from the books he had chosen to read, which would have at least covered two of the three Rs. In a more practical sense, during his years at the Ralstons' he had become an expert rider and had gained knowledge about caring for livestock of all sorts, especially horses, which would be of great value to him in his future endeavors.[8]

It was at about this time that Harry's oldest brother, Elwood, left home to become a whaler on the ship *Mary & Helen*, based out of San Francisco. Harry and Elwood had enjoyed a close relationship, and the departure of his brother must have hit Harry hard. He would faithfully keep in contact with his brother, and the two would get together occasionally over the years to come.[9]

Harry's other brother, Harvey, stayed around home and worked as a day laborer and carpenter, like his father. One of the projects that Harvey was hired to work on was the now-famous Boardwalk at Atlantic City, New Jersey. Sister Emma remained unmarried and established a successful seamstress company at a time when women were rarely independent or owned businesses—and she would eventually change the spelling of her last name to protect her business from being discriminated against for the crimes committed by her famous outlaw brother. The sibling whom Harry had bonded with more than the others, however, was his oldest sister, Samanna.[10]

Samanna had married Oliver Hallman, who owned a foundry and blacksmith shop that specialized in ornamental wrought iron. In his early teens, Harry had upon occasion worked for his brother-in-law Oliver, and learned ironworking skills to go along with his horse wrangling expertise. Samanna kept the business books for her husband, and over the years within those pages would make handwritten notations about family happenings, especially with respect to Harry. She had been like a mother to Harry as he grew up, and tried to keep track of her wayward brother as best as possible as the years passed. Her closeness to Harry did not go unnoticed by the Pinkerton Detective Agency, which maintained a file on her, and would go as far as to pay a postal clerk to open her mail and spy on her residence located near the post office.[11]

In 1882, at the age of fourteen, Harry accompanied Uncle Michael on a canal boat trip for the purpose of finding a decent job. This excursion could probably be attributed to an intrinsic restlessness that affected Harry, rather than the lack of jobs in his hometown. There would have been plenty of positions around Phoenixville available for such a hardworking, energetic youngster, but for some reason he had decided to seek employment far from home. Samanna noted in the company business books: "Phoenixville June 1882—Harry A. Longabaugh left home to seek employment in Ph. [Philadelphia]. And from their [sic] to N. Y. C. from their [sic] to Boston and from their [sic] home on the 26 of July or near that date."[12]

Either Harry had been unable to secure a job to his liking or there were none available, or there was another, more provocative, reason why he had returned home—as evidenced by Samanna's next entry: "Phoenixville Aug 30th 1882 Harry A. Longabaugh left home for the West. Left home at 14—Church St. Phoenixville below Gay St."

Fourteen-year-old Harry was about to visit the Wild West that he had read and dreamed so much about and was surely itching to experience. He would willingly leave his family and the familiar behind and, barely into his middle teens, travel alone from the train depot in Phoenixville to western Colorado at the invitation of a distant cousin, George Langenbaugh.

George had recently moved his pregnant wife, Mary, and son, Walter, from Illinois to Colorado by covered wagon. He had settled initially in Durango, Colorado, to work on the fledgling town's new irrigation system, but within a year had decided to homestead land about fifty miles to the west near Cortez.

Young Harry arrived at George's southwestern Colorado property to help his cousin raise crops, breed horses, and improve his land by constructing outbuildings and corrals. At this time, Harry once again became the student of a trade, and was taught the finer points of the horse business—trading, breeding, and how to purchase and sell the animals at a reasonable price.[13]

One neighbor of George Langenbaugh was the sprawling LC Ranch, which was situated in nearby McElmo Canyon. This ranch was comprised of unsettled and primitive pastureland that was ideal for grazing the outfit's five thousand head of cattle. Harry was hired on part-time by foreman Henry Goodman, and split his time between the LC bunkhouse and continuing to work now and then for his cousin.

Harry Longabaugh, the boy from Pennsylvania, was on the verge of earning his spurs and becoming a card-carrying member of the Western cowboy fraternity.

The job of cowboying has been romanticized to the point that the perception of a cowboy has become fact. In truth, real cowboys of the Old West bore little resemblance to those dime-store cowboys depicted in motion pictures, television, and most Western novels. In the world of entertainment, these swashbuckling, indestructible men wore big white ten-gallon hats, skintight clothing, and fancy boots, and they sported a six-shooter hanging low on each hip. Not only that, these cowboys spent a great deal of time chasing bad guys, rescuing pretty girls, tearing up saloons, and fighting Native Americans. Rarely did they have time left over to perform the job for which they were paid—herding and tending to cattle.

Honest-to-goodness cowboys wore ordinary work clothes of the day—loose-fitting cotton or flannel shirts and heavy-duty woolen pants, often with buckskin sewn around the seat and upper thighs to help them wear longer. Not until the 1890s did Levi's become popular and replace regular trousers. Serviceable boots featured pointed toes to make it easier to slip the feet through stirrups, along with high heels to hold the boot securely in place. Boots were usually custom-made—cowboys stuck up their noses at ready-made pairs—and would cost about a month's wages. The hat was designed for practicality. The wide brim shaded eyes from the sun, protected the face from rain or low branches while riding, and had common uses, such as fanning a fire or signaling across long distances. Hat designs were exclusive to each region of the country, and a seasoned cowhand could tell what part of the Western range a stranger was from just by looking at the size of the brim and the crease of the crown of his hat.

Other vitally necessary items worn by cowboys were chaps, which were leather pants a cowboy stepped into that protected his legs when riding through mesquite and chaparral thickets, and spurs, worn on the boot heels to encourage a horse to move faster when necessary. As far as six-guns were concerned, most cowboys rarely carried a sidearm, and never two like in the movies, but if a cowboy did have one it was worn high on the hip and used mainly to kill rattlers and other pests or as a means with which to signal. Last but certainly not least was the trademark brightly colored bandanna that protected the neck from sunburn, or served as a dust mask on trail drives, or as earmuffs in the cold, or a tourniquet for snakebites or accidents, or as a washcloth, or as a blindfold to help calm a skittish horse.

But more than simply by dress, a real cowboy was distinctive by the job he was expected to perform—not chasing outlaws or dance hall girls, but working with cows to turn grass into beef for the market. Fourteen-hour days, and often longer, were spent in the saddle or on the ground working with cows—doctoring, herding, branding, and protecting them from predators and rustlers.

Most cowboys were wanderers who were always on the move looking for better range, often changing jobs with the seasons. Young and single, usually in their late teens or early twenties, these men were just not yet ready to settle down, and many adventure seekers who went west to become cowboys were soon disillusioned. Cowpunching was not the glamorous endeavor they had envisioned or read about in dime novels. Quite a few young men worked less than a year before changing careers, while others stayed for perhaps six or seven years before finding a job in a town or saving up a grubstake to start their own spread. Only a few stalwart men would remain in the bunkhouse for more than a decade.

The reason for this short period of employment can be found in the job description. Cowboying was a tough, sweaty, dirty, dangerous, low-paying job that offered little compensation other than the coveted title of "cowboy." This reward was earned for backbreaking work that extracted from the normal human countless gallons of sweat, often pints of blood, if not layers of flesh and other knuckle-busting physical agonies. Why? Because the cowboy was the cow's natural-born enemy, and that made for an adversarial relationship that created incidents detrimental to both of them.

Cowboys ruled over cows, and put those beasts through paces

they did not want to go through—like chasing them from pasture to pasture whooping and hollering and swinging a rope in their faces, or cramming medication down their throats when needed, or notching their ears and sticking a hot poker on their hide for identification, or lopping off their horns or other body parts more private and personal. The cowboy was required to do those necessary things because a cow could not be trained, or bribed, or coaxed, or reasoned with.

Quite frequently, the cow sought revenge. It would target the cowboy to stomp, gore, kick, trample, or whip with its tail without the slightest provocation or twinge of conscience or fear of retaliation. It was difficult to work around cattle for long without developing a complete vocabulary of colorful curse words and phrases.

But the benefits—in addition to the pay of $30 to $40 a month—included the satisfaction that the job was meaningful, that food was being provided for hungry people. The cowboy was his own boss, able to come and go as he pleased from job to job. He was also privileged to breathe fresh air and feast his eyes daily on scenes of natural beauty most people only dreamed about. Cowboys were truly alive to the sights, smells, and sounds of the outdoors, preferring this free-roaming lifestyle to one among those who marched through life in step at society's pace.[14]

Harry Longabaugh was anxious to fit the description of a cowboy in every respect. He was young and had a yearning to wander, and it was possible that his cowboying travels brought him in contact with his future Wild Bunch partners in crime.

Although the exact dates or places cannot be determined, it was probable that during this time Harry would have known that living, working nearby, or passing through the territory were the likes of Tom McCarty, Matt Warner, Bill Madden, and the man with whose name his would be indelibly linked throughout history, Bob Parker, alias Butch Cassidy. McCarty's cabin, where Tom, Matt, and Bob would brainstorm their criminal activities, was located less than a mile from Cousin George's place.

Harry must have heard about the exploits of Betty, the famous racehorse owned by Matt Warner, and the shoot-out over the Ute horse named White Face. Horse races were often held in McElmo Canyon, where the LC was located, and Harry likely attended as a spectator. Several of the men, including Bob Parker, may have worked briefly for the LC Ranch and occupied the same bunkhouse as Harry Longabaugh. And, just as Bob Parker had received an education from Mike Cassidy on the LC Ranch, Harry would have been tutored by the yarns spun by the hard-riding, worldly cowhand bunkies whom he desired to emulate.[15]

Harry may have also run across Bob or Matt—or renewed acquaintances—in Telluride, which lay about eighty miles north of Cortez. Satisfying a need for good horseflesh in the flourishing community, George and Harry likely drove a herd of horses up to that mining city on occasion and sold them to the mine companies.

Another chance meeting of the future partners could have happened through Bob Parker's brother Dan. While Harry was working at the LC Ranch for Henry Goodman, the outfit was embroiled in a feud with the rival Carlisle Ranch, where Dan Parker worked as a hand. Some LC sheep turned up missing, and were found slaughtered with the hides hung out to dry. Suspicion rested on Dan Parker and a coconspirator, in some reports. The Carlisle foreman found the skins and hid them in a cabin in town. An LC cowboy noticed the hides and reported the theft to his boss. Allegedly Dan Parker caught wind of that report, and quickly switched the LC hides with hides wearing the Carlisle brand. Foreman Henry Goodman arrived to find only Carlisle hides, and angrily ordered their return, which ended the episode. Although no evidence exists—nor rhyme or reason for a few historians to point to his involvement—some accounts report that Harry Longabaugh had been an accomplice of Dan Parker in the theft.[16]

The question of whether Harry had met Bob, Matt, or Tom around that time cannot be answered, but what was certain was that Harry had grown restless around Cortez. He was anxious to ride over the horizon and explore this Western range about which he had read so much.

At this point in Harry Longabaugh's life, his movements are virtually impossible to accurately document. Historians are rarely able to follow the lives of vagabond cowboys, or, when they become notorious, the comings and goings of outlaws—and Harry, like Bob Parker, was no exception. He was living in the shadows as far as history was concerned. Even Harry's sister Samanna did not know where Harry had wandered during this period.

He may have taken a job as a cowhand to the south near Springer, New Mexico, where the outfit he signed on with was in the midst of a cattle war. Could it have been that Harry used his six-gun in a meaningful manner for the first time to defend his employer's interests? Probably not. No evidence can be found to support such a premise. It appeared that Harry either found New Mexico unappealing or he had no taste for that range war. The job in New Mexico was short-lived, and he soon returned to Cortez. At that time, he may have participated in a ranch posse that pursued thieves who had made off with some of the LC's best animals. During the chase, one of the LC men was shot and killed, which could very well have been Harry's first encounter with violent death.

Harry may have signed on temporarily, as a wandering cowboy, with other outfits both near and far—possibly the Pittsburgh Land and Cattle Company or the Suffolk Cattle Company in Wyoming—before deciding to drift back to Cortez again.

His next departure from his home base was made convenient when he happened upon an outfit from eastern Montana—the N Bar N—that was in the midst of a trail drive from Perico Creek, New Mexico, back home to Little Dry Creek. Pushing seventeen thousand cattle, the outfit's drive was so large it required fifteen chuck wagons that served twelve riders each. Harry was hired on, and headed north on his quest to find his rightful place in the West.[17]

It would usually take four to six months, depending on conditions, to push a herd of cattle from Texas or New Mexico to Montana. Several trails—the most popular being the Chisholm Trail—were well-worn dusty pathways offering water holes and plenty of grass, but they were also rife with danger. Cattle had a tendency to panic during river crossings, and something as insignificant as the flick of a matchstick could send a herd of thousands stampeding in the dark of night. Other perils could come from outlaws, hostile Native Americans, predators, or just a settler with a rifle protecting his fields from passing cattle. Riding accidents were prevalent—and the most common cause of death—and more cowboys were killed by lightning out on the open prairie than were ever killed by outlaws or Native Americans.

Cowboys on horseback surrounded the herd to keep them plodding along toward their destination. The men skirted the edges of this wavering sea of beef and chased strays while shouting at the animals to encourage them to maintain their pace. At night with the cattle bedded down, cowpunchers stood watch and rode slowly around the herd, often singing, humming, or softy whistling, much like a mother would do to calm her baby.

The trail drive may have had a few brief episodes of excitement along the way, but for the most part it was monotonous and uneventful. The cowboys would ride mile after mile eating dust, enduring the blazing sun, ignoring blisters and abrasions, fighting saddle soreness, and dreaming about the end of the trail, when they could let loose in town to celebrate their freedom.[18]

For Harry Longabaugh that end of the trail was pasture owned by the N Bar N Ranch in the vicinity of Miles City, Montana.

The Home Land & Cattle Company—the N Bar N—had been established in 1885 in Missouri by brothers William F. and Frederick G. Niedringhaus. The brothers were involved in a St. Louis enameled-kitchenware company as well as a silver mine in Utah, both highly profitable enterprises. They had used capital from those businesses to invest in a Montana ranch, then known as the Anchor THL, located at Little Dry Creek about sixty miles north of Miles City, and soon changed its name to the N Bar N.[19]

The brothers had established satellite ranches in the south where they would buy the cattle, then winter them on ranges in New Mexico, and drive them north in the spring. In the first year the ranch was under its new owners, more than sixty-five thousand head of cattle were fattening up on Montana pastures under the watchful eye of about 150 cowboys.

There was a distinct possibility that Harry was riding for the N Bar N at the same time that Bob Parker was either residing in Miles City or was employed as a cowpuncher for that same huge N Bar N enterprise or at another local ranch. One provocative notion would be that Harry and Bob may have ridden together and shared a bunkhouse at this time, or at least reacquainted themselves from their days in southwestern Colorado. The two men did possess a mutual love of horses, a factor that could have brought them together at any time. In either case, Bob could have been riding on the wrong side of the law in Montana, and, as far as it was known, Harry had not yet chosen to break the law.

Circumstances could change in a heartbeat, however, and perhaps every man possesses a heart of larceny when his survival is at stake. In the case of Harry Longabaugh, a desperate situation would call for desperate action, and this boy from Pennsylvania was about to make a decision based on desperation that would change his life forever.

CHAPTER FOUR
SUNDANCE

My friends and relations, they live in the Nation,
They know not where their boy has gone,
He first came to Texas and hired to a ranchman
Oh, I'm a young cowboy and I know I've done wrong.

Go gather around you a crowd of young cowboys,
And tell them the story of this my sad fate;
Tell one and the other before they go further
To stop their wild roving before 'tis too late.

—"The Cowboy's Lament"

Western ranchers for decades had bred their cattle not only for beef-bearing characteristics but also for qualities that would enable the animals to survive in the worst of weather. Although spring flooding and summer droughts took their toll, winter was extremely difficult for the health and well-being of cattle. Mostly on their own on the open range, the animals fended for themselves for food, grazing through snow and icy conditions. Cowboys had no way to deliver hay to herds over such far-reaching distances. When the snow was deep, younger and weaker animals struggled to find enough subsistence to survive. Stronger stock could paw through the snow and expose anything edible, albeit meager pickings, unless the snow melted under the sun and then froze again to form a hard crust that could not always be adequately penetrated.

Either way, the rancher would put out his stock to pasture and then hold his or her breath, praying for the months to pass and a warm Chinook wind from the southwest to arrive and melt the snow. There would always be winter losses, occasionally in the hundreds, but no one was prepared for the devastation of that legendary winter of 1886–87.

The hot summer of 1886 brought no rain, creating drought conditions and choking the life out of great numbers of livestock. Many desperate ranchers dumped cattle they could not feed on the market for whatever price they could get. Others drove herds up from Texas, overgrazing already stressed pastures.

Consequently, prices fell dramatically, and cattlemen could do nothing but hope to weather this dire situation until the market rebounded. To make matters even worse, wildfires during autumn scorched the dry, tinderbox prairie and devoured what little remained of the grass that cattle desperately needed for grazing. Then came "the Big Die-up," as it was informally called—or, more commonly, the Great Blizzard of 1886–87.

On November 16, an arctic wind blew in, lowering temperatures to twenty below, and at least six inches of snow fell to blanket Wyoming and Montana. Three weeks later another severe blizzard struck with the full force of nature's wrath. On January 9, a third major blizzard arrived and dumped an inch of snow an hour, while temperatures plummeted to as low as sixty-eight degrees below zero in some places throughout the region. Worse yet, just when the skies would begin to clear, the clouds would build up again and heavy snow would intermittently fall. It did not make a difference whether cattle were located in distant pastures or close to the home ranch. There was little or no feed for them, natural or grown hay, and if there had been some, there was no way to get it to them through the deep snow, barbed-wire winds, and freezing temperatures.

On January 15, thermometers at the N Bar N and most of eastern Montana read forty-six degrees below zero. On January 28, heavy snow fell for seventy-two hours straight without stopping or even easing up. Never before had this area endured such low temperatures combined with constant, driving snows. Ranchers were aware that something dramatic was happening, and could only hold their collective breath and fear the worse. Still, they hoped for the best when the skies turned blue and they prepared to ride out and investigate the damage.

By the end of February, a Chinook finally arrived with its warm, dry wind that pushed out the cold and thawed the snow. Skies continued to clear, and the snow steadily melted. Within a week the cattlemen had their answer—and no one was prepared for what was revealed.

The devastation was like nothing before seen, not even in the worst of winters by veteran ranchers. The open range was littered with tens of thousands of dead or dying cattle, their bloated carcasses dotting the landscape for miles and miles—virtually everywhere anyone could ride. Every avenue to pastures remained blocked by snow, and they could only imagine the dreadful scene in those places. Snowdrifts had piled up to heights of more than one hundred feet in many areas, filling ravines and gulches and laying waste to the vulnerable grasslands. Some ranch houses, barns, and outbuildings were completely buried under the snow.

In addition to bodies of cows and horses, searchers encountered more macabre scenes—corpses of cowboys, sheepherders, and Native Americans who had frozen to death. No figures have been calculated, and true numbers could never have been determined, but suffice it to say that countless people who never returned home that winter fell victim to nature's fury.

An estimated 90 percent of range stock in Wyoming and Montana had perished in the snow and cold, and many ranchers were permanently out of business or compelled to sell what remained to big corporations or foreign-owned outfits. The huge N Bar N Ranch reportedly lost about 75 percent of its herd—around forty thousand head—but the Niedringhaus brothers vowed to rebuild.

Desperation forced honest men to turn to rustling in an effort to hold on to their homesteads. The day of branding mavericks was back. Countless cowboys who had been laid off from their jobs did whatever necessary to survive. They would often steal mavericks, use a running iron to brand them, and then drive the animals to buyers near railroad towns, where no questions were asked about ownership.[1]

One interesting story that emerged from that Great Blizzard was about Jesse Phelps, foreman of the OH Ranch in the Judith Basin of central Montana, and one his cowboys. The cow boss had received a letter from Louis Kaufman, the ranch's owner, who lived in Helena, Montana, asking how their herd had weathered the winter. Phelps was struggling over how to break the news to the owner that his animals had been wiped out. As he wrote the letter, one of his cowboys handed him a sketch depicting a single steer standing alone and forlorn in deep snow with its backbone and every rib showing. Wolves lurked in the background, and the steer's tail had been chewed to a nub.

Phelps was so impressed with the drawing that he decided to forget about writing the letter and just sent the artwork to Kaufman. The cowboy, Charles M. Russell, named the rendering *Waiting for a Chinook (The Last of the 5000).*

Kaufman gave the sketch to a saddle-maker friend named Roberts, who displayed it in the window of his shop. Eventually, Roberts printed and sold thousands of postcards of Charlie Russell's most famous work.[2]

There was a good chance that by the time of the Great Blizzard of 1886–87, Harry Longabaugh had already been laid off by the N Bar N. The previous summer's drought had sent many cowboys riding the grub line from ranch to ranch looking for a job, and he was probably one of them. By his own admission—whether truthful or not—Harry claimed that he had headed for the Black Hills region of South Dakota during this period to work for food and shelter until cattle markets improved and the big ranches were hiring again.[3]

At the time of the winter meltdown during February 1887, however, Harry, now destitute and desperate for work, had decided to head back to the N Bar N and see whether he could get his old job back, or at least reach friends who might stake him until jobs were available. His ride from the Black Hills took him right through the heart of the Three V Ranch, or Western Ranches, Inc.—known for its VVV brand—which was located in the northeastern corner of Wyoming, with range that extended to the borders of South Dakota and Montana. This spread was owned by a group of English investors, and managed by John Clay, an influential member of the Wyoming Stock Growers Association and the exclusive Cheyenne Club.

During these hard times, Harry Longabaugh certainly fit the picture of a down-and-out saddle tramp, a cowboy who had sold most or all of his personal belongings other than necessities in order to eat. All he wanted was the chance to work cattle once again. Harry directed his horse north, passing through the winter quarters of the Three V, located on Crow Creek, north of the town of Sundance, Wyoming.

On February 27, 1887, Harry, presumably out of desperation, stole a light gray horse with a J branded on the left shoulder, a saddle, and a bridle that belonged to Three V wrangler Alonzo Craven, along with a revolver owned by another cowboy named Jim Widner. The novice outlaw lit out with his ill-gotten loot, hightailing it northwest toward familiar surroundings at Miles City, Montana.[4]

Three V Ranch manager John Clay possessed a special dislike for wandering cowboys who rode the range from job to job rather than becoming respectable and honest ranch hands who settled down and took root in one place. Clay reported the theft to Crook County sheriff Jim Ryan, and made it clear in no uncertain terms that he expected Ryan to ride down this thief without delay.

The perpetrator of the crime had been described as a "smooth-faced, grey-eyed boy," which certainly fit twenty-year-old Harry to a T. Although descriptions of Harry Longabaugh varied at this time, he was probably about five feet, ten inches in height with a light facial complexion, light hair, and blue or gray eyes. Ryan dispatched a description of the young thief, along with a description of the stolen horse with the J brand on its shoulder, to towns around the region.[5]

It was not long before his efforts were rewarded. In early April, word was received in Sundance that this alleged horse thief, along with the stolen horse, had been spotted in Miles City, almost three hundred miles away. Ryan, likely at the urging of ranch manager John Clay, immediately dropped everything else and traveled to that city to apprehend the culprit.

On April 8, 1887, Sheriff Jim Ryan placed Harry Longabaugh under arrest for the Three V thefts. Ryan temporarily housed his prisoner in the Miles City jail, located at Main and Seventh streets on the north side of the courthouse. Apparently Harry did not put up any resistance and went along quietly to the local jail, where he was locked inside a cell for the first time in his life.[6]

Harry would have had plenty of time to reflect on his criminal behavior, but there was no indication that he was remorseful or had resigned himself to his fate. He had been a wandering cowboy, free of any encumbrance, and accustomed to laying his bedroll wherever he pleased and then moving on at will. His thoughts would have been of the wide-open range, and how he could get back to this vast frontier where he was always comfortable and secure.

On April 12, four days after Harry was taken into custody, Sheriff Ryan, accompanied by a shackled and handcuffed Longabaugh, boarded a Northern Pacific train and embarked on what could only be called an unexplainable odyssey. Instead of returning directly to Sundance, Wyoming, this train was headed for St. Paul, Minnesota, nearly seven hundred miles away.

The *Yellowstone Daily Journal* considered this roundabout itinerary quite odd, to say the least. The newspaper reported on April 12: "Sheriff Ryan departed with the prisoner this morning bound for Sundance. The route taken by the sheriff would seem to be a long one; Miles City to St. Paul. St. Paul to the railroad terminus in the Black Hills and thence by stage to Sundance, a distance of nearly 2,000 miles. Sundance is less than 300 miles across country from here." Possibly Sheriff Jim Ryan had pressing business around the St. Paul area—personal or otherwise—and viewed this trip on official business as an opportunity to attend to those matters. No explanation has ever been given for this strange behavior on the part of the sheriff.[7]

Ryan's apparent nonchalance about bringing his prisoner along on this long journey worked to the advantage of Harry Longabaugh. While the train rolled down the tracks somewhere near Duluth, Minnesota, Sheriff Jim Ryan felt the call of nature and retired to the restroom in the back of the coach. Harry hurriedly picked the locks on his shackles and handcuffs and made his escape—by leaping off the moving train.

Evidently no one in the coach wanted to play hero and try to detain the escaping prisoner. Some accounts suggest that Harry had an accomplice, perhaps even Butch Cassidy, who may have been in Miles City at this time, but there was no evidence to confirm that theory. In addition, Harry would demonstrate his ability to escape handcuffs in the future.

Sheriff Ryan ordered the train stopped immediately, and a frantic search of the area was conducted. But Harry Longabaugh was nowhere to be found. The train had a schedule to keep, and the sheriff was informed that they could wait no longer. A disgusted and disheartened Jim Ryan reboarded the train and resumed his journey. He would eventually return to Sundance, Wyoming, and place a $250 reward for the capture of horse thief Harry Longabaugh.[8]

Harry did not make his way to a secure hideout in Robbers Roost or ride out of the territory entirely. Instead, he inexplicably returned to Miles City, the very same place where he had been arrested and temporarily incarcerated.

No explanation has ever been offered for this questionable course of action. Harry assuredly was not a fool or a person who would flaunt himself before the law and dare them to catch him. But considering that decision, there could be only one reason why a healthy twenty-year-old man would risk arrest by returning to the place where he had recently been taken into custody—a girl. No evidence exists to confirm this theory, but the raging hormones of an infatuated male of the species have been known to provoke rash behavior. And Harry Longabaugh had been undeniably rash in risking a return to Miles City, where the certainty of his capture was only a matter of time.

It cannot be determined whether Harry was aware at this point in time that his mother, Annie Place Longabaugh, had died during May. He did not return home for the funeral, but was lying low while concentrating on keeping out of the hands of the law. His eventual capture in a place where he was quite well-known, however, was inevitable.

The arrest occurred on June 6, when Harry was located by Deputy Sheriff E. K. "Eph" Davis and stock inspector W. Smith on the N Bar Ranch in Powderville, Montana. The N Bar was neighbor to the N Bar N, and although Harry was not employed there at the time, he would have been familiar with the lay of the land. He had probably been fingered by a cowhand he had ridden with while working at the ranch. The *Miles City Big Horn Sentinel* reported on June 11, 1887: "Lombaugh

[sic], the man who escaped from Sheriff Ryan in Sundance was arrested at the Newman ranch, on Powder River."[9]

The hour was late, so Deputy Sheriff Davis and Stock Inspector Smith handcuffed the prisoner and escorted him to an N Bar line shack, where they shackled him to the wall. The three men would spend the night there at that cabin on the stage route between Miles City and Deadwood and wait until morning for the next stage. Harry Longabaugh, however, was about to attempt another "Harry Houdini" act. What happened next was reported in the *Yellowstone Daily Journal* under the headline:

HE PLAYED 'POSSUM
How Deputy Sheriff E. K. Davis
Fooled a Fly Young Criminal
He Had in Charge

THE ASTONISHING RECORD OF CRIME
Perpetrated By Harry Longabaugh
In Three Weeks

On Saturday, Deputy Sheriff Davis, together with Stock Inspector Smith, made a most important arrest near the N-bar ranch on Powder River. After his escape from Sheriff he [Harry Longabaugh] made his way back to Montana. After Mr. Davis had made the arrest he took three six-shooters from the bold young criminal and shackled him and handcuffed him with some patent lock bracelets which were warranted to hold anything until unlocked by the key and which the manufacturers offered a premium if they could be opened otherwise. Eph Davis had heard a good deal of Longabaugh's prowess in effecting escape, and after taking all due precautions when night closed in upon them he lay down in one corner of the shack and

Mr. Smith in another, the kid between them. Smith was tired out and soon fell to sleep and Davis played "possum," keeping an eye on the prisoner. Soon as he thought everyone was asleep the kid, shackled and manacled as he was, managed to free himself and rising stealthily approached the window and raised it and was about to make a break for liberty when sly old Eph thought it was time for him to take a hand and rising on his elbow with a cocked six-shooter in his hand he said in a quiet tone of voice, 'Kid, your [sic] loose, ain't you?' then called to Smith. The kid dropped back as though he was shot and it is needless to add that the officers did not sleep at the same time during the rest of the night. Resolving not to lose his prisoner or reward this time, Sheriff Irvine telegraphed Sheriff Ryan asking what he will give for the Kid laid down in Sundance. Talk about the James boys, this fellow has all the necessary accomplishments to outshine them all and Tom Irvine considers him one of the most daring and desperate criminals he had ever had to deal with.[10]

That was quite an embellished reputation for a young man who had only the alleged theft of a horse, a saddle, and a six-gun and an escape on his criminal record. Both the newspaper and Deputy Davis had developed an interest in Harry, however, due to a rash of robberies at ranches around the Miles City area that had coincidentally occurred during the month after Harry had escaped from the train. The items taken were the same as those Harry had stolen at the Three V Ranch—horses, saddles, and six-shooters. Naturally, Harry came under suspicion for those thefts, and the newspaper had practically come right out and accused him of being the culprit.

Harry, sitting in his solitary cell at the jail, read the newspaper article about himself and was highly offended. He took umbrage at the accusation that he was one of the most dangerous outlaws in the West. Taking up pen and paper, he responded with a letter to the editor that read:

In your issue of the 7th inst. I read a very sensational and partly untrue article, which places me before the public not even second to the notorious Jesse James. Admitting that I have done wrong and expecting to be dealt with according to the law and not by false reports from parties who should blush with shame to make them, I ask a little of your space to set my case before the public in a true light. In the first place I have always worked for an honest living; was employed last summer by one of the best outfits in Montana and don't think they can say aught against me, but having got discharged last winter I went to the Black Hills to seek employment—which I could not get—and was forced to work for my board a month and a half, rather than to beg or steal. I finally started back to the vicinity of Miles City, as it was spring, to get employment on the range and was arrested at the above named place and charged with having stolen a horse at Sundance, where I was being taken by Sheriff Ryan, whom I escaped from by jumping from the cars, which I judged were running at the rate of 100 miles an hour. After this my course of outlawry commenced, and I suffered terribly for the want of food in the hope of getting back south without being detected, where I would be looked upon as I always had been, and not as a criminal. Contrary to the statement in the Journal, I deny having stolen any horses in Canada and selling them near Benton, or any place else, up to the time I was captured, at which time I was riding a horse which I bought and paid for, nor had I the slightest idea of stealing any horses. I am aware that some of your readers will say my statement should be taken for what it is worth, on account of the hard name which has been forced upon me, nevertheless

it is true. As for my recapture by Deputy Sheriff Davis, all I
can say is that he did his work well and were it not for his
"playing possum" I would now be on my way south, which I
hoped to go and live a better life.

Harry Longabaugh[11]

Harry's letter had tainted the jury pool to the point that it would have been unlikely to convict him for any crime around Miles City. Consequently, Davis wired Sheriff Jim Ryan and told him that if he still wanted this desperado named Harry Longabaugh, he could come get him. Ryan arrived on June 19, and headed back to Sundance with his prisoner. This time Ryan took the direct stage without any detours.

The *Yellowstone Daily Journal* reported: "Longabaugh was securely shackled and handcuffed, the shackles being made of steel and riveted with steel rivets, and as they got aboard Ryan informed the kid that he was going to land him or his scalp in Sundance jail. The kid gave him fair warning that he intended to escape and told him to watch him but not be too rough on him." Whether Harry would have actually forewarned the sheriff was questionable, given his future actions. But he certainly was not done any favors by that newspaper that wrote their articles in the style of dime novels.[12]

The two men arrived at their destination without incident on June 22. Harry Longabaugh was placed in a jail cell, and booked on suspicion of larceny for stealing from the two Three V cowboys. Harry was not idle in his cell, however, and continued his attempts to escape. At one point, he and a fellow prisoner named William McArthur were able to remove a bolt from a hinge on their cell door, but were discovered before they could open the door. The jail was only three months old and likely had the latest devices to hold a prisoner, which would have presented a challenge for Harry. After that bolt incident had been discovered, Sheriff Ryan undoubtedly doubled his efforts to watch Harry Longabaugh.[13]

On August 2, 1887, the fall judicial term of the U.S. District court for the Territory of Wyoming was called into session. The following day, Harry Longabaugh was indicted by the grand jury on three counts of grand larceny:

> True Bill #33—Indictment of Grand Larceny. One horse of the value of Eighty Dollars ($80.00) of the personal goods and chattels of Alonzo Craven then and there being found, then and there feloniously did steal, take and carry away, ride away, drive away and lead away contrary to the form of the Statute in such case made and provided and against the peace and dignity of the Territory of Wyoming.
> True Bill #34—Indictment for Grand Larceny. [No particulars given.]
> True Bill #44—Indictment for Grand Larceny. One Revolver of the value of thirty Dollars of the personal goods and Chattels of James Widner, then and there feloniously, did steal, take and carry away contrary to the form of the Statute in such case made and provided and against the peace and dignity of the Territory of Wyoming.[14]

Judge William L. Maginnis determined that Harry could not afford to pay for an attorney, and appointed Joseph Stotts, who would later be elected to the state legislature, to defend him. Stotts was opposed by prosecutor Benjamin F. Fowler, who would go on to become a U.S. attorney for Wyoming and state attorney general.

Harry initially chose to plead not guilty to the charges, but his lawyer wisely advised him not to risk a jury trial. Horse thieves were not the most popular defendants in Western towns, and he just might find himself sentenced to a lengthy term in prison at a jury trial. But if he would agree to plead guilty to just one indictment, number thirty-three, horse stealing, the other two indictments would be dropped in a plea-bargain agreement. This would be his first conviction—as far as anyone knew—and the judge would take that fact into consideration. Harry agreed to plead guilty to that one count.

On August 5, 1887, the court transcript pertaining to Harry's case read: "The defendant Harry Longabaugh was this day brought before the court, and having been asked by the court if he had anything to say why judgment and sentence should not be pronounced against him upon the plea of guilty in this cause says he has nothing to say; the court thereupon pronounced sentence upon said plea as follows: the sentence of the court is that you HARRY LONGABAUGH be confined in the place designated by the penitentiary commissioner of the Territory of Wyoming as a penitentiary for the term of eighteen months at hard labor."[15]

Harry had caught a break with the date of his sentencing. Had he been sentenced prior to March 8, 1887, he would have been shipped to Joliet, Illinois, for incarceration due to an agreement with the Territory of Wyoming and the State of Illinois for prisoners with terms longer than six months. As it was, the penitentiary at Laramie was overcrowded, and the Wyoming Board of Penitentiary Commissioners had designated certain Wyoming counties as "territorial penitentiaries," one of which was the newly built jail at Sundance, and the local sheriffs as "wardens." Harry Longabaugh would be serving his sentence in familiar surroundings right there at Sundance, Wyoming.[16]

Incidentally, Harry's court-appointed public defender received $25 for each of the three indictments, and the judge was paid $10.95 from the coffers of the Territory of Wyoming.[17]

Harry was placed in a jail cell at Sundance with William McArthur, a fellow horse thief who had also been sentenced to eighteen months. Harry was a known commodity when it came to escape attempts, and for that reason Sheriff Jim Ryan made certain that he was under constant surveillance. But on May 1, 1888, when the jailor, a man named Daley, was delivering the evening meal, Harry and another prisoner, Jim O'Connor, jumped him.

The *Sundance Gazette* reported: "Just before 6 o'clock, as Jailor

Daley was taking supper to the prisoners in the county jail, he was suddenly assaulted in the hallway by Jim O'Connor and Harry Longabaugh, two of the prisoners who had effected their escape from the cells. Mr. Daley grappled Longabaugh (the 'kid') and succeeded in overpowering him and returned him to his cell. Longabaugh, or 'the kid' is the slippery cuss who gave Sheriff Ryan so much trouble, while bringing him to this place from Miles City. He is serving out a sentence of 18 months for stealing a horse on Crow Creek two years ago." O'Connor did escape, but was captured within a few hours and returned to jail.[18]

There would be a couple of other futile escape attempts by Harry, which probably contributed to the fact that he did not receive a pardon and an early release. Bill McArthur, for example, served only fourteen months of his eighteen-month sentence due to good behavior.

Apparently Harry did keep his nose clean throughout the final part of his sentence. In January 1889—one month before his scheduled release date—a petition was filed requesting a full pardon for horse thief Harry Longabaugh. The present Crook County prosecutor, H. A. Alden, wrote to Governor Thomas Moonlight and Colin Hunter, the secretary of the Board of the Prison Commission, with an endorsement from the sheriff, stating in part: "We have forwarded to the Governor a petition for the pardon of Harry Longabaugh whose term will expire on the 5th of February. I should have sent it to you but fearing that you might be away from home and not get it in time I forwarded it directly to him. The Sheriff tells me that you will assist in obtaining a pardon so that the boy may be restored to his civil rights."[19]

It was not until February 4, one day before Harry was released from prison, that the governor responded. "He is still under 21 years of age, and his behavior has been good since confinement, showing an earnest desire to reform. Therefore, I do hereby grant Harry Longabaugh a full and complete pardon."[20]

Harry probably never laid eyes on the pardon document, which would not have arrived before his jail cell was unlocked and he walked out a free man. Whether it would have mattered to him was also questionable. He had walked out of jail to freedom, and probably did not care whether his rights had been restored or not at that precious moment.

The *Sundance Gazette* wrote on February 8, 1889: "The term of 'Kid' Longabaugh expired on Tuesday morning, and the young man at once hired [sic] himself to the Hills, taking the coach for Deadwood."[21]

The newspaper report was correct. Harry bought a stagecoach ticket for Deadwood, the closest town offering all the pleasurable vices a twenty-one-year-old could want after being locked up for eighteen months. He probably had friends in Deadwood from his stay a couple of years earlier. Whether these friends were reputable or not can be answered by his next brush with the law.

On or about May 17, Harry was staying at a dugout on Oil Creek, thirty-five miles north of Sundance, with three men of questionable character. One of his associates, Bob Minor, also known as Buck Hanby, was a wanted man—wanted for murder, no less. Without warning, the men in the dugout were surprised by the presence of lawmen who had come to arrest Minor for his crime. Minor did not intend to go quietly, and went for his gun. Deputy Sheriff James Swisher, however, was faster on the draw. Swisher slapped leather and fired his six-shooter. Minor fell dead.

Harry Longabaugh and his companions did not intend to get shot for defending Minor, and kept their hands away from their revolvers. Harry, however, was affected by the killing enough to utter a threat toward Deputy Swisher. The deputy backed away from the volatile situation, and returned to town. Once there, he swore out a warrant for Harry's arrest on the charge of threatening a peace officer. This was a minor offense in Wyoming Territory, and rarely resulted in a conviction. But Harry was not about to take chances. By the time Swisher had sworn out the complaint, Harry had ridden out of the territory rather than face arrest and incarceration.[22]

The next movements of Harry Longabaugh cannot be accurately chronicled. One source wrote that he returned to his cousin George's ranch in the Cortez, Colorado, area, and then may have teamed up with Bob Parker, Matt Warner, and Tom McCarty to rob the San Miguel Valley Bank in Telluride. A remote possibility exists that Harry could have been an accomplice to that robbery, but it is highly unlikely.[23]

Harry was probably spooked enough by the shooting of Bob Minor—and the knowledge that his threat to the deputy who had killed his companion would not be taken lightly—that he thought it best to go straight for a while. Eighteen months was a long prison term for a young man, and he wanted to experience life on the outside—and perhaps his conscience got the best of him. After all, Harry had been raised in the Phoenixville Baptist Church, and his mother, now deceased, had always preached to him about right and wrong. Witnessing the killing of another man, especially a friend or companion, could make any man reflective and thoughtful about his future pathway in crime.

Harry rode north, finding a job as a cowboy with the John T. Murphy Cattle Company near Lavina, Montana, about fifty miles north of Billings. The following spring he moved to a ranch near Malta in Valley County, Montana, where he broke wild broncos.[24]

After that stint, Harry moved north of the border to Alberta, Canada, and broke broncos for the Bar U Ranch, located near High River, about thirty-five miles south of Calgary. One of the biggest spreads in the province, the Bar U had a government contract to provide beef for the Blackfoot tribe. Harry may have landed his job due to his prior friendship with the foreman, Everett Johnson, with whom he had been acquainted at the Powder River Cattle Company in Wyoming. In November 1891, Harry would serve as best man at Johnson's marriage in High River. Harry also hired on part-time with a railroad contractor who was building track from Calgary to Fort Macleod.[25]

Harry's reputation in Canada was one of a respected cowhand, but telltale signs gave some suspicions about this young man. One fellow cowboy noticed the hacksaw blade that Harry had hidden under his saddle, and assumed that such a tool would be used only by a burglar or escape artist.[26]

Also, in August 1891, Harry had a warrant sworn out against him in Calgary on the charge of "cruelty to animals." Someone may have taken offense to the way he went about breaking a certain horse, and complained to authorities. Although the Northwest Mounted Police arrested Harry, evidently nothing came of the warrant or the arrest.[27]

Otherwise, Harry was a model citizen, even a minor hero. According to fellow cowhand Fred Ings, Harry was a "thoroughly likeable fellow . . . a favorite with everyone," and "no one could have been better behaved or more decent." Perhaps the glowing character reference the cowboy offered had something to do with the fact that Harry had acted with bravery when Ings found himself in dire trouble.[28]

Harry and Fred were out on a large roundup at the Bar U when an unexpected blizzard blew in. Apparently Harry made it to safety, but Ings became lost in the ensuing whiteout.

Risking freezing to death in the frigid storm, Harry Longabaugh rode through the blinding, drifting snow and located his friend. Visibility by that time was near zero, and Harry advised Ings that they should just let their horses have their heads and hope their instincts would take them back to the camp. It was a frightful ride that took most of the night, but, sure enough, the horses and their snow-covered, frozen riders found their way, and the two men were saved. Harry had courageously put his own life on the line to make sure that Fred Ings returned safely.[29]

Harry's next venture would suggest that he had stashed away some money, or had saved wisely. In early 1892, he bought into a saloon at the Grand Hotel in Calgary, with partner Frank Hamilton. The partnership soon went sour, however, when the two men became embroiled in a dispute over a horse that Harry had purchased from Hamilton. Harry pulled his gun on his partner, grabbed what money from the till he thought was owed him, and headed out of town. He drifted back to Montana, likely working for a ranch breaking horses before being laid off and returning to Miles City.[30]

Around this time, Harry either renewed acquaintances or met for the first time a man named Bill Madden, who may have been involved in the Telluride bank robbery with Bob Parker and the other men. Miles City was a magnet for out-of-work cowboys, especially with winter approaching and few jobs to be had. Harry whiled away his time in the saloons—drinking, playing cards, and romancing the young ladies. He was a handsome man, with blond hair and a mustache, and flashing blue eyes, and he paid particular attention to his clothing, preferring the most stylish fashion of the day and always embroidering his garments with an "HL." His only physical flaw was his small feet, which turned in when he walked and gave him the appearance of being slightly bowlegged.

Harry and Bill would have commiserated about their lean prospects for winter work, a season when more stable cowhands were rewarded with available jobs. The leftovers would be the less desirable endeavors, such as mucking out stalls, swamping saloons, or washing dishes. But the two had other ideas about their business opportunities. They had decided that there was only one logical course of action to take to replenish their empty wallets—they would rob a train.

Harry Longabaugh was about to make his final transition to the other side, and ride the outlaw trail for good. He now would not be known simply as the "kid," as the newspapers had always called him. Instead, as a result of the time spent in the Sundance jail, he would now be known as "the Sundance Kid," a fitting nickname for a Western outlaw and gunslinger.

CHAPTER FIVE
RIDING THE OUTLAW TRAIL

I danced with a gal with a hole in her stockin',
And her heel kep' a-rockin' and her toe kep' a-knockin',
I danced with a gal with a hole in her stockin',
And we danced by the light of the moon.

Buffalo Gals, won't you come out tonight,
come out tonight, come out tonight?
Buffalo gals, won't you come out tonight,
And dance by the light of the moon?

—"Buffalo Gals"

When it came to criminal activities, trains and stagecoaches were relatively easy and less dangerous to rob compared to banks. Railroad and stage lines ran on a predictable schedule. A stagecoach had only a driver and shotgun guard aboard, while trains always had problems providing adequate security. Most outlaws avoided banks in favor of other, less risky endeavors. The brazen act of robbing a bank, with all its romance, danger, and adventure, however, has become another enduring myth about the Western frontier.

Hollywood and dime novels have time and time again hoodwinked the public into envisioning a group of riders wearing heavy, dark dusters—despite 110-degree summer temperatures—who would ride into town in broad daylight, tie up their horses to a hitching rack near the bank, and inconspicuously scan the cityscape in search of law officers. Several of these strangers would casually enter the bank, while the others stood nonchalantly outside taking in the sights, smoking, and tipping their hats to the passing womenfolk.

The men inside the bank would suddenly brush aside their dusters to display their six-guns in a menacing fashion, force the terrified cashier or the indignant bank president to open the safe, stuff all the cash into saddlebags, back out the front door, maybe fire off a warning shot or two, run to their waiting horses, and gallop out of town with their loot, perhaps jubilantly wasting more ammunition as they went. The sheriff would organize a posse of townspeople, but the bank robbers made their getaway and holed up at some desolate hideout, or visited a Mexican town where they could celebrate in a cantina with their newfound riches.

What could possibly be wrong with that pulse-quickening picture of Western drama? Just about everything. Bank robberies rarely happened like that romantic celluloid example or the depictions found within the pages of Western novels. That fact alone demonstrates the brilliance and uniqueness of the robbery of more than $20,000 from the San Miguel Valley Bank in Telluride by Bob Parker, Matt Warner, and Tom McCarty. The three men must have been quite proud of their criminal achievement—and they had a right to gloat. Records reveal that history was stacked against them when they had entered that bank with guns drawn and demanded cash.

Some historians claim that the first bank robbery in the United States took place in Liberty, Missouri, at the Clay County Savings and Loan on February 13, 1866. Several gunmen, believed to be members of the James-Younger Gang, entered the bank, killed a nineteen-year-old student, and escaped with about $60,000. This bank has even established a museum to commemorate that groundbreaking event. There was also said to have been an earlier robbery reported on December 15, 1863, when a man stole $5,000 at gunpoint from the Middlesex County Massachusetts Bank and shot dead the young bookkeeper. Previous robberies that took place during the Civil War, such as one at St. Albans, Vermont, which was likely perpetrated by rebel soldiers, were considered acts of war and not official bank robberies.[1]

None of these incidents, however, can stake its claim as the first bank robbery in America's history. That honor goes to City Bank on Wall Street in New York City in 1831, when Edward Smith stole $245,000. Smith was readily captured, tried and convicted, and given a sentence of only five years in Sing Sing prison.[2]

Countless bank robberies, successful and unsuccessful, were pulled off after Edward Smith's theft, and the legendary James Gang were probably the best-known bank robbers in the Old West. The gang has become part of American folklore as modern-day Robin Hoods who stole from the rich and gave to the poor. Actually, no evidence exists to suggest that the James Gang ever gave a dime to the less fortunate; rather, they selfishly kept all the loot for themselves. In addition, Jesse

James was anything but chivalrous and good-hearted—he was a callous, cold-blooded killer who murdered unarmed victims.

The gang raided a handful of banks during the decade after the Civil War—among them Lexington, Missouri; Richmond, Missouri; Russellville, Kentucky; Gallatin, Missouri; and Corydon, Iowa—and made off with small amounts of cash. Their career as bank robbers came to an end, however, in Northfield, Minnesota, on September 7, 1876, when townspeople virtually shot to pieces the James-Younger alliance with gunfire.

The James brothers enjoyed limited success, but the act of robbing Western banks with the frequency represented in popular culture can be dismissed as historical myth. More bank robberies are attempted in modern-day Rhode Island in a year than there were in a decade or more in the Old West. This does not imply that outlaws in those days were any less greedy or bold compared to robbers of today. It simply points out that banks back then were not as easy to rob as might be imagined, and the success rate was quite low.

Contrary to myth, it has been established that few outlaw gangs or lone gunmen could simply sashay into a town in broad daylight, stroll into the bank in the middle of a bustling downtown, part their dusters to reveal their drawn sidearms, and depart with the contents of the safe or cashier's cage without the townspeople filling them full of bullet holes. The money held in trust in that bank belonged to those working people—many of whom were Civil War veterans and most of whom were always armed—and they were not about to allow some stranger or strangers to make off with their precious assets without a fight. Potential bank robbers were aware of the zeal with which towns protected their banks, which usually discouraged even the most experienced and determined criminal.[3]

The banking business in the Old West was intentionally planned to instill confidence in those wary pioneers who settled fledgling prairie or mountain towns. Small-town banks were primarily owned by a man who came from the East and first established another type of business, usually a general store. A banker needed the trust of the public, and that trust had to be earned over time. Setting up a business that traded fairly and gained confidence and respect from the community was a prelude to opening a bank. That was why the marketplace in some towns was for all intents and purposes owned by one man—occasionally with partners—whose holdings might include the general store, the livery stable, the best hotel, the saloon and gaming house, the biggest ranch outside of town, the funeral parlor, and, of course, the bank.

This banker-to-be had to portray himself as a wealthy man, and play the role to the hilt. This meant that he had to look the part in appearance and mannerisms to impress his potential customers. He would wear only the most expensive fashions shipped out from the East—garments made of materials that were generally unavailable to the common man—and he would add gaudy accessories, such as gold watches on gold fobs, diamond stickpins and pinkie rings, silver gem-studded buckles, and custom-made boots and hats that virtually reeked of personal prosperity. He was often overweight and out-of-shape from eating too much imported rich food and not being required to lift a hand at any labor, which left his pink palms without calluses. In addition, he always sported manicured fingernails, a fresh shave, a meticulous haircut, and smelled of a pleasant fragrance rather than those odors associated with the workingman in a Western town.

This banker was compelled to construct a sturdy and stately building of eye-appealing architecture that would be situated right in the center of downtown. This building featured double-reinforced walls and a secure place to store cash and other valuables, such as the latest technology in iron safes, possibly a large walk-in safe. This walk-in safe was often left open during the day to allow the customers to peek inside and verify that their money was indeed within those walls. Not every banker trusted a safe, however. There are stories of bankers who kept the bank's assets in a crate with rattlesnakes inside; or placed the money in a wastebasket at night, thinking that thieves would never look there; or even took the cash and valuables home with them at closing time and hid them under a bed, under the floorboards, or somewhere else inside their houses.

After constructing the secure and majestic building, the banker was obliged to ostentatiously decorate and furnish the interior of his bank with custom wooden counters, ornate furniture, brass or gold finishings, exquisite chandeliers, marble floors, luxurious carpeting, and other elegant accoutrements intended to awe the eye of the public. The building had to be regarded by the townsfolk as a sacred financial cathedral that conveyed the message that the institution was stable and thriving and that the depositors' money was safe from any and every threat, especially bank robbers.[4]

The banking industry was reserved exclusively for males until after 1900. The first bank owned by a woman in this country finally opened in November 1903, when Maggie Lena Walker, an African-American entrepreneur, started the St. Luke Penny Savings Bank in Richmond, Virginia.[5]

Of all the crimes Bob Parker would commit in his lifetime, the Telluride robbery of 1889 was perhaps the crown jewel of the outlaw's career—and it established the methodology he would use for years to come. The heist, pulled off with Matt Warner and Tom McCarty, attests to their remarkable skills in planning and executing a bank job, especially by setting up relay stations to assist in getting a head start on any posse that might be formed.

Although the Telluride bank caper epitomized all the romance, danger, and excitement portrayed by Hollywood's stereotypical Old West bank robbers—perhaps they even wore black dusters—the safe getaway of the perpetrators was anything but guaranteed. Bob Parker, Matt Warner, and Tom McCarty were riding hell-for-leather to put as much distance as possible between themselves and the San Miguel Valley Bank.

The exact escape route and itinerary taken by these outlaws has been a matter of speculation, with countless conflicting accounts related by alleged horse handlers at relay stations and old-timers passing on local legends. Suffice it to say that the relay station system worked quite well, and the posse was made to eat dust far behind the fleeing outlaws.

One mistake in their plan—the accidental meeting of an acquaintance on the road—had branded them as outlaws. Their chances of working as honest cowboys in that part of the Western range had vanished along with the dust that they hoped would cover their tracks. But that was the least of their worries. They sensed a posse on their trail that would not be easily discouraged. Further, it was feared that these men were dogged in their pursuit, and were perhaps even gaining on them.

On their second night on the run, somewhere between the Dolores and Mancos rivers, the bank robbers gave fodder to dozens of future Hollywood scripts. When it was determined that a posse was indeed following them, they found a stray pony, tied branches to its tail, and drove it toward the path of the posse. The posse took the bait and futilely chased the pony in the dark. The resultant frustration with their gullibility and inability to gain on their quarry coaxed them to give up the hunt and return to Telluride.[6]

The fugitive trio hid in a remote corner of the mountains near Dolores or thereabouts in southwestern Colorado for a short period of time before heading into Utah, where they took refuge in a cave in the Blue Mountains while their horses rested. Later, they crossed the Colorado River at Moab by ferry—paying the $1.50 fee with a ten-dollar gold piece—and rode north across the southern edge of the Salt Valley, with its maze of breathtaking arches, hidden canyons, and view-obstructing bluffs.[7]

Parker, Warner, and McCarty were well aware that they were not out of harm's way, and that they would have to remain vigilant. Colorado may have given up the chase, but authorities in Utah could have sent out a posse of their own. The jagged pillars that rose from the ground in the Salt Valley afforded many hiding places for men on the run, but also provided ambush sites for law officers trailing the three outlaws.

The desperadoes soon became paranoid as they journeyed through the valley, where they could find themselves easily trapped and with few sources of potable water available. Matt Warner made it a point to stop every now and then to scan the landscape with a pair of field glasses. Their paranoia was for good reason. Eventually, Matt's eyes captured a disturbing sight—about three miles behind them was a posse from Utah that had joined the hunt for the notorious Telluride bank robbers.

"From then on," Warner related, "it was hell proper. It wasn't the case of just one outfit of deputies trailing us, but posses was out scouring the whole country, and we was running into fresh outfits every little while and had to suddenly change our direction, or dodge into a rock or timber hide-out, or backtrack, or follow long strips of bare sandstone where we wouldn't leave our tracks or wade up or down streams long distances so they would lose our tracks."[8]

The three outlaws had a close call in Whipsaw Flat, south of Thompson Springs. They were riding along a trail that was gradually veering into a high cliff face to their right. Their pursuers were riding to the left and steadily gaining on them. Suddenly, the cliff opened to reveal a canyon—a box canyon, with rock walls on both sides. The trio realized that they could be trapped in that canyon, but, perhaps against their better judgment, rode inside nonetheless. They pulled out their Winchesters, placed their fingers on the triggers, aimed at the canyon entrance, and anxiously waited for the posse to ride into view. They had decided to shoot it out with their pursuers and settle the issue once and for all.

But no one appeared on the trail at the canyon's mouth. Tense moments passed, and still nothing stirred. What had happened? they wondered. The outlaws had expected and prepared for a gunfight, but there was no sign of their adversary. Had the posse halted outside the canyon and set up an ambush?

The answer soon became apparent. The Utah horsemen had misread the terrain. Observing the three outlaws riding into the canyon, they continued north, not knowing that it was a box canyon and thinking that it had an opening on the other side where they could set up an ambush. Bob, Matt, and Tom finally understood what had happened and high-tailed it out of there, eluding the dangerous posse.[9]

The posse did know, however, that the bank robbers were heading north, and would have notified Colorado authorities. With that in mind, the fleeing outlaws stayed away from settlements and large ranch houses. They camped without a fire at night or in a location well off the trail within the protection of rock outcroppings. The horses were left saddled and staked by a length of rope tied near their bedrolls.[10]

The stolen cash soon became a peculiar problem. Each man had stuffed his share into a money belt strapped securely around his waist. They could not chance tying the belts to their saddles or placing them in saddlebags in case their horses were shot out from beneath them. After days on the trail, the heavy belts rubbing against their flesh became unbearable.

"The sweat would roll down our bellies and backs," Matt Warner wrote, "and the hard, heavy money belts would gall a ring clear around our bodies, and the money got heavier and heavier and the sore rawer and rawer every mile we rode, till we thought we couldn't stand it any longer. More than once one or the other of us let loose and acted like a crazy man, swore like a trooper, pawed at his belt, and threatened to tear the damned thing off and throw it away."

Evidently, the life of a bank robber was made much more difficult by successfully stealing a large amount of money.[11]

After crossing into Colorado, they encountered a friendly band of White River Utes, and traded for fresh horses. Before the new mounts were broken in, however, another posse had taken up their trail. The three men raced back toward Utah, leaving the lawmen behind, crossed the Green River, and headed northeast toward the rugged wilderness known as Brown's Park, where relative safety awaited.[12]

Brown's Park was a forty-mile-by-six-mile valley with layered terraces of forests and grasslands that straddled the borders of Colorado, Utah, and Wyoming. The natural wonders of the valley— its abundant wildlife, mild winters, and excellent grazing land—had attracted settlers who had moved there for a fresh start. These farm-ers had put up fences and planted crops on the bottomland along the

Green River, all the while being protected from the cold wind by surrounding mountains that served as a natural barrier.

Brown's Park had been named after a French Canadian trapper,
Baptist Brown, who had been one of the first white men to discover
the area in 1827. Trappers had quickly flocked to this valley with plentiful game, especially beaver, and in 1837 a trading post was built on
the Green River near the entrance to Lodore Canyon. The post closed
down when the beaver played out, and the Park, as it became known,
was virtually abandoned until the 1870s, when settlers could ride the
train on the transcontinental railroad to a point some sixty-five miles
to the south and travel the rest of the way by wagon or horseback.[13]

Brown's Park was also a place—a no-man's-land—where a stranger
would be left alone as long he behaved like a good citizen and did not
cause any trouble or draw negative attention to himself, which made it
ideal as a hideout for Bob Parker, Matt Warner, and Tom McCarty.

A small number of honest cattlemen ranched in the Park, but
many of the cows that found their way to the valley had been driven
in by rustlers, often Texas cowboys on a cattle drive who had abandoned their own herd in favor of profiting from stolen stock or range
mavericks. It was no secret that Brown's Park was a relatively safe
haven for rustlers and outlaws. Lawmen generally avoided following
lawbreakers into the area for fear of being ambushed in the twisted
jungle of rock formations—as well as for questions of jurisdiction
stemming from fact that it bordered three states.[14]

Matt Warner had raised horses at Diamond Mountain, and was
familiar with the Park. He led his companions to the remote horse
ranch owned by Charley Crouse, a hard-drinking, hard-riding former
Virginian who had no problem associating with men on the run.
Crouse's spread was located at the mouth of a small stream on the
south side of the Green River about three miles west of the Colorado-
Utah border. Bob, Matt, and Tom welcomed the respite from the hot,
dusty trail—not to mention relief from the pursuit—and rested up for
several days.

On the fourth day word arrived that a posse was on the way,

searching for the Telluride bank robbers. The three men saddled up immediately, and headed toward what they hoped would be a safe haven—Robbers Roost in southern Utah.[15]

Matt Warner wrote only that they had headed for Robbers Roost, but whether or not they actually arrived and hid out there cannot be determined. After all, this was the end of June or the first part of July, and that desolate place, with its thousands of rocky cliffs, buttes, and canyons, although fed by a number of natural springs, could be a virtual broiler. Consequently, the whereabouts of the three men that summer of 1889 was anybody's guess.

It was possible that Bob Parker became homesick, and at some point during late summer seriously considered visiting his family home in Circle Valley. According to his sister Lula, he rode as far as Beaver Creek, but then had second thoughts about returning. He believed that his presence, if discovered, would cause his family further shame now that he was a known outlaw.

Bob did venture to the town of Milford—where he was known as a jeans thief—and, by prearrangement or by complete surprise, met up with his brother Dan. The brothers celebrated the happy reunion with lunch at a tavern. Afterward, however, Bob was certain that he had made the right decision not to visit home. Dan had likely informed him that everyone in Circleville had heard about his robbery of the bank in Telluride. Bob rode away from Milford, and dismissed for the present any thought of seeing his beloved mother, father, and siblings.[16]

It was at this time that Bob Parker decided to change his name. He had been known as Bob or Roy Parker in Telluride, but now that he had abandoned hope of becoming a solid citizen, he chose to honor Mike Cassidy, the man who had taught him the ways of the outlaw. He would now be known as George Cassidy—the nickname "Butch" would be added later. Apparently he had earlier chosen "George" to add confusion to his identity on account of another George Parker living in Rock Springs, Wyoming, who, Lula wrote, was "frequently stirring up some devilment." Also, the brother of the original George Parker was a lawman.[17]

The three bank robbers may have sought safe refuge together outside of Robbers Roost, but finally split up that fall and went their separate ways. Bob Parker chose to return to the Brown's Park area, perhaps hoping to work for Matt Warner's friend Charley Crouse. Instead he found employment as a ranch hand at the nearby Bassett Ranch. The Bassetts were not in the habit of asking questions of strangers, rather offering their hospitality to those in need who appeared at their door.[18]

Herbert and Mary "Elizabeth" Bassett had come to the West from Hot Springs, Arkansas, in 1878 to find a healthy climate for Herbert, who was asthmatic. Herbert, who had at first worked as a schoolteacher and bookkeeper in Green River, had a brother who had homesteaded Brown's Park and eventually decided to join him. The Bassett boys had grown up on a farm, and, despite his health condition, Herbert was confident he could succeed. His ranch on the north side of Vermillion Creek, where the Vermillion ran into Green River, however, was operated mainly by his wife, Elizabeth, who had the reputation of being quite capable of performing that task. The Bassetts were parents to five children—Josie, Sam, Ann, Eb, and George.[19]

The Bassett family, Bob's sister claimed, reminded the young outlaw of his own family, and he felt right at home. The Bassetts had a well-stocked library from which Bob was encouraged to borrow, and he spent his spare time with his nose in a book. Religious services were held on Sunday mornings, and social gatherings were frequent— their home was known as the center of society in the valley. Eleven-year-old Ann Bassett always found a way to tag along with Bob while he was working. Rumors later surfaced that Bob might have courted fifteen-year-old Josie, but when asked in later years she would neither admit nor deny it. She referred to him as a "big dumb kid who liked to joke," and that they were simply "good friends." Josie did, however, later call Bob her "Brown's Park beau."[20]

Horse races and dances served as the primary means of entertainment. Serving as a jockey in a race with about $3,000 and two horses at stake, Bob won the contest by several lengths. Ann Bassett later wrote:

"A dancing party was given at the Charles Allen ranch to celebrate the winning of a race. The youthful jockey stabled the horse, joined us at supper, then went quietly to bed, without sharing in the jubilant merry-making that went on until dawn streaked the sky." Apparently Bob, usually outgoing and affable, preferred not to attract attention to himself on that occasion.[21]

Bob demonstrated his skill with horses in another way while at Brown's Park. Charley Crouse's daughter, Minnie Crouse Rasmussen, wrote: "I was a teenager when Cassidy rode into the yard one day, and saw that we were trying to get a newborn colt on its feet. He helped us get the colt walking and stayed around for several minutes to make certain it was up to stay, before he walked into the house to talk with father."[22]

Early one morning after an extended stay with the Bassetts, before the family had arisen, Bob saddled up and rode away. His departure was reminiscent of the morning in June 1884 when he had left home with a heavy heart but a burning anticipation. Once again he demonstrated that good-byes were difficult for him. He had made the decision to move on to greener pastures, and perhaps he did not want anyone to try to dissuade him from leaving.

Bob rode to Rock Springs, seventy-five miles away to the north, and discovered that the only work available was in the coal mines, which did not appeal to him. His sister wrote: "Looking around town for work, he bumped into a man by the name of William Gottsche who ran a butcher shop. He needed someone reliable. This was better than coal mining; so Bob took the job. My brother had a disarming way with people. It wasn't long before he had befriended nearly everyone in town. He always gave good measure with the meat, and housewives had the highest confidence in him; children adored him."[23]

Bob had acquired his skill as a butcher from his cattle-rustling days. Rustlers would steal the calves, butcher them in the field, and then sell the meat to general stores. In fact, butcher shops were often associated with rustlers, who would herd the cattle to slaughterhouses owned by the retailer.[24]

• • •

There have been countless theories and disagreements with respect to whether or not Bob Parker—or George Cassidy—assumed his nickname "Butch" from this butcher job in Rock Springs. Historians have written that he received the nickname from Tom McCarty after having problems operating a rifle that knocked him down, or that he earned the nickname when he was responsible for providing meat for a camp cook on a cattle roundup, or that his sister simply made up the story about the job in the butcher shop.[25]

Another version of Lula's story was written by writer Kerry Ross Boren, who claims that his grandfather once asked Bob Parker himself how he had come by the nickname "Butch." Bob said that he had been given the handle "a long time ago when I first came to this area. I took a job in Rock Springs in the butcher shop when I needed to lay low for a while. Matt Warner nicknamed me Butch; he thought it was a big joke." Warner made no mention of that story in his book.[26]

Regardless of how he received the nickname, the immortal name Butch Cassidy had been created. Robert Leroy Parker, Bob Parker, Roy Parker, and George Cassidy will now be retired in this text in favor of the name that has endured as one of the Old West's premier outlaws—Butch Cassidy.

Butch enjoyed to the fullest the winter that he resided in Rock Springs. Regional historian John Rolfe Burroughs writes that Butch "walked pretty much on the wild side of life, spending his spare time and money drinking and gambling in Rock Springs's numerous saloons and paying far more attention to the ladies than was his custom."[27]

He resigned his position at the butcher shop and eventually went to work as a cowhand for the EA Outfit, a 240-acre ranch on Horse Creek in the Wind River area of Wyoming. The EA was owned by a man named Eugene Amoretti, who also owned a bank in Lander, and ran about forty thousand head of cattle for a distance of about one hundred miles. It was at this ranch that Butch became friends with another young cowboy by the name of Al Hainer.[28]

Little biographical material can be found about Al Hainer, if that indeed was his real name, but he may have been another wayward boy from the Mormon Empire in Utah. Butch and Al became fast friends, and it was not long before they had purchased a piece of property together and planned to go into the business of raising horses. Their spread on Horse Creek in northern Fremont County was located in the Upper Wind River area just north of the modern-day town of Dubois. Butch possibly supplied most of the money for this venture from his share of the Telluride bank robbery.[29]

The ranch with a two-room cabin was known for its sagebrush flats, rolling hills, and red-walled mountains, not an ideal place to raise livestock. Ranchers thereabouts were fond of saying that "when there was rain in the Wind River Basin—an event that happened about as often as a birthday—wagons were stopped in their tracks."[30]

The hostile environment had discouraged many homesteaders and ranchers from settling nearby, which may have been the intended purpose of Butch and his partner. To his few neighbors Butch was friendly and helpful. His closest friends were John and Margaret Simpson, whose son William, another local rancher and lawyer, was the grandfather of future Wyoming United States Senator Alan Simpson.

The Simpsons operated a ranch and the local post office on the Wind River near Jakey's Fork Creek, four miles southeast of Horse Creek. Butch and Al were frequent visitors at the post office, and became favorites of the elder Simpsons, especially when Butch would pitch in to help fill water buckets and chop wood.

Butch not only assisted the Simpson family with chores, but came to the rescue of the entire territory during an influenza epidemic that winter of 1889–90. Margaret Simpson prepared homemade remedies out of herbs for flu sufferers. Butch, apparently immune to the illness, rode to the Simpson ranch weekly to get the medicine and then distribute it to people as far away as twenty-five miles. When one of the Simpson children had contracted the flu and homemade remedies failed to work, Butch rode to Fort Washakie, a 120-mile round trip, to obtain medicine from a doctor.[31]

Butch attended social gatherings as well, accepting an invitation that first winter from Will Simpson's wife for a Christmas dinner. Most of the residents of the Wind River Basin were present at this soiree, but Butch made the biggest impression.

According to A. F. C. Greene, Al Hainer kept mainly to himself, but Butch became the life of the party as he played with the children. "Cassidy had the spirit of frolic within him. Before dinner was on the table, those who had grinned in silence were beginning to laugh out loud. The children hovered close about him. In the afternoon there was an eggnog, and then they had games. There are old-timers who tell to this day how the cowboys of Wind River roared with laughter, and the children shrieked with mirth, and how Butch Cassidy set the pace, with his tow-colored hair in wild disorder and his puckered blue eyes blazing." Butch was somewhat of a showoff, occasionally engaging in dangerous stunts, like performing acrobatic feats on a bicycle for the entertainment of everyone.[32]

Butch became known as a ladies' man around the town of Lander and neighboring ranches. He attended dances with various girls, including Dora Lamorreaux, who became his steady girlfriend for a time. The two would go as a couple to dances and take horseback rides together. Later, when Dora was asked whether the two had "necked," she indignantly replied, "I'll have you know he was a gentleman and I was a lady."

Another relationship that may have grown serious was between Butch and a girl named Mary Boyd. But Butch was apparently hesitant to settle down. Mary would later claim to have been Butch's common-law wife, but no evidence exists to verify that the two had ever lived together.[33]

This gregarious and kindhearted man calling himself George Cassidy denied having Mormon roots and told everyone that he hailed from New York City, although it was suspected that he was from Utah and had been raised a Mormon. This lie about his origins, which he would repeat later to the law, may be an indication of why he had refused to take a wife. Aware that one day it could become necessary to reveal his shady past—that he was a rustler and bank robber—he feared the reaction and consequences. He may have known that he would continue his criminal ways, and did not want to subject a wife and family to the shame they would surely endure. Destined to ride the outlaw trail or spend time in prison, his future could not include a proper lady.

Butch and Al Hainer worked alongside their neighbors for the spring roundup of 1890, but upon returning to their ranch on Horse Creek the two men sold their herd, closed up the cabin, and rode away to parts unknown without an explanation.[34]

On the afternoon of December 29, 1889, two mounted men—Tom Ricketts and William Brown—held up a stagecoach at gunpoint north of Muddy Station on the Dixon-to-Rawlins, Wyoming, route. The robbers rummaged through the U.S. mail, stuffing the contents of letters and packages into their pockets. They tossed the mail sack back into the coach, fired several shots under the horses to start off the team, and rode away with their meager pickings. In September 1890, both men were captured and held in the Wyoming State Penitentiary to await trial. On April 7, 1891, Ricketts and Brown were tried, convicted, and sentenced to spend the rest of their lives in prison at hard labor. The man calling himself Tom Ricketts was soon found to be using an alias; his real name was Daniel Sinclair Parker, the brother of Butch Cassidy.

Max and Ann Parker lobbied long and hard for their son, and finally in 1894 the governor pardoned Dan. He would never again commit a felony.[35]

Butch eventually made his way to Johnson County in the Powder River country of northeastern Wyoming. It was a rustler's paradise, with many horses and cattle available to thieves and nothing to worry about from the law. Thousands of head of livestock were stolen there during the late 1880s, with few rustlers caught and prosecuted.[36]

The opportunities for a rustler with Butch's talent were so promising in Johnson County that he bought a 160-acre piece of property on Blue Creek. This narrow, winding ribbon of water meandered through a valley about ten miles northwest of the Hole in the Wall, a famous refuge for outlaws. Located about sixteen miles southwest of Kaycee,

Wyoming, this desolate, parched ancient riverbed, which featured red sandstone canyon walls, featured few cabins. There was not exactly a "hole" as such in this protective canyon wall, rather a V-shaped notch near the rim of a steep cliff that was large enough to run horses or cattle through. The Hole in the Wall was assuredly not a place peace officers would dare to enter without the support of an army battalion.

Butch put his efforts into improving his property, soon adding 420 acres to his original purchase. He built outbuildings and corrals, planted trees, and dug irrigation ditches—every element necessary to make it an ideal place to hold stolen horses and raise their offspring. To the casual observer, the spread looked to be a legitimate horse ranch. Butch's rustling operation was said to have extended from Wyoming to the Dakotas, stealing and selling animals in Utah, Colorado, and Montana as well.[37]

All good things must come to an end, however, and for Butch word came in late December 1890 that the law was targeting Johnson County. Stock detectives hired by the large cattle ranchers, along with local law enforcement officers, would soon be paying him a visit that could very well land him in jail, or even worse. Butch hastily sold his land to a neighbor and rode out of the county on a fast horse.[38]

During 1891, Butch Cassidy likely lived off and on at his Horse Creek ranch with partner Al Hainer. But their visits to the ranch were so infrequent that neighbors assumed the two men had abandoned the property.[39]

Butch kept tabs on happenings in Johnson County, and was angry to hear that the big cattle companies were squeezing out small ranchers from the best bottomland by establishing illegal homesteads. This process was called "straw man homesteads," which entailed having one of their cowboys file a claim on the land and then sell it cheaply to the large outfit. Perhaps Butch's outrage was merely a way in which he justified his rustling, but he wondered whether he had departed Johnson County too soon and should have stayed to fight. Regardless, with so many law officers present he was not about to risk returning.[40]

In the summer of 1891 Butch reunited with old pals Matt Warner and Tom McCarty. Leading packhorses laden with everything neces-sary to run a serious cattle- or horse-rustling operation—cooking utensils, extra rope, food, bedrolls, and, of course, branding irons—they traveled from Ten Sleep to the west bank of the Powder River, roping strays and mavericks, all the while dodging the "shoot-first-ask-questions-later" mentality of the big ranchers. Those outfits had banded together to hire large groups of heavily armed regulators to sweep through the territory, swoop down on suspected rustlers, and mete out justice at the end of a rope tossed over a tree branch.[41]

One hot, dry summer day, Butch and his two associates were driv-ing a stolen herd of about fifty cows through a grassy valley some-where north of the Washakie County line. Halting to rest, the men unsaddled and picketed their horses to graze. Moments later, Butch noticed a disturbing sight on their back trail—at least ten armed rid-ers were galloping directly toward them. He shouted a warning. The trio of rustlers abandoned the cattle herd and packhorses, leaped aboard their mounts, and raced away.[42]

The mysterious riders quickly closed to within shooting distance, and sent bullets from their Winchester rifles whistling dangerously close to the outlaws' heads. Armed only with six-guns, Butch and his companions knew their weapons were useless against the Winchesters. Worse yet, there was nothing within that pastureland to hide behind and make a stand. They could only urge their horses on to greater speeds and try to outrun their pursuers.

At sundown, their mounts weary and struggling, the outlaws reached a stand of timber somewhere near the Wind River and decided to split up. Now that the rustlers had reached a wooded area, the riders who had been chasing them found it necessary to exercise caution. Butch and the others could easily set up an ambush in this thicket of green and inflict devastating damage even with six-shooters.

Butch's specific escape route through this wooded area and be-yond cannot be determined. According to Matt Warner, the report of Winchesters could be heard throughout the timber for some time. In the end, the three men managed to elude capture. Their rustling days in that territory, however, had ended for now.[43]

Butch should have accepted this close call as a dire warning to put his rustling activities behind him and turn to legitimate means to satisfy his interest in horses. Not only was he an excellent jockey, but, with a little patience, he could have built up a thriving business breeding, raising, training, and selling and buying quality horseflesh. Something within his character, however, caused him to scheme in criminal ways instead of endeavoring to nurture a lawful business.

Due to his propensity for living on the wrong side of the law, Butch Cassidy was on the verge of making a mistake that could put him behind high concrete walls and iron bars for a long, long time.

CHAPTER SIX
CRIME AND PUNISHMENT

When slumbering in my convict cell my
    childhood days I see,
When I was mother's little child and
    knelt at mother's knee.
There my life was peace, I know, I knew no
    sorrow or pain.
Mother dear never did think, I know, I would
    wear a felon's chain.

When I had grown to manhood and evil
    paths I trod,
I learned to scorn my fellow-man and
    even curse my God;
And in the evil course I ran for a great
    length of time
Till at last I ran too long and was condemned
    for a felon's crime.

—"The Convict"

It would not have been unusual for fledgling outlaws the likes of Harry Longabaugh—the Sundance Kid—and Bill Madden to contemplate robbing a train. Newspaper articles about holdups of trains were quite common, and the result of these robberies was usually good news for the bad guys. Railroad security was a difficult proposition, and robbers were almost never caught in the act, and rarely tracked down afterward.

Early train robberies had taken place only on trains parked at railway stations or freight yards, a relatively safe approach that changed after the Civil War.

The first holdup of a moving train took place in Jackson County, Indiana, on October 6, 1866, when the Reno Gang—four Reno brothers and their associates—made off with more than $10,000 from an Ohio & Mississippi train. The Reno Gang enjoyed success at their criminal craft, including the heist of $96,000 in cash and valuables near Marshfield, Indiana—until December 1868, when they were captured by Pinkerton agents and locked up in the New Albany jail. The gang members never went to trial. On December 12 a vigilante mob stormed the jail, escorted three of the brothers and another man outside, and strung them up. The surviving brother was already serving time in another prison.[1]

The daring exploits of the Reno Gang, however, encouraged other would-be outlaws to plan and execute holdups of moving trains all across the American West. The Western economy was booming, and express cars often carried bank deposits, large payrolls, and precious metals such as gold and silver shipped by mining companies. Robbers could easily stop or board trains in remote locations where the population was sparse and witnesses were few. Peace officers were usually far away and would not learn about the robbery until the train arrived at its next stop or destination, which afforded the outlaws a huge head start on any posse. In addition, there were numerous isolated places to hide should a posse take to the trail after them.

Another factor in the criminals' favor was that law enforcement officers and even judges were frequently hesitant to arrest and put on trial suspected robbers who had friends and relatives in the area, for fear of retaliation. Members of the community were often sympathetic toward the outlaws, and would refuse to cooperate or occasionally assist in the getaway. The public had little use for big corporations, such as express companies, and railroad moguls, who had amassed great wealth. The robbery of one of these entities was frequently cause for celebration.

Train robberies had an extremely high success rate in the decade following the Reno Gang's first heist, and the modus operandi was quite simple. Regardless of Hollywood's propensity for the dramatic and dangerous, outlaws would rarely jump from their horses onto a moving train. They would either board the train at a station and wait for an opportune time to strike, or, more often, they would place an obstruction on the tracks—a fire, logs, or boulders—and derail or force the train to stop. Other methods included loosening a rail or signaling the engineer with a fake emergency. Some robbers ambushed the train crew at an isolated water tank or station and rode off with the loot. There were so many effective methods and techniques to pull off the theft that it was only a matter of proper planning and execution with respect to the vulnerabilities of the particular targeted train.

Express companies that shipped valuables were slow to respond to the threat of robbery. Companies normally required their messengers, who guarded the safe, to provide their own weapons. These messengers would lock express car doors, but the wooden structures were no match for a determined outlaw, who could simply drill out the lock with a brace and bit. Safes were of no consequence, either. They could be blown up with black powder or, after 1889, dynamite. Also, the company messenger could be persuaded at gunpoint to open the safe or suffer dire consequences.

The first train robbery west of the Rocky Mountains took place near Verdi, Nevada, in 1870, when four or five men surreptitiously jumped aboard a Central Pacific train as it was departing the station. The bandits entered the cab of the engine and held the crew at gunpoint, ordering them to keep the train moving. When they arrived at a remote stretch in Truckee Canyon, the robbers broke into the express car and rifled the safe to the tune of $40,000. They were never captured.[2]

The James-Younger Gang was known to terrorize trains throughout western and southwestern Missouri and surrounding states. On the evening of July 21, 1873, they committed their first train robbery, which took place near Council Bluffs, Iowa. Jesse and his companions had pulled away the track with a hawser just before the approach of the Chicago, Rock Island and Pacific Railroad train. The engineer spotted the broken track in his headlights, and immediately slammed his brakes into reverse. His actions were too late—momentum carried the train across the open section and it toppled over. The engineer was scalded to death. Jesse James and his cohorts leaped out of the darkness, firing their revolvers—in Jesse's case his Navy Colt—and yelling like rebels on the attack. They entered the express car and were outraged to find only about $2,000 inside the safe. The $100,000 shipment of gold they expected had passed through on an earlier train. The angry gang then raided the passenger cars, stealing rings, watches, and cash from the riders as they went. They departed the scene amidst a volley of pistol shots.[3]

The take from express cars was usually downplayed by the railroad, but probably averaged around $30,000. A larger prize, however, went to the notorious Sam Bass and his gang, which stopped a Pacific Express train at Big Springs, Nebraska, in 1877. Bass and his confederates boarded the train, forced the crew to jump off, and rummaged through the safes and passengers' pockets, taking an estimated $60,000 in cash and valuables. Bass and his boys gained a stellar reputation over time as skillful train robbers. Sam Bass met his end the following year in Round Rock, Texas, however, when he and his gang assembled to rob a bank and were ambushed by authorities after one of their own informed on them.[4]

Three years later, in October 1881, an unknown gang of bandits attacked the express car attached to the Colorado and Southern Railway near Colorado Springs. Reportedly $105,000 in cash was taken from the safe, and another $45,000 removed from the possession of the passengers. The perpetrators of this crime were subsequently captured, but the loot was never recovered.[5]

By the early 1880s, express companies began to take action to thwart robberies, making the crime measurably more difficult. The doors of express cars were fortified, many with boiler iron, and safes were made tougher to open. Messengers were hired who had experience with arms and were not afraid to shoot first should they be subjected to a robbery attempt. To be fair, part of the diminishing losses at this time can be attributed to the advent of the money order, which was now commonly used by express companies. Bank transfers and payrolls, however, continued to be shipped by rail.[6]

These improvements in security were short-lived. By the late 1880s train robbers had adapted to the changes and it was business as usual. In 1886, $59,000 was taken from a westbound St. Louis and San Francisco express, and soon after that same railway line was struck for another $67,000. A year later, the International and Great Northern was robbed of $50,000, and the Southern Pacific lost $240,000 in cash and negotiable bonds.[7]

Now it was November 1892, and the Sundance Kid and Bill Madden had set their sights on robbing a train. The two men whiled away long hours in Alex Black's Saloon in Malta, Montana, where they secretly planned their heist and commiserated about their financial woes with other cowboys who were without work for the winter. Train robbery was at least a three-man job, and sometime that winter they made the acquaintance of a man named Harry Bass. This out-of-work cowboy was no relation to the famous train robber Sam Bass, but may have hinted at some sort of kinship to bolster his credentials.

Malta, which lay fifty miles south of the Canadian border, was a cattle shipping depot for local ranches on the route of the Great Northern Railroad. Consequently, it was decided that there was no better place than home to stage a holdup. Sundance, Madden, and Bass likely trudged through the bitter cold from the saloon to the train yard upon occasion to covertly learn schedules, security, and, most of all, which trains might be carrying cash and other valuables. After much deliberation, they chose as their target Great Northern No. 23, an early morning passenger train that ran from St. Paul, Minnesota, to Butte, Montana.[8]

At three a.m. on November 29, the temperature had dipped to sixteen degrees below zero, and the stretch of the Milk River that ran through Malta had frozen over. The Great Northern westbound express No. 23 had arrived at the station for its regular mail and water stop, and the train robbers were ready for it.

One of the three bandits rode out about a mile west of town, built a huge bonfire near the tracks, and secured the lead ropes of the horses he and his partners would ride to make their escape. The remaining two outlaws covered their faces with bandannas and climbed aboard the blind baggage car while the No. 23 was taking on water.

The passenger train soon departed Malta and picked up speed. The two masked men wasted no time climbing over the coal tender and into the engine compartment. They ordered the engineer at gunpoint to apply the brakes near the bonfire, where the third robber was anxiously waiting.

The horse holder trained his six-gun on the engineer and the fireman while the other two jumped off the train and sprinted toward the express car. Along the way, they encountered the conductor and brakeman, who were headed forward toward the engine to investigate the stoppage. The two railroad men were ordered to raise their hands, and were brought along with the outlaws to the mail car. The conductor was then ordered to tell the mail clerk to open the car door.

The mail clerk, a man named Rawlins, complied, but nothing of value could be found in the bags of mail. The bandits and the railroad men continued on to the express car, where the conductor was told to ask the messenger, Jerry Hauert, to open up. Hauert obediently opened the express car door, and one of the robbers—described as being about five feet, ten inches tall and wearing a fur overcoat over blue overalls—leaped aboard. The other outlaw kept his six-shooter trained on the conductor and brakeman.

Hauert was ordered to open the "through" safe—one with a variable combination sent to destinations by telegraph. The messenger replied that he had not been provided the combination for this safe. There was another safe, however, and the messenger opened up this one. Inside, the train robber in the fur coat found two checks, two packages, and less than $20 in cash. Cramming the money and one of the packages into his overalls pocket, he turned to Jerry Hauert and ordered him once again to open the big safe. The messenger pleaded that he did not have the combination, to which the robber replied, "You open the safe or you die!" Hauert was clearly frightened, and managed to croak, "Very well, then, I suppose I've got to die."[9]

The outlaw was clearly taken aback by the messenger's reply, and judged him to either be telling the truth or willing to put his life on the line for his meager paycheck. Murder was not on the mind of this train robber, however. He nodded good-bye to the messenger—one version says he toasted the crew with a drink—and leaped back to the ground. He signaled to his partners, and the three men mounted up and rode off into the darkness. Jerry Hauert reached for his Winchester, but by that time the robbers had already vanished.[10]

At a press conference, the express company estimated that the package taken by the train robbers was worth no more than $50, which would have brought the grand total of the robbery to around $70. The bandits had overlooked the passengers in their quest to hit the safes, which was a mistake for them. One passenger was carrying $2,000 in cash that he had intended to keep safe in the express car, but had arrived too late to store it back there. In addition, the train robbers never realized that the train had departed St. Paul on a Sunday, which was not a banking day, so they could not have hoped for bags of deposits.

The express company offered a $500 reward for the arrest of each of the outlaws, and the governor of Montana agreed to match that amount. One newspaper wryly mentioned that the reward was worth more than the robbers had stolen and that "the affair occurred in less time than it takes to relate it."[11]

Not only did the robbers fail to steal much money, but their bandannas had a habit of sliding down to expose their faces during the heist. Descriptions of these men were quickly sent around the territory, especially in Malta, the scene of the crime.[12]

The dissemination of the descriptions of these desperadoes became a factor when Bill Madden and Harry Bass inexplicably returned to Alex Black's Saloon two days later. Unaware that they had been identified, the two men were subsequently arrested and tossed into jail. Under questioning, Madden implicated Bass and a man named Loungbo in the robbery. A wanted poster was printed for the arrest of this third man. The express company and the law intended to send a message that train robbers would not be tolerated.

$500 REWARD

The above reward will be paid by the Great Northern Express Company for the arrest and detention of Harry Loungbo [sic], who in the company with others held up and robbed the west bound train on the Great Northern Railway, near Malta, Montana, on the morning of November 29th, 1892.

Description—Height, 5 feet 11 inches. Dark complexion, short dark mustache, dark hair. Age, about 25 years. Slender and erect, with slight stoop in head and shoulders. Short upper lip, exposing teeth when talking. Teeth white and clean with small dark spot

on upper front tooth to right of center. Wore a medium size black soft hat. Dark double breasted sack
coat. Dark, close-fitting pants with blue overalls.
When last seen was riding bay horse branded Half
Circle Cross on left shoulder.[13]

By this time, the Sundance Kid was nowhere to be found around
Malta, Montana. It was rumored that he had headed for familiar
ground in Wyoming, where he hid out at the Hole in the Wall for a
while before moving on to Brown's Park. Whether it was luck or
smarts that had saved him from the same fate as his not-too-bright
partners cannot be determined. There is always the possibility that he
may have initially remained in the area—there is some indication that
he was apprehended but released due to confusion over an assumed
name he used—and then fled only when his accomplices had been
taken into custody.

In any case, Harry Longabaugh, alias the Sundance Kid, now
vowed to seek a job as an honest, hardworking cowhand and, at least
for the near future, leave his criminal endeavors behind. All things
considered, he had not exactly had much success trying to make a living on the wrong side of the law. Perhaps these Malta train robbers
had consumed too much liquor when planning their heist, or they
were just not cut out to be outlaws. Regardless, Sundance had been
given a lucky reprieve, and he was not about to make another mistake
anytime soon.[14]

In late December, Bill Madden and Sam Bass appeared before
Judge Dudley Dubose of the Tenth Judicial District in Fort Benton.
Charged with "burglary in the nighttime" in connection with the
Malta train robbery, both defendants pleaded guilty, and were immediately sentenced by Judge Dubose. Madden, who had not only confessed to authorities but had implicated Harry Longabaugh in the
robbery, was sentenced to eight years in the state penitentiary. Bass
apparently never talked, and was given ten years. The two men were
remanded to custody, and transported to the Deer Lodge penitentiary
on a chilly Christmas morning.[15]

• • •

The Sundance Kid had heeded the warning of his close call with justice, but his future partner, Butch Cassidy, had not yet experienced a sufficient threat to discourage him from criminal activities.

Butch had returned with partner Al Hainer to the ranching—or some would call it rustling—business. Despite numerous transactions, the two men had little stock on hand at the Horse Creek ranch to show for their efforts. Perhaps taking into account the easy money to be made by rustling, a legitimate business requiring markedly harder work had completely lost its appeal.

Townspeople noted that the two men did not spend much time at their ranch, yet always had plenty of cash on hand for supplies and spending sprees—including high-stakes games of faro and monte—at the saloons. Local ranchers came to suspect that Butch and Al were rustling cattle and horses to finance their lifestyle, and implemented an effort to catch them and other thieves.

In August 1891, Butch and Al purchased three horses at Mail Camp from Joseph "Billy" Nutcher, a young man from Lander known to ride with a gang of rustlers. Butch later claimed that he never suspected the horses had been stolen, believing they had been traded for cattle in Johnson County, which was perfectly legal. In truth, he assuredly would have known those horses were stolen, and simply had been careless in buying them—at a huge discount that should have been a warning—from a questionable third party.

Cassidy and Hainer had fallen into a trap set by the ranchers, and now it appeared that the noose was tightening around them. Peace officers, encouraged by the big ranchers, were gathering evidence against the two men. Butch and Al caught wind of their possible detainment, and were not about to make themselves available for questioning or arrest by the authorities. They left behind everything, and hightailed it away as fast as their horses could take them. They would eventually hole up at a remote ranch near the town of Auburn in Lincoln County, Wyoming.

John Chapman, a Big Horn Basin rancher, volunteered to track down the two horse thief suspects, but his quest was deterred by the onset of winter. The following spring, notified that Cassidy and Hainer had been seen in Lincoln County, Chapman took off after the two men, bringing along a deputy sheriff named Bob Calverly, who had the reputation of being hell on rustlers.

The two-man posse arrived in Auburn, and received a tip that Butch and Al were hiding outside of town. Further, the rustlers had engaged a girl named Kate Davis to run errands into town for them. Chapman and Calverly located the girl, and either persuaded her to take them to the ranch where the fugitives were holed up or simply followed her out there.[16]

The rancher and the deputy—in the company of local law enforcement officers—rode out to the ranch hideout of Butch Cassidy and Al Hainer on April 11, 1892. They found Hainer working at a small sawmill on the property, and easily took him into custody. An unwitting Butch Cassidy was said to have been lounging about the bunkhouse, and was immediately on high alert when he heard footsteps approaching. Calverly shouted that he had a warrant for Butch's arrest, and Butch called back, "Well, get to shooting!"

Calverly burst through the door with his six-gun drawn, pointed the weapon at Butch's stomach, and squeezed the trigger. The .45-caliber revolver misfired. Butch grabbed his six-shooter, but before he could get off a shot he was smothered by the other lawmen who had entered the bunkhouse. Calverly had continued snapping the trigger of his gun. On the fourth snap, the gun discharged and the bullet struck a glancing blow to Butch's forehead.

The stunned Butch Cassidy was disarmed and placed in handcuffs and shackles. The two accused horse thieves were taken back to Lander and placed in jail.[17]

A complaint dated July 15, 1892, charged George Cassidy and Al Hainer with two counts of grand larceny for stealing a horse valued at forty dollars from the Grey Bull Cattle Company, as well as another horse valued at fifty dollars from Richard Ashworth. Bail was set at $400, but neither had the cash and remained in the Fremont County jail for two months, until local citizens arranged bail.[18]

Surprisingly, the case was delayed for a year due to witnesses being absent and unable to testify. Until they were required to turn themselves in to stand trial, Butch Cassidy and Al Hainer were free to travel about the countryside.

Butch decided to move from his Horse Creek ranch to a cabin on Owl Creek, some seventy miles north of Lander. He immediately blended into the community and befriended the locals, as had always been his custom.

One special friend was Christian Heiden, who was about fifteen years old. Heiden's father owned a saloon near the M-Bar Ranch, and Butch and Al Hainer were frequent customers. Young Christian had obtained a job driving a stage on the Greybull River road. Butch would ride shotgun with his "wicked-looking Colt .45 with a big wooden handle" and a bottle of blended whiskey—his favorites were said to have been Mount Vernon and Old Crow—in his hip pocket. The boy enjoyed the company of the outlaw, remembering him as being quick-witted and a fun companion to have along on the monotonous ride, not to mention being a capable guard if danger presented itself.[19]

Butch may have moved from his ranch on Horse Creek up to Owl Creek for practical reasons. Facing enormous legal fees for his defense when he went to trial, his potential for making money was much better away from the prying eyes of those who had already trapped him. Butch may have run a horse- and cattle-rustling operation on Owl Creek, stealing livestock from those same Big Horn Basin ranchers who had had him arrested. These ranchers would unknowingly be paying for Butch's defense when he went to trial.[20]

One story has Butch taking a trip to San Antonio, Texas, during this period between arrest and trial. He visited Fannie Porter's house of ill repute, where he happened upon a girl said to be only sixteen years old. Believing that she was too young to be working in such a place, Butch decided to take her along when he rode out of town. Supposedly, she willingly accompanied him to Wellington, Utah, where he placed her in the care of a devout Mormon family. There has been speculation that the girl was Etta Place, who would one day become the companion of the Sundance Kid, but there is no evidence to confirm the identity of the girl.[21]

Butch must have contemplated never reporting back to Lander for trial. The West was a vast wilderness, with countless places to hide— Robbers Roost, Brown's Park, and the Hole in the Wall among them. He had made friends around Owl Creek, and from all indications business was good. He could safely hide out with good friends and neighbors to assist him and the rugged terrain to conceal him.

Regardless, Butch Cassidy rode into Lander on June 20, 1893, prepared to face the music. He would gamble with his freedom by standing in judgment before a jury of his peers, hoping that his popularity with the majority of the townspeople would outweigh the evidence.

Butch's attorney was Douglas A. Preston, a well-known and respected trial lawyer. The rustler and the lawyer had become acquainted when Butch lived in Rock Springs, Wyoming. Preston was involved in a barroom brawl one night, and Butch had come to his aid, perhaps saving his life. Preston showed his appreciation by promising that he would defend Butch in court should he ever get into trouble. True to his word, Douglas Preston arrived in Lander to mount Butch's defense.[22]

Another person well-known to Butch Cassidy was involved in the prosecution. James Vidal, who had brought the original charges against the two men, had been defeated in the last election by up-and-coming lawyer Will Simpson, brother of old Jakey's Fork friends John and Margaret Simpson. Will Simpson excused himself from this trial, however, and was replaced by a special prosecutor, former judge M. C. Brown. Judge Jesse Knight would preside over the trial.

The trial was brief. The state presented its evidence and rested. The defense rested without offering any witnesses or evidence to clear the two accused. Remarkably, two hours later the jury returned and announced that they had voted for acquittal. In the minds of the jury, there had been no positive identification of the alleged stolen horse, and ownership of the animal had not been conclusively proved—both factors necessary for a conviction.[23]

The ranchers were incensed by the verdict, but were pacified when it became known that three days before the trial the prosecution had anticipated losing and had sworn out another complaint against Cassidy and Hainer. Preston probably argued that a second prosecution constituted double jeopardy—that his clients could not be subjected to a second trial for the same crime. The state had anticipated that motion as well, and had charged Butch and his accomplice with the theft of a different horse, a separate crime.[24]

Due to a full court schedule, this new trial did not begin until late June 1894. Butch was once again released on a surety bond, and likely headed up to Billings or Miles City, Montana, to spend the winter. During this time, Butch and Al Hainer probably had a falling-out. Whether it was over their business or a personal issue is not known. Eventually, Butch became suspicious of his codefendant, who had kept his distance, and began thinking that Hainer had worked out a deal for himself with the authorities.

Butch returned to Lander to face prosecutor Will Simpson, who this time chose to try the case himself. Conspicuously missing from the witness list was Billy Nutcher, the known rustler who had sold the stolen horse to Butch. Nutcher was incarcerated at the penitentiary in Laramie on account of a horse rustling conviction in July 1893. No reason was given for his absence at the trial. Simpson went ahead with the state's evidence, establishing the ownership and the value of the horse, and explaining that the animal had become missing from the owner's property and was later found in the possession of Butch Cassidy and Al Hainer.[25]

Douglas Preston thought he had a solid defense to refute the state's case, especially with the seller of the stolen horse not testifying. He held what he believed would turn the case in Butch's favor—a bill of sale signed by a prominent Nebraska horse trader that was obviously a forgery. Just as Preston was ready to introduce the document into evidence, he was approached by a man who whispered in his ear: "See that big man in the middle of the fourth row? He's the fellow whose name is signed to your bill of sale. The prosecution brought him here." The bill of sale, promised to be the magic bullet that would shoot holes in the prosecution's case, was now a useless scrap of paper.[26]

The case went to the jury, and a decision was reached late in the day on a Saturday. Judge Knight announced that the verdict would be sealed and read in open court on Monday morning.

The wait had the town in an uproar, and the sentiment was assuredly in favor of Al's and Butch's innocence. Hainer, who, with Butch, was out on bail, horsewhipped a man who had testified against him at the trial. Rumors spread that as many as ten of Butch's friends, led by Matt Warner, were camped outside of town, prepared to instigate trouble if Butch was convicted.

A meeting of concerned citizens convened at the jewelry store to talk about this possible threat by Warner. The consensus opinion was that they should form a posse and roust the troublemakers, if they indeed were even camped out there. Will Simpson advised these people to simply calm down and maintain vigilance. The town remained on edge, but no one saddled up and rode out after the alleged outlaws.[27]

Another violent incident occurred that night when prosecutor Will Simpson was accosted by three drunken men—Al Hainer; a Mexican named Armento, who had a case before Simpson; and a man named Lamareaux. The three drunks tried to pull Simpson off his horse near the livery, with obvious intentions of dragging him into the stables and beating him senseless.

Simpson, however, managed to remain aboard the frightened animal, which furiously bucked and in the process slammed Lamareaux hard against the wall. Simpson then drew his six-gun, which caused the three attackers to flee into the night.

Fremont County sheriff Charley Stough came running to Simpson's aid as the men disappeared down the street. The sheriff reported the incident to Judge Knight, who ordered the arrest of the three assailants, as well as the arrest of Butch Cassidy for good measure. This mayhem had gone on long enough, and the judge wanted to send a warning that the town would put up with no more of it.

Monday morning arrived, and court was convened. The courtroom was a virtual combat zone, as the sheriff and his deputies, concerned citizens, and even the judge—with a six-shooter hidden under his robe—were armed to the teeth and ready for anything the outlaws might try. Strangers were prohibited from entering until the verdict had been read.[28]

George S. Russell, the jury foreman, unsealed the written verdict and read it to a hushed courtroom. "We the jury find the above named defendant George Cassidy guilty of horse stealing, as charged in the information, and we find the value of the property stolen to be $5.00. And we find the above named defendant Al Hainer not guilty. And the jury recommends the said Cassidy to the mercy of the court." Although no transcript is available, Al Hainer's lawyer likely convinced the jury, through some deal, that it was Butch, not Al, who had purchased the stolen animal.[29]

Judge Jesse Knight immediately sentenced Butch Cassidy for his crime of stealing a $5 horse, and as recommended did show a measure of mercy. Butch could have received as many as ten years in the penitentiary, but Knight sentenced him to only two.

Douglas Preston filed for a new trial on the grounds that Butch had not been tried for "grand larceny," which was the crime of which he had been accused. Judge Knight refused the motion without comment.

Butch and Al Hainer had mortgaged their Horse Creek property to banker and friend Eugene Amoretti Jr. to pay for their defense. Preston signed a receipt in the amount of $76.40 from Amoretti dated January 6, 1894, "on the account of George Cassidy and Al Hainer, the same received on standing order of George Cassidy and E. Amoretti, Jr." Amoretti would eventually file a title on the property.[30]

There was an uncommon happening in Lander the night of that verdict. Butch Cassidy was being held in the county jail for transport to the Wyoming State Penitentiary in Laramie. Sheriff Charley Stough was out of town, and clerk of the court Ben Sheldon was approached by the county jail deputy while at home watering his garden. "Butch Cassidy wants me to let him loose tonight," Sheldon was told. "He says there's something he wants to tend to, and that nobody in town will see him. He promises he'll show up by daybreak." Sheldon was said to have replied, "If Cassidy said so, he'll keep his word."[31]

On his last night of freedom, Butch visited the home of Will Simpson, likely spending more time with Simpson's wife and mother rather than the man who had sent him to prison. This was not a "no hard feelings" visit, however. The family—and likely Butch—never completely forgave Will Simpson for prosecuting the case. Years later, it has been written that Simpson spotted Butch in town and "stayed under cover, fearing reprisal."

True to his word, Butch was back in his jail cell by dawn.[32]

On July 15, 1894, convicted horse thief Butch Cassidy and five other prisoners were transported by wagon from Lander to Rawlins, and from there by train to the Wyoming State Penitentiary in Laramie. Extra security was in force, with Sheriff Charley Stough, Deputy Sheriff Harry Logue, and Lander town constable Henry Boedeker leading the entourage of law enforcement officers.

They were met at the gate by warden W. H. Adams, who noticed that one of the prisoners, George Cassidy, was not wearing leg shackles. Adams, a stickler for rules, demanded to know the reason. Before any of the peace officers could answer, Butch muttered, "Honor among thieves, I suppose." His notable sense of humor had not been affected by the seriousness of the circumstances.[33]

The Wyoming State Penitentiary was an impressive facility. This forty-two-cell fortress made with two-foot-thick limestone and sandstone walls and a high surrounding wooden stockade had been built in 1872, and was separated from the town of Laramie by the Big Laramie River. The complex included two cell blocks, warden's office, guard's quarters, a dining hall, a blacksmith's shop, boiler houses, a bakery, icehouses, a broom factory, and barns and pens for livestock. Cells measured at six by eight feet in the north wing and five by seven feet in the south wing. Two prisoners in each cell slept on canvas hammocks. When Butch arrived at the prison, the population was approximately 115 inmates.[34]

His prison file read: "Number 187; Name, George 'Butch' Cassidy;

Received 7-15-94; Age, 27; Nativity, New York City; Occupation, cow-boy; Height, 5'9"; Complexion, light; Hair, dark flaxen; Eyes, blue; Wife, no; Parents, not known; Children, no; Religion, none; Habits of life, intemperate; Education, common school; Relations address, not known; Weight, 165 pounds; Marks scars; features, regular, small deep set eyes, 2 cut scars on back of head, small red scar under left eye, red marks on left side of back, small brown mole on calf of left leg, good build."

George "Butch" Cassidy—convict number 187—would begin to serve his two-year sentence at hard labor. He was now a member of a brotherhood of hardened criminals who lived in an environment that offered little rehabilitation but plenty of schooling in the finer points of lawbreaking.

CHAPTER SEVEN
DAY OF THE OUTLAW

I hate to see the wire fence
A-closin' up the range;
And all this fillin' in the trail
With people that is strange.

We fellers don't know how to plow,
Nor reap the golden grain;
But to round up steers and brand the cows
To us was allus plain.

—"Bronc Peeler's Song"

After hightailing it out of Malta on the fastest horse he could saddle, escaping the clutches of the law following a train robbery, Harry Alonzo Longabaugh, alias the Sundance Kid, decided to lie low and seek an honest job as a cowboy.

But the land on which Sundance rode had changed dramatically from his earlier days as a cowpoke. Open-range roundups and long cattle drives had passed into history. A new method for controlling livestock and protecting fields now stretched across the prairie—barbed wire.

Homesteaders all over the West found that large areas of garden or pasture could now be easily and cheaply fenced off with barbed wire, which would protect their property. Cattle ranchers soon strung their own wire across miles and miles of formerly open plains. Cows could no longer wander freely or be driven long distances, but rather were confined to expansive fenced pastures, making simpler the task of managing a herd. Roundups that had once ranged over hundreds of miles were now held within barbed-wire pens. The only driving that cowboys on horseback engaged in now was pushing the herd from one enclosure to another or to the railroad for shipment.

Part of the reason ranchers accepted the confining barbed wire was the lessons learned from the devastating winter of 1886–87, which changed forever the cattle industry in Wyoming and Montana.

Outfits able to rebuild their herds not only rounded up their cattle and placed them inside barbed-wire fenced ranges, but they also provided sheds, windbreaks, and barns to protect their animals against the harshest of elements. Ranchers planted and grew hay in sufficient quantities to be stored and fed to the penned-up cows during the lean winter months. If no streams or other water sources were available within the fenced pasture, ranchers dug wells and erected sturdy windmills to pump water into tanks for the thirsty animals. No one expected such a harsh winter anytime soon, but the tragic incident had been a warning that even the largest rancher could be wiped out during a single season of severe weather.[1]

In addition to his normal duties of doctoring, branding, notching, and castrating cattle, a cowboy's job now included stringing and fixing fence, digging wells, repairing windmills, constructing sheds and windbreaks, as well as planting, mowing, and baling hay. These new tasks were "ground work," and anything that could not be accomplished from the back of a horse was against the nature of the cowboy and regarded as highly distasteful. The days of the wide-open range and unbridled freedom had indeed been transformed forever with the advent of barbed wire.[2]

After his escape from Malta, the whereabouts of the Sundance Kid are impossible to accurately trace. He likely remained somewhere in Montana, keeping a low profile as he worked at ranches such as the RL, the Circle Bar, and the N Bar. He never let the dust settle under his boots for too long, and warily watched his back trail. Strangers approaching on horseback might indicate a posse coming to arrest him.

By early 1895, Sundance had returned to work at the Niedringhaus brothers' N Bar N, which had rebuilt its herd following the devastating blizzard and moved its headquarters to Wolf Point, Montana. Sundance had the pleasure of sharing the bunkhouse with two cowboys of historical significance. Harvey Logan, a small-bodied, vicious man and a natural-born killer, would take the name Kid Curry and later ride the outlaw trail alongside Sundance. The other man was the future famous artist Charles M. Russell.[3]

Years after rendering his masterpiece depicting the carnage

wreaked by the blizzard of 1886–87, Charlie Russell still held his day job as a cowboy and, during his off hours, sketched and painted romantic scenes of ranch life. N Bar N co-owner William Niedringhaus soon became an important mentor for Russell, giving him commissions, promoting his artwork, and encouraging his cowboy to take up painting full-time. The Niedringhaus family would eventually own a large collection of Russell paintings.

Sundance soon rode away from the N Bar N and drifted south to Wyoming. He found employment as a horse wrangler with several outfits, including the Beeler Ranch and later at Albert R. Reader's Stone Wall Ranch.

During this time, he dropped his surname and went simply by Harry Alonzo—likely the result of an effort to turn a page in his life and leave the criminal past of Harry Longabaugh behind. He had failed twice in his endeavors as an outlaw, and perhaps was nagged by his Baptist upbringing that played with his conscience and preached right over wrong. His two forays as a lawbreaker had been motivated by desperation—when he was out of work and broke. He may have told himself that he could and would live a decent and lawful life as long as he was gainfully employed, and cowboying came naturally to him.

From all indications, Harry Alonzo was keeping his promise to himself. He became known and well liked in the Little Snake River Valley, where he was respected by the citizens as an honest man and capable ranch hand. His expertise with horses in particular was noted by his fellow cowboys at the Beeler Ranch, and Jean Beeler Russell described him as "quiet and soft-spoken, a very agreeable person . . . congenial."[4]

Harry counted among his friends at that time Oliver St. Louis, a store clerk in nearby Slater, Colorado. St. Louis wrote that Harry "used to go to dances . . . he was a straight man . . . he was one of the strongest men . . . we used to wrestle together and all I could do to throw him." Harry was also remembered by John F. Gooldy, whose ranch was in the Valley: "He rode mean horses, and could ride about any horse anyone else could ride. He behaved himself pretty well."[5]

At some point, however, Harry became involved in a confrontation with his boss, Ed Wren, which resulted in his arrest by Deputy Sheriff "Big" Perkins. Harry, as he had proven in the past, had an aversion to handcuffs. But this time, instead of slipping out of them, he whacked Perkins across the face with the metal bracelets.

Apparently no charges came of the arrest—or the assault with the handcuffs—but the deputy sheriff did start to make inquiries about this stranger named Harry Alonzo, one of which was sent to the Pinkerton Detective Agency.

The Pinkerton National Detective Agency, which began as the North-Western Police Agency, was formed in 1852 by Allan Pinkerton, who had been a deputy sheriff in Chicago. As the nation's first detective agency, Pinkerton enjoyed immediate success. The agency, employing undercover tactics and infiltration, solved a series of train robberies during the 1850s. They were then hired to guard President Abraham Lincoln during the Civil War, and in 1861 foiled an assassination attempt on the president. Lincoln asked Allan Pinkerton to set up the spy system for the Union, which became the Federal Secret Service, a concept later copied by the Federal Bureau of Investigation. The agency also brutally put down several episodes of labor unrest—including busting the Texas and Pacific Railroad strike in 1888 and the Coeur d'Alene mine strike in 1892—while working for management against unions.

The Pinkerton Agency was also known as a shadowy organization that hired its agents out to the highest bidder, and was ruthless in its execution of justice—as judged by the Pinkertons themselves. Result-oriented at any cost, the agency was said to be not above committing crimes—voter fraud, bribery, jury tampering, intimidation, and by some accounts even lynching and other murders—to satisfy the demands of their clients.

On the facade of the Pinkertons' three-story Chicago headquarters was the company slogan, "We Never Sleep," along with their logo—a huge black-and-white eye. The Pinkerton logo was the origin of the term "private eye."

After Allan Pinkerton died in 1884, the agency was taken over by his two sons, Robert and William. The brothers opened an office in Denver, and set their sights on ending the criminal careers of every Western outlaw and hooligan who dared target Pinkerton clients.[6]

The inquiry by Deputy Sheriff Big Perkins was taken seriously by the Pinkertons, which was always interested in gathering information for its files. Before long, the Little Snake River Valley was under the watch of Pinkerton agents, who began checking into anyone and everyone, whether they were an honest rancher or a wandering cowboy. The agents resorted to their tried-and-true method of infiltration, and also developed a network of local informants. Dossiers were opened on ranchers, horse breeders, saloonkeepers—and Harry Alonzo. It was an anxious time in the Valley, as residents wondered who was a criminal among them and who might be an informant.[7]

Harry was aware that wanted posters referencing his train robbery had been widely circulated. He was now faced with the predicament of running, which would have been interpreted as an admission of guilt, or steeling his nerves and going about his business as a cowpuncher and hoping to avoid Pinkerton interest. For the time being, he decided to stay put and take his chances. He no doubt blended into the landscape of the hundreds of nameless, faceless cowboys in the area, but was prepared to ride away at any sign that he was about to be apprehended.

While the Pinkertons investigated potential crime in the Little Snake River Valley, inmate Butch Cassidy had been attending an informal school of crime at the Wyoming State Penitentiary.

Butch's fellow inmates ranged from thirty-nine-year-old Isaac Winkle, who had killed another man's bull and been sentenced to two years, to Bill Wheaton, a twenty-three-year-old fellow cowboy from Utah serving eight years for manslaughter, along with the usual assortment of horse thieves, brawlers, and bandits.

Butch's best friend on the inside was Abraham "Rocky" Stoner, a fifty-one-year-old sheep rancher from Cokeville, Wyoming, serving four years for larceny. Butch would later hide stolen loot from robberies at Stoner's ranch upon occasion while making a getaway.[8]

Butch, sentenced to hard labor, spent his days working at physically demanding jobs, like mucking out barns and pens that were home to the prison livestock, laboring at various building projects, tending to crops on the prison farm, or making brooms in the workshop. He may have participated in construction that added four feet to the prison stockade, as well as the completion of three additional watchtowers.[9]

Daily work was purposely strenuous, designed to wear out the prisoners and make them more apt to obey rules—and they faced severe punishment for misbehaving. The prison had a "dungeon," where unruly or chronically offending inmates were shackled to handcuffs suspended from the ceiling and fed a diet of only bread and water. Minor rule violations could result in a prisoner's being placed in solitary confinement inside a windowless cell or locked in handcuffs attached to a door. The normal cuisine was a far cry from their mother's home cooking, with shortages of fresh fruit and other dietary necessities, and suspected water contamination would often cause diarrhea and stomach ailments.

Prison life was not all hardship, however. Holidays were treated as special, and inmates enjoyed various forms of entertainment on those occasions. On Independence Day, 1894, an opera company performed a rousing show that offered a colorful glimpse of the outside. Other diversions from the daily routine featured rodeos, which, considering the makeup of the inmates, must have been quite spirited and competitive. Baseball games, the most-liked national sport next to horse racing, were also a favorite form of recreation. Other privileges for good behavior provided for extra free time to participate in activities in the prison yard.[10]

Perhaps the inmates locked up at that point in history were fortunate even to be receiving three hot meals and a place to bed down at the expense of the state. The outside world was in turmoil, with the Panic of 1893 fueling a severe depression.

The economic crisis had been sparked by the collapse of the

Philadelphia and Reading Railroad and the National Cordage Company. A panic erupted in the stock market as foreign investors sold off American stocks to obtain American funds backed by gold. The stock market finally crashed on June 27. Banks began calling loans, which affected businesses that had borrowed money to expand. People rushed to withdraw their money from banks, causing a run on many institutions, and credit was nonexistent for most people. The value of silver dropped, rendering many silver notes worthless.

An estimated fifteen thousand firms—as well as about six hundred banks and seventy-four railroads—fell into bankruptcy and ceased to exist. Farmers were impacted, with drastically falling prices for export crops such as wheat and cotton. The workingman felt the effects of the crisis as unemployment soared to twenty to twenty-five percent. By the middle of 1894, more than four million people were unemployed and looking for work. The once-secure middle class lost their life savings, and people were forced to simply walk away from their homes. Homelessness and hunger struck American cities, as families were turned into the streets when they could not pay their rent or mortgages. Bands of jobless men, loosely organized into "armies," roamed the countryside. Strikes, often involving violence, were commonplace, including the famous Pullman Strike, which shut down the transportation industry.

President Grover Cleveland and his administration decided to tackle the crisis with a strategy of doing absolutely nothing at all. Cleveland was of the opinion, as were both major parties, that this adjustment of the economy was a natural occurrence that should not be meddled with by politicians.

Many people abandoned their homes in the East and headed west for what they hoped would be a fresh start. Populations rose dramatically in railway destination towns like Seattle, Portland, Salt Lake City, San Francisco, Los Angeles, and Denver, as well as many smaller communities in between. But the West was having its own problems as the ripple effects of the failed economy spread to every part of the country with the roar and peril of a cattle stampede.[11]

Wyoming's struggling livestock industry—both beef and wool—had almost brought down the Union Pacific Railroad, which filed for bankruptcy. Denver was also hit hard when the mining industry in the nearby mountains went bust. No state or territory was protected or exempted from this recession that set in like a shroud of doom over the nation.

On an individual basis, property values plunged, as did cattle prices. In Utah, Butch Cassidy's home state, the depression, coupled with severe drought, caused the price of beef to fall from $75 to $30 a head all the way down to $8. Once-mighty cattle spreads, like the LC and the Pittsburgh Cattle Company, were abandoning their ranges and having a hard time staying afloat. This devastation of the live-stock industry had a domino effect, and soon many business and min-ing interests had joined in the failure. By 1895, four of the seventeen banks in Wyoming had gone under. Dollars had become difficult to come by, and more and more people found themselves unemployed and hopeless.[12]

It would be four years before the economy began to show signs of recovery. Republican William McKinley would be elected president and restore confidence—helped by the Klondike Gold Rush.

Perhaps of a more personal interest to Butch Cassidy, who was not worried about seeking employment at the moment, was the news from the Big Horn Range. British cattle baron Richard Ashworth was the owner of the horse Cassidy had been imprisoned for stealing. In February 1895, Ashworth was the target of an assassin's bullet. He was inside his ranch house shortly after dark when a shot was fired through the window of the front room. The bullet was deflected ever so slightly by the thick pane of glass in the window—enough to cause it to miss Ashworth by several feet.

Initial suspicion predictably pointed the finger of blame at associ-ates of Butch Cassidy who may have sought revenge for his conviction and incarceration. It was later concluded, however, that the shot had been fired by Ashworth's ranch foreman, Wilfred Jevons. Apparently Jevons had been distraught over a relationship, or the lack thereof, with a young lady who was staying at the ranch. Before authorities had a chance to question him, Jevons committed suicide.[13]

Butch's sentence was set to expire in July 1896, but shortly after Christmas 1895, he learned that there was a chance that he could be released early. He had been a model prisoner, and, citing a clean record as reason for a shortened sentence, he petitioned the governor for a pardon. Governor William A. Richards had already issued a record number of pardons—to the ire of some opponents—which was all the more reason for Cassidy to seek an early release. To Butch's delight, Governor Richards agreed to a personal interview.

The governor was of a mind to release the young convict—few inmates with good behavior served their full sentence—but worried about the reaction of his cattleman friends, who were opposed to the move. "If it is your intention to go straight after you get out," the governor told Butch, "perhaps it could be arranged. You're still young, and smart enough to make a success in almost any line. Will you give me your word that you'll quit rustling?"

Butch supposedly answered, "Can't do that, Governor, because if I give you my word I'd only have to break it. I'm in too deep now to quit the game. But I'll promise you one thing: if you give me a pardon, I'll keep out of Wyoming."

The governor was said to be so impressed with Butch's truthfulness, or he saw the pardon and release as a way to be rid of an outlaw inside his borders, that he granted the request.[14]

More than likely, the above conversation was simply another of the countless myths that have been passed down through the years about Butch Cassidy. There is a pretty good chance that Butch told the governor exactly what he wanted to hear and nothing more. If the above conversation actually took place, time would tell whether or not he kept his alleged promise to stay away from Wyoming railroads and banks.

Regardless of particulars, on January 19, 1896—under the watchful eye of the governor, who was visiting the prison that day—Butch Cassidy, now almost thirty, walked out of the Wyoming Territory

Prison a free man. Butch would later remark that he was a petty criminal before entering prison, but his experience behind bars had hardened him into an outlaw. This stretch in the pen, for the record, would be the only time that he would be imprisoned in his lifetime.[15]

Butch headed directly to the outlaw refuge of Brown's Park, where friend Matt Warner had a cabin on Diamond Mountain. Matt had recently wed Rose Morgan, an eighteen-year-old Mormon girl from Star Valley. Rose had not known of Matt's criminal activities when they married, and at one point had left him in disgust with their daughter, Hayda. Matt was able to persuade Rose to return, but only if he promised to give up his outlawing ways. Rose suffered from cancer that eventually caused one of her legs to be removed. She and Hayda subsequently moved to Vernal, Utah, where she could keep regular doctor appointments, while Matt remained alone at the ranch.[16]

Butch Cassidy was a welcome sight to Matt Warner, and was invited to move into the ranch house. Butch helped out with chores, but he had no intention of remaining there. Although Matt likely tried to convince Butch to go straight, the newly minted ex-con was not about to give up his outlaw ways. One of his first acts to celebrate his freedom was to ride into Vernal and buy a new .45-caliber, single-action Colt revolver.[17]

Butch was pleased to run into another old acquaintance, a young man named Ellsworth "Elzy" Lay, who had ridden for the Bassett Ranch back in 1889. The tall, good-looking cowboy was a flashy dresser who favored wearing jewelry—diamond stickpins in particular—and was a favorite with the ladies.

Twenty-eight-year-old Elzy, a native of McArthur, Ohio, had come west with his family in the early 1870s, settling in northeastern Colorado. He left home at eighteen and traveled to Denver, where he was the driver of a horse-drawn streetcar. One day, he was on the job when a man attempted to molest a woman passenger. Elzy threw the man to the pavement so hard that he thought he had killed him. Fearing arrest, Elzy Lay panicked and fled the city. He eventually found his way to Brown's Park, where he began a new life. Incidentally, one of his new experiences was attending school one winter with the Bassett children and their friends, although he was in his early twenties. Josie Bassett described him as "the finest gentleman I have ever known."

Elzy Lay was a now-and-again resident of Brown's Park. He would depart upon occasion to commit some petty crime, such as counterfeiting, and return to hide out. Elzy had earlier been linked romantically with Josie Bassett, but when Butch arrived in Brown's Park early in 1896 he was head over heels in love with Maude Davis, whose father owned a ranch on Ashley Fork near Maeser, Utah. Elzy moved in with Butch, while Matt spent more and more time in Vernal as his wife's condition worsened.[18]

One day in May, Matt Warner visited Vernal's Overholt saloon and ran into an old friend, Bill Wall, a gambler whom he and Butch had known back in Telluride. Also at the bar that evening was a prospector and mining promoter named E. B. Coleman. Coleman was shutting down his claim, and offered the men $100 to help pack up the equipment.

But the packing chore was not the only activity on the minds of the three men as they rode out of town. In truth, Coleman had hired the two men to scare off some other prospectors who'd found the same vein Coleman was following up in the Uintah Mountains, one with prospects of leading to a gold deposit.

Upon their arrival at the mine, a gunfight broke out between Warner, Wall, and Coleman and the alleged intruders. When the smoke had cleared, Warner, Wall, and Coleman had shot to death two men. The three of them were subsequently arrested and charged with murder.[19]

Matt and his associates were at first locked up in the Uintah County jail at Vernal, but threats on their lives by the vigilante committee forced the sheriff to transport the prisoners to Ogden, where they would stand trial. Matt had no funds with which to pay for a legal defense. His friend Butch Cassidy told him not to worry. He would find the money to hire the best lawyer available, Douglas A. Preston. Butch had a plan, and called on Elzy Lay and a man named Bob Meeks to assist him. He would secure the funds to hire Preston by robbing a bank.[20]

Wilbur "Bob" or "Bub" Meeks, a cowboy from Fremont County, Wyoming, had also been hanging around Brown's Park when Butch arrived. Butch and Meeks had probably met back when Butch and Al Hainer owned the ranch on Horse Creek, and Bob's father, a devout Mormon, owned property nearby. Bob was always up for whatever would lead to a payday.[21]

The bank Butch selected was located in Montpelier, Idaho, a town cradled in the bosom of the mountains in the southwestern corner of the state. Founded by Mormons, the town had grown considerably with the coming of the Oregon Short Line Railroad, but the growth spawned by the tracks included business inconsistent with Mormon beliefs. Montpelier split into two districts—with a gate as a dividing line.[22]

On Thursday, August 13, 1896, Butch, Elzy, and Bob rode into town and tied up their horses outside the general store. After a brief visit at the store they mounted and walked their horses down the street to the hitching posts outside the bank.

It was three p.m. when two of the robbers stepped inside, their six-guns drawn, while the third man waited with the horses. The robbers ordered everyone to raise their hands and line up with their faces against the wall. Two town councilmen were among the several customers, along with three bank employees, all of whom complied with the demand.

One of the bandits, later described as blond and stocky and acting like the leader, remained at the door. The taller man moved behind the counter and ordered the teller to hand over all the money. The teller swore that he had none. The robber answered by whacking the unarmed man on the head with his six-shooter, an act that apparently angered the leader by the door, who told his associate not to strike the man again.

The tactic worked, however, and the teller began stuffing bills into a sack provided by the tall bandit. The robber then moved to the vault, where he found more money. Upon exiting he noticed a stack of coins behind the counter, and dumped them into the bag. His last act was to reach up and remove a Winchester rifle from the wall.

The blond bandit held his position as the tall man ran outside with the loot and the rifle and tied them to his horse. The leader then told everyone to stay in the bank for at least ten minutes or there would be severe repercussions. After assuring himself that his partners were ready to leave, the blond man exited the bank. The three robbers rode at a normal gait until reaching the edge of town, where they urged their mounts into a gallop and headed toward the Wyoming line, fifteen miles away.

The men rode as far as Montpelier Pass, where, according to plan, they had fresh mounts waiting. Butch had once again employed the relay system, and, just as in the past, the tactic allowed the three men to easily outdistance the posse. In this case, their pursuers gave up the chase, and the robbers were not pressured to keep riding hard. This bank robbery demonstrated the modus operandi of what was the signature holdup designed by Butch Cassidy—quick and well planned.[23]

There was one interesting twist to the story, however. The sheriff and his deputy rode on after the posse of townsfolk turned back, and were thought dead from an ambush when firing was heard coming from Montpelier Canyon. The gunfire was never explained and the two peace officers returned safely to town—but not before the *Montpelier Examiner* reported their deaths in its Saturday edition.[24]

The amount of money that Butch's gang made off with has never been determined. Estimates range from $5,000 to $16,500. Whatever the true figure, most of the bills, coins, and gold were turned over to Douglas Preston to pay for the defense of Matt Warner on murder charges.

The trial began on September 8, 1896, and the following day an article appeared in the *Salt Lake City Herald* that read in part: "It is alleged that the bank was robbed by Cassidy and his gang to secure funds for Warner's defense and that one of the attorneys in the case had already received $1000 of bank money. Attorney Preston from

Rock Springs says that inference is a malicious falsehood. He received his fee before the Montpelier robbery occurred. He was not employed by Cassidy or any of the alleged Cassidy gang."[25]

Matt Warner thought his and his codefendants' chances were pretty good with Douglas Preston as their defense attorney. In one respect, Preston was able to disprove the theory that Matt fired first, lessening the charge from first-degree murder. The jury, however, convicted Matt and Bill of involuntary manslaughter, while somehow acquitting Coleman. The two men were sentenced to five years at hard labor in the Utah State Penitentiary.[26]

After the robbery, Butch and Elzy had holed up in a cabin somewhere north of Vernal. That fall, Elzy married his longtime girlfriend, Maude Davis, whose parents lived not far away. Maude moved into the cabin with Elzy, Butch, and Butch's female companion, thought to be Ann Bassett.[27]

The living arrangement was soon disrupted, however, by word that the law was coming to arrest the two men for the Montpelier bank robbery. The four headed for Brown's Park, where Butch had always been welcomed and Ann Bassett's family could provide refuge.[28]

The Sundance Kid likely heard about Butch Cassidy's release from prison and return to Brown's Park. News like that would have been prime gossip around every bunkhouse and saloon in the territory. Not that there was a connection, but evidence indicates that the man now known as Harry Alonzo departed his job in the Snake River Valley at least long enough to visit the Bassett ranch in Brown's Park for a traditional Thanksgiving celebration in 1896. Among the thirty-five visitors who attended the gathering was none other than Butch Cassidy.

The men were dressed formally in dark suits with white starched collars and bow ties at the dinner party. Butch and Harry were among those who served as waiters. There is no indication that Butch and Harry planned any mischief or even chatted at length during this time. There is a distinct possibility that it was a girl—as yet unknown—who lured Harry to Brown's Park, and his attention was paid to her.[29]

After Thanksgiving, rumors spread that the law was planning to roust Butch and Elzy from Brown's Park and arrest them for the Montpelier robbery—enough information for the two men and their ladies to head to Robbers Roost. They found a place in a desolate location near Horseshoe Canyon in northern Wayne County, Utah.

That winter, Butch played host to a number of transients, every one of whom would one day ride with him. But the young bandit had plans percolating that called for only Elzy Lay and himself to pull off another brazen robbery as soon as the snow melted.[30]

In April 1897, Butch and Elzy rode into Castle Gate, Utah—home to the Pleasant Valley Coal Company—on horses Butch trained not be startled by a train whistle. One of the largest mining enterprises in the entire state, Pleasant Valley Coal virtually owned the town, employing nearly every able-bodied man.

As a precaution against theft, the company varied the day of the week on which it would pay its workers. The strangers from Robbers Roost, unaware when the next payroll would arrive, had to loaf around town for several days, which may have become uncomfortable given the fact that they were cowboys in a town full of miners, many of them foreigners. Nonetheless, Butch was determined to steal the payroll whenever it became available, and tried to remain as inconspicuous as possible.

On the twenty-first day of the month, Butch and Elzy were mingling with about one hundred other men who were hoping to pick up their paychecks. Today was the day, Butch judged. While Elzy tended to their horses, Butch, dressed in denim overalls and a brown coat, hung around the stairway leading to the company offices—the only entrance to the paymaster's office.

At noon, the D&RG passenger train No. 2 arrived on its biweekly trip from Salt Lake City. Paymaster E. L. Carpenter and his clerk T. W. Lewis descended the steps from the upstairs office and hurried to the train station. Carpenter signed for two cloth sacks, one holding $1,000 in silver, the other $860 in silver and $1,000 in currency, as well as a leather satchel containing $7,000 in gold—a total of $9,860.

Butch nonchalantly moved over to the side of the building near the stairway and watched as Carpenter and Lewis departed the station carrying the heavy sacks and satchel. Elzy tensed up as he untied the horses. He swung into his saddle and held ready the reins to Butch's horse.

Carpenter had just placed his foot on the bottom step of the wooden stairs when Butch stepped forward. His six-gun in the paymaster's face, Butch calmly and quietly instructed him to drop the sacks and hold up his hands. The astonished man complied as his frightened clerk ran inside the nearby Wasatch Company store, still clutching the bag containing $1,000 in silver.

Butch grabbed the satchel and two bags of loot and made a mad dash for Elzy and the horses. He tossed the sacks to Elzy, who inadvertently dropped the reins to Butch's horse to catch them. The terrified animal bolted down the street. Butch, on foot with a horde of confused miners closing in on him, remained cool. He displayed his six-shooter, and acknowledged the crowd by saying, "Don't anybody make a mistake; everything's going to be all right."

By this time, Elzy had captured the escaped horse and ridden back. Butch quickly mounted and the two men spurred their animals out of town. Several shots fired by Pleasant Valley Coal Company employees whistled past them, but there was no immediate pursuit.

E. L. Carpenter ran back to the train station to telegraph the sheriff in the nearby town of Price, but the line was dead. Butch or Elzy had earlier climbed a pole outside of town and snipped the wire. The paymaster then ordered the engineer of the waiting train to cut loose the locomotive from the rest of the train and head for Price without delay. The train rolled down the tracks, its whistle splitting the silence of the countryside to herald the robbery.

The outlaws dropped the sack containing silver and currency to lighten their load and fled with $7,000 in gold. Butch, having planned their getaway from Castle Gate with his usual precision, had fresh horses waiting for them down the trail. The two men easily eluded the posse that was eventually formed, cutting more telegraph wires as they rode on, and finally took refuge back in Robbers Roost, where few lawmen dared enter.[31]

Butch had not panicked but demonstrated calmness under fire when confronting the paymaster, as well as when his horse had bolted. Apparently the Sundance Kid had not panicked either when the Pinkertons came snooping around. He had remained on the job— with a few absences—as a wrangler at the Reader Ranch.

On January 9, 1897, the Craig, Colorado, *Courier* reported that "Harry Alonzo and Bert Charter went to the Lower Snake River last Monday to establish a winter camp and look after the cattle of the Reader company till spring." One week later, the newspaper wrote: "Reader's outfit left last Monday for the lower country for the winter. Bert Charter, Harry Alonzo, and Mr. Fillbrick were with the horses."[32]

But by springtime, Harry had larceny on his mind. Monotonous days, stretching into months, cooped up in a winter line shack without much companionship or many vices, likely convinced Sundance that he had little future working for such low wages and enduring the aches and pains of cowboying. A place of his own or a better life as he got older was nothing but a pipe dream on cowboy wages. Or, as was the case with Butch Cassidy, he could have simply had robbery in his heart and could not help himself. In any event, Sundance decided to partner up with several shady acquaintances who hung around Brown's Park and try his hand at robbing a bank.

The town of Belle Fourche, South Dakota, was a thriving cattle community located on the railroad across the Wyoming border at the confluence of the Belle Fourche and Redwater rivers—hence the town's name, which in French means "beautiful fork." The town lay only about twelve miles away from the Three V Ranch, the place where Harry Longabaugh committed his first crime in 1887.

Beginning on June 24, 1897, Belle Fourche hosted a weekend re-union of Civil War veterans, a welcome boom that had money flowing to the town's merchants. That year's reunion was a marked success, and the vault at the Butte County Bank bulged with extra dollars deposited by retailers. Given the economic desperation around the West, the cash bonanza had likely aroused the interest of more than one criminal mind. Acting upon that interest was another matter altogether.

Shortly before ten a.m. on June 28, six strangers—said to include Harvey and Lonnie Logan, Tom O'Day, "Flatnose" George Currie, Walt Punteney, and the Sundance Kid—rode their horses down State Street and halted at Sixth Street, across from the two-story limestone building that housed the bank. With strangers filling the saloons and the streets full of activity, during the weekend no one paid much attention to the nondescript riders.

The newcomers tied up their mounts at the side entrance of the bank on Sixth Street. Two of them sauntered across the street and tried to act inconspicuous. One of the remaining group of four stayed with the horses, while the other three—Harvey Logan, George Currie, and the Sundance Kid—wasted no time entering the lobby of the bank.[33]

The three robbers had their pistols drawn as they burst through the door to encounter head cashier Arthur R. Marble, his assistant Henry Ticknor, and five customers. One of the armed intruders shouted for everyone to raise their hands high, an order readily obeyed.

Within moments, however, while the attention of the outlaws was elsewhere, Arthur Marble reached for a pistol he had secreted under the counter. Slowly lifting the weapon, he aimed at Harvey Logan and pulled the trigger. The hammer struck metal with a loud snap—a misfire.

Logan swung around, ready to fire, but by then Marble had dropped the gun and raised his hands high above his head. Oddly enough, Harvey Logan, the known cold-blooded killer, did not shoot. Perhaps he had not actually observed the gun in the hand of the head cashier, who now wore a sheepish grin.[34]

Meanwhile, George Currie passed a sack among the customers, ordering them to toss all their cash inside, amounting to $97 from shopkeeper Sam Arnold.

Alanson Giles, the owner of the hardware store across the street, happened to glance out his front window to notice that the customers inside the bank were standing with raised hands. Giles hurried outside and stepped into the street to get a closer look. He then turned and ran back toward his store, shouting, "They're robbing the bank!"

George Currie reacted to the alarm by firing a shot through the front-door window. The bank robbers had apparently prepared for the possibility that shots would be fired. The two men stationed across the street hooted and fired their six-shooters into the air, hoping to convince any bystanders that they were just a couple of drunken cowboys celebrating Civil War days. The gunshots served to spook the waiting horses, however, and the handlers were compelled to wrestle with the frightened animals in an effort to calm them.

Now that they had been discovered, the robbers inside the bank dashed out the front door and made a break for their horses. Five of the six outlaws swung into their saddles, dug their spurs into their horses' flanks, and raced away down Sixth Street in the direction of the railroad tracks. Tom O'Day, who was said to have been drunk, was unable to mount his frightened, bucking horse. The animal broke away and raced down the street, chasing the escaping riders. O'Day was left behind at the mercy of the aroused townspeople, who were at that moment grabbing their rifles. O'Day was later taken into custody.[35]

When the retreating bandits noticed that Tom O'Day was missing, they pulled up on a small rise to see what had become of him. Just then, one of the visiting Civil War veterans opened fire at the robbers with an old .44-caliber rifle, but the rounds fell short. Other townspeople began shooting as well, while blacksmith Joe Miller, packing a rifle, raced his horse toward the hill where the five men waited. He was partway up the hill when disaster struck—his mount was mistakenly shot out from beneath him by Frank Bennett, who was firing from a second-story window of his nearby flour mill. The aggressiveness of the citizens of Belle Fourche, however, persuaded the outlaws to abandon their hopes of reuniting with Tom O'Day, and they spurred their horses and dashed away.

Apparently the bank robbers had been spooked out of the bank by the shouts from the hardware store owner and the resultant gunshots before accomplishing their mission. They galloped away from town with little more to show for their brazen act than the $97 taken from the deposit bag of shopkeeper Sam Arnold. This definitely was not a Butch Cassidy trademark robbery.

The outlaws made a dash for Wyoming, with Butte County sheriff George Fuller and his posse in hot pursuit. At some point, Sheriff Fuller was able to get off a shot at the escaping outlaws, and brought down the horse ridden by the Sundance Kid. Remarkably, Sundance still managed to somehow escape the posse and make it on foot to Newcastle, Wyoming, ten miles west of the South Dakota line. Newcastle was a county seat; thus the authorities would have been notified of the bank robbery and been on the lookout for strangers.[36]

According to Elizabeth Griffith, the granddaughter of Ben F. Hilton, publisher of the Newcastle newspaper, the Sundance Kid broke into her grandfather's office just as he was closing for the night. The Kid was tired and hungry, having likely traveled quite some distance on foot without food or sleep. He held his six-shooter on Ben Hilton and offered him a deal: If the publisher would hide him in his attic and bring him food, no one in the Hilton family would get hurt. After a couple of days to rest up, the outlaw would be on his way. Hilton had no choice but to accept those terms. At one point, Hilton's daughter, Edith, heard footsteps upstairs and guessed the identity of the visitor. Hilton supposedly asked her to keep quiet about it, and she obliged.[37]

Another story casts doubt that Sundance was even one of the participants in the robbery. Allegedly, Snake River Valley rancher John Gooldy claimed Sundance was still working at the Reader ranch at the time of the robbery. His story was confirmed by two clerks at a general store in Slater, Colorado, one being Oliver St. Louis. This evidence may or may not be valid, given the fact that both Gooldy and St. Louis were known to be good friends of the man they knew as Harry Alonzo. It would not be the first time that friends have banded together to help out another friend by offering an alibi for a crime—or the two men simply could have been confused about the time frame.[38]

One fact is true, however: Harry Alonzo Longabaugh was headed to a hideout populated by criminals, and he planned on staying awhile. Leaving behind once and for all a life of wrangling, the Sundance Kid would soon become a full-fledged member, along with Butch Cassidy and a cast of dozens, of the outlaw gang destined to become known as the Wild Bunch.

CHAPTER EIGHT
THE WILD BUNCH

Oh, a man there lives on the Western plains,
With a ton of fight and an ounce of brains,
Who herds the cows as he robs the trains
And goes by the name of cowboy.

He laughs at death and scoffs at life;
He feels unwell unless in some strife;
He fights with a pistol, a rifle, or knife,
This reckless, rollicking cowboy.

—"The Cowboy"

During the years before and after Butch Cassidy's release from prison, notorious desperadoes from across the West made their way to Robbers Roost, or Brown's Park, or Hole in the Wall, those secluded badlands of breathtaking mesas, winding trails, and ragged rock formations, to seek refuge from the law. Most of these wanted men soon made the acquaintance of Butch, the Sundance Kid, and whoever else with a kindred soul may have been hanging around those safe havens.

Many had heard about the mastermind Butch Cassidy, whose reputation was without peer when planning a heist, and wanted to throw in with him and his partners for adventure and profit. The loosely organized group rarely had more than ten or so members operating together at one time, but likely numbered as many as one hundred or more different outlaws over the years. Members of the gang would come and go depending on whether or not Butch needed their help with a robbery or if their own criminal endeavors beckoned them elsewhere.

The majority of these men were in their thirties, and most had worked off and on as cowpunchers. Some had taken to the outlaw trail following the blizzard of 1886–87, when ranch jobs were nonexistent. Butch sized up these men for his heists, and each and every one chosen to participate had to demonstrate his trustworthiness, loyalty, and fearlessness, as well as his ability to use a firearm, if necessary. Remarkably, no one in this gang of illustrious cutthroats would have ever considered betraying the gang leaders or their associates, even when rewards rose to a small fortune.

Butch reportedly wanted to call this gang the "Train Robbers'

Syndicate," but the name failed to catch on. Eventually, a name that would perfectly describe this elite corps of ruffians and manslayers would emerge from various sources—saloonkeepers, newspaper articles, the Pinkerton Detective Agency, and the American Bankers Association among them. No one knows its true origin, but the colorful moniker was destined to live in infamy—the Wild Bunch.[1]

Law enforcement had little knowledge with respect to descriptions or the real names of the gang members. The ever-changing group was adept at using aliases, and it would be some time before authorities were able to match up names with faces—often after the outlaw had died a violent death.

The roster of this diverse collection of desperadoes who were committed to criminal activities and comprised the nucleus of the Wild Bunch reveals horse and cattle thieves, bank and train robbers, and a handful of cold, calculating killers.

Perhaps the most dangerous character involved with the Wild Bunch was Harvey Logan, alias "Kid Curry." A diminutive man—five-foot-seven and 140 pounds—with dark blowtorch eyes, brown hair, and a bushy mustache, Logan made up in ferocity what he lacked in size. His first murder came two days after Christmas, 1894, in Montana, when he engaged in a fistfight with a man named Pike Landusky. Logan, although the smaller of the two, was winning the brawl when Landusky, who feared that he might be beaten to death, went for his six-gun. Unfortunately for Landusky, the piece misfired. Logan drew his own pistol and shot Landusky dead. The deceased man was well liked around town, and Logan was compelled to flee for his life.

Everyone associated with Harvey Logan was aware that he possessed a split personality, and was not a man with whom to trifle. On one hand, he was a charming and polite gentleman who was known to always treat women—no matter their profession—with the utmost respect. The other hand exposed the dark side of a vicious psychopathic killer, who would draw and fire his Colt Peacemaker at the slightest provocation. During his lifetime, he would be wanted on warrants for fifteen murders, but it was well-known that he had killed at least twice that number.

Sundance had worked with Logan at the N Bar N Ranch, and both had participated in the bank robbery at Belle Fourche. Butch Cassidy would be able to rein in the fiery temperament of the Kid during robberies, but if shooting occurred there was a good chance Logan was involved or had initiated it. William Pinkerton, head of the Pinkerton Detective Agency, wrote of Harvey Logan: "There is not one good point about Logan. He is the only criminal I know of who does not have one single redeeming good point."[2]

Although it was usually spelled differently, Logan had taken his alias from an outlaw named George Currie (sometimes spelled "Curry"), whom he greatly admired. Currie was known as "Flatnose" or "Big Nose" due to a nose that had lost its cartilage along the ridge. One lawman remarked, "George's nose was so flat between his eyes that standing at his side, one could see his eyelids standing higher than the bridge of his nose."

George Currie was born on Prince Edward Island, Canada, in 1871, but his Scottish Presbyterian family soon migrated to a farm near Chadron, Nebraska. Currie rebelled against the hard work and the strictness of his father, and ran away from home at age fifteen. He made his way initially by stealing livestock, and then graduated to larger crimes like armed robbery as he aged. He had likely met and worked as a rustler with Butch Cassidy when Butch had his ranch on Blue Creek in Johnson County. Before throwing in with the Wild Bunch, Currie, with enforcer Harvey Logan, led the largest gang in the West. The group was responsible for sheep, cattle, and horse rustling, and the robberies of banks, post offices, and trains in Montana, Wyoming, South Dakota, and Utah. Currie became a role model for Harvey Logan by demonstrating a hair-trigger temper and a complete disregard for human life. He reportedly killed at least nine lawmen during his illustrious career.[3]

William "News" Carver was born in Coryell County, Texas, in 1866, and gained his outlaw reputation by robbing banks and trains in

Texas and New Mexico while a member of the Black Jack Ketchum Gang. After the Ketchums were captured and hanged, News Carver hightailed it for Hole in the Wall, where he was welcomed by the gang. He was a handsome man, fast with a gun, and usually happy-go-lucky except when he was drinking, which made him moody and dangerous. His nickname was bestowed upon him because of his thrill at seeing his name splashed across newspapers after a heist. While staying with the gang, Carver supposedly took up with Josie Bassett, and later Laura Bullion.[4]

Then there was Ben "the Tall Texan" Kilpatrick, a dapper man who stood six feet, two inches in height. He possessed an amiable nature, liked practical jokes, and was slow to pull his six-shooter. Ben had been born in Coleman, Texas, in 1874 into an outlaw family of horse thieves and cattle rustlers. Kilpatrick always ordered ham and beans for dinner in a saloon or restaurant due to being illiterate and unable to read a menu. Harvey Logan called the handsome Tall Texan the "lady killer" of the gang.[5]

Harry Tracy committed his first crime in 1892, when he was fifteen. He stole some geese and served twenty days in jail. He was so dangerous at that time that police had been afraid to arrest him single-handedly. He left home after that to find work in the goldfields of Colorado, but soon moved on to Provo, Utah, where he was arrested for breaking into a house and other petty offenses. He was sentenced to a year in prison, but escaped from a labor gang—killing a guard in the process—after serving less than three months. Tracy went on a crime spree across the West, committing offenses that ranged from kidnapping to murder.

Tracy eventually traveled back to Colorado, where he was an accessory to the murder of a young man committed by Swede Johnson. He was arrested for the crime, but escaped from jail. He was trailed by peace officers to Brown's Park, where he sought refuge. Along the way, Tracy shot and killed Valentine Hoy, a member of the posse who was well liked in the Park. In what was dubbed the "Battle of Brown's Park," Tracy and his cohorts eventually surrendered without a shot. It has been reported that Butch Cassidy was one of those who was not enamored of the exploits of Tracy, and at one point personally ordered him to leave Brown's Park. Tracy's alliance with the Wild Bunch was minimal, but his name does make the roster.[6]

Patrick Louis "Swede" Johnson, a Missourian who was not Swedish, was a hard-drinking rustler and murderer. He was a friend of Harry Tracy's, and shared the same trait—they were both pathological killers. Johnson was in the company of Tracy in March 1898 in Wyoming when a witless sixteen-year-old named Willie Stang accidentally dumped part of a pitcher of water onto Johnson. Swede did not rebuke the boy, but rather went berserk and emptied his six-gun into Stang's body. Johnson was eventually captured at the Bassett ranch in Brown's Park, and extradited to Wyoming to stand trial for that shooting. He was acquitted due to lack of evidence.[7]

Camilla "Deaf Charley" Hanks was deaf in one ear and had a habit of cocking his head to the left to favor his good ear. He had been born Orlando Camilla Hanks in San Augustine, Texas, in 1863, and may have been a grandnephew to Nancy Hanks Lincoln. He was known as a quiet man who had experienced his share of action, as evidenced by the numerous scars from bullet and knife wounds that marked his body. Hanks had fled to Montana and Wyoming to work as a cowboy after killing a man in a brawl in New Mexico. He was an excellent horseman and a cool hand with a gun, and had served time at the Deer Lodge penitentiary in 1892 for robbing a Northern Pacific train at Big Timber, Montana. Harvey Logan said: "I brought Charley in because he was a good man on the outside." Logan was alluding to the ability of Hanks to capably cover an entire railroad car of passengers.[8]

Dave Atkins was a Texas train robber and murderer who was known to be fast on the draw. This man who walked with a slouch was wanted for murder in San Angelo, Texas, and had a $300 bounty on his head when he joined the Wild Bunch. Little is known about Atkins's involvement with the gang, other than a confrontation he had with Harry Longabaugh, the Sundance Kid. Sundance had an affinity for Ralston cereal, and Atkins once teased Sundance about that craving. The Kid did not take kindly to the razzing, and, while his hands rested on his two holstered six-shooters, he invited Atkins to try a bowl of the cereal. Atkins blanched, then complied with the request, afterward professing that it was the best cereal he had ever tasted.[9]

William "Bill" Cruzan stood only five feet, one inch tall, but was known to have enormous physical stamina. This Texan was the best horse thief of the Wild Bunch, and knew every out-of-the-way canyon where horses could be safely hidden. He was said to be as skillful as an Apache when covering his back trail.[10]

Jesse Linsley was a handsome man—except that most of his front teeth were missing. This convicted horse thief had worked for the railroad and supplied the gang with inside information about engines and procedures. It seemed that he had little gumption for robbing trains, however, and left the gang rather than participate in those holdups.[11]

Walter "Wat the Watcher" Punteney, who was with Sundance for the Belle Fourche bank robbery, was known as an excellent horseman, crack shot, and expert reconnaissance man due to his ability to blend in at any town he visited. He was one of the robbers who remained outside during the Belle Fourche bank robbery, and fired his six-shooter while pretending to be drunk as a diversion.[12]

Sam "Laughing Sam" Carey was a train and bank robber who rarely smiled, hence the nickname. He once arrived at Hole in the Wall with three bullets in his body, which were removed by another gang member. One week later, Carey was back in the saddle.[13]

Texan Joe Walker, born in 1850, had worked as a cowboy and at a sawmill, but came to the attention of authorities when he began rustling horses and cattle and then shot up the town of Price, Utah, which caused considerable property damage. He escaped from a Price town posse to Robbers Roost after a fifteen-mile running gunfight, and threw in with the Wild Bunch. There is a possibility that he may have helped Butch and Elzy Lay with the Castle Gate robbery by cutting telegraph wires outside of town.[14]

And there were other known members of the Wild Bunch who had tired of the hardscrabble life of a cowboy and turned to crime: Joe Chancellor, Dick Maxwell, Dave Lant, Will Roberts, Tom O'Day, Jack Bennett, Bob Lee, Lonnie Logan (Harvey's brother), Bob "Bub" Meeks, the incarcerated Matt Warner, and Butch's first partner, Elzy Lay.

The undisputed head of this band of rogues was Butch Cassidy, known as a fun-loving, easygoing cowpoke who did not by any means fit the stereotype of a ruthless criminal. He preferred to use his brains rather than his six-shooter, and professed throughout his life to never having killed a man. Butch was a natural-born leader who had proved himself over the years as being quick-witted, shrewd, and sensible, which was why the gang deferred to his wishes in the planning and execution of a holdup. He had a knack for choosing the right time and place for a robbery, as well as knowing enough to put as much effort into the all-important getaway as into the heist itself.

No matter how much money was jingling in his pockets, Butch's tastes were those of the common cowboy of his day, which was the profession in which he always had worked during respites from rustling or other unlawful endeavors. Butch enjoyed the occasional night on the town at the saloon drinking and gambling, but he rarely drank to excess. He was loyal to a fault, and always rewarded those who remained loyal to him. One time a friend loaned Butch $25, which Butch promised to repay as soon as possible. Within a year, Butch had sent $100 to repay the loan with a note that read: "If you don't know how I got this, you will soon learn someday." Butch also welcomed the company of young ladies, and was rarely without their companionship, even when in hiding, and enjoyed an on-again, off-again romance with Ann Bassett.[15]

Ann Bassett was twelve years younger than Butch, and as an eleven-year-old had followed him around like an adoring puppy dog when he had worked at the Bassett ranch in Brown's Park. At that time, rumor had it that Butch was more interested in her older sister, Josie, who was fifteen, but it appears that Ann finally got her man now that Butch had returned to the Park after prison.

Both Bassett girls had been taught how to ride, rope, shoot, spit, and curse as well as any man by their father, Herbert. In return, the girls helped their father with the profitable family business of harboring outlaws and selling them horses and supplies. Their mother, Elizabeth, the matriarch of the family, was like a big sister or even a mother to Butch and Sundance and some of the other boys. Her ranch house maintained an open-door policy for the Wild Bunch.

Ann and Josie had been educated at a prominent boarding school in Boston and were intelligent girls, but chose to return to the remote ranch after school. In 1896, a group of wealthy cattlemen, especially those of the Two-Bar Ranch, made an attempt to buy the Bassett ranch, but Herbert and Elizabeth refused to sell. Thus these ranchers, who wanted to control Brown's Park, ordered their cowboys to rustle Bassett cows in an effort to run the family out of business. Ann and Josie returned the favor and took to rustling stock from their adversaries.

A feud erupted, with famed regulator Tom Horn being brought in by the cattlemen to assist them. Horn eliminated several known rustlers, but for some reason stayed away from the Bassetts. It was rumored that Harvey Logan had paid visits to certain people employed by the cattlemen and warned them to leave the Bassett family alone.

At this time, Ann became known from newspaper accounts as "Queen Ann Bassett," and was something of a folk figure to the public. Both Josie and Ann have been linked romantically with Elzy Lay, Ben Kilpatrick, News Carver, and with Butch. But after Butch's release from prison, he and Ann evidently became a steady pair in a relationship that may have lasted as long as seven years.[16]

If Butch was the brains of the gang, the man who ascended to stand at Butch's side with six-guns in his hands was Harry Longabaugh. In the role he played as the gunslinger known as the Sundance Kid, Harry was often called "the fastest gun in the West." Although that compliment may have been an exaggeration, it was said that by the time of his days with the Wild Bunch he had indeed developed a lightning-fast draw. Sundance was moody, shy around strangers, and often quick-tempered and unapproachable. There was a hard edge to him that was missing in his good-natured partner, Butch Cassidy. Those who knew him best, however, say he was an extremely likable and friendly man who would always stand up for his friends or associates, no matter the risk.

Sundance did have his share of vices, however. He loved to play cards, oftentimes drinking to excess while doing so. He also nursed a guilty conscience throughout his life for turning his back on his childhood Baptist teachings, and made a concerted effort to conceal from his family the true nature of his profession. Sundance was a handsome man, with blond hair, a matching blond mustache, and intense blue eyes. He had been quite the ladies' man, but his carousing days ended when he fell in love with a strikingly beautiful yet enigmatic young woman who called herself Etta or Ethel Place.[17]

Little is known about this lady whom the Pinkertons described as "about 27 years old, five feet four inches in height, weighing about 110 pounds, medium complexion and wears her brown hair on the top of her head in a roll from forehead. She appears to be a refined type." Etta or Ethel Place simply does not exist in the pages of history except during the days of her relationship with Sundance and the Wild Bunch. It would be futile to research the surname "Place." Place was the maiden name of the Sundance Kid's mother, and its likely origin as an alias. Sundance occasionally called himself "Harry Place" and would check into hotels with Etta as "Mr. and Mrs. Harry Place." It is not known whether the couple was ever legally married or in a common-law relationship, but they always presented themselves as husband and wife.

The now-famous photograph taken in New York in which Etta is standing with Sundance portrays a delicate beauty who hints of proper high teas, Central Park carriage rides, and evenings at the theater—and assuredly not a crude cabin in some desolate canyon of Brown's Park. The big screen has portrayed Etta as an innocent and pure schoolteacher who fell madly in love with Sundance. Many historians have implied, however, that she was simply a working girl from Fannie

Porter's sporting house in San Antonio, Texas, which the gang was known to frequent. Then there was always the story that Etta was that young girl whom Butch saved from a house of ill repute years earlier and placed with a Mormon family. Another theory rife with faults and lacking facts that has been tossed around was that Ann Bassett and Etta Place were one and the same person—that Butch and Sundance had shared a girlfriend. There is no evidence to support any one theory over another.

So much effort has been consumed seeking the origins and identity of this elegant beauty that no one has speculated about what coaxed Etta Place to travel the outlaw trail. Was it wanderlust, or had she been born into the role, or did the love of a man named Harry Longabaugh lead her astray? No one will ever know the truth. Etta Place will remain a romantic figure who has been the subject of more speculation than perhaps anyone in Old West history. For more than a century, historians have attempted to ascertain the true identity of this young lady, but she has eluded scholars with the same proficiency that Butch and Sundance eluded lawmen.[18]

Ann and Josie Bassett and Etta Place were not the only women associated with the gang. The Wild Bunch had a revolving roster of females who for one reason or another were attracted to the outlaw life. A number of these young ladies had worked as prostitutes at Fannie Porter's in San Antonio, and others were merely ranch girls seeking adventure and excitement. Only a few were ever invited to stay for any period of time at the gang's hideouts.

Laura Bullion had been born in Knickerbocker, Texas, into a family of outlaws. Her father, Ed Bullion, had been killed during a train robbery. Laura first became the common-law wife of "News" Carver, but later took up with Ben "Tall Texan" Kilpatrick, who was said to have won her in a dice game. She has been called "the Rose of the Wild Bunch," and used such aliases as Clara Hays, Laura Casey, and Della Rose.

Annie Rogers made the acquaintance of Harvey Logan while working at Fannie's in San Antonio. Reportedly, Annie was infatuated with this swarthy killer with tobacco-stained teeth, but made the mistake of trying to reform him. She wanted to leave her profession and become a wife and a mother. Harvey would have none of it, and Annie was compelled to follow him around, writing love letters and hoping for a change of heart in him.

Callie May Hunt, better known as Lillie Davis, a working girl from Palestine, Texas, was the girlfriend of Will "News" Carter. Lillie would became known for betraying the Wild Bunch, and eventually spilling her guts to the Pinkertons about everything she knew or had witnessed—locations of their hideouts, aliases, descriptions, and who had been involved in specific crimes. She also mentioned that Butch Cassidy was an expert bicycle rider, the sport that had become a fad throughout the West.

Other ladies, such as Maude Davis, the comely Mormon girl from eastern Utah who married Elzy Lay, were not involved in crime but were affiliated with the gang only by being romantically attached to an outlaw member. Not so Della Moore, who traveled with Harvey Logan until her arrest for laundering money from one of his robberies.

Many of the girls who become involved with the gang were working at the aforementioned Fannie Porter's brothel at 505 South San Saba Street, on the corner of Durango Street in San Antonio, Texas. Fannie's house was the most popular destination for outlaws throughout the Old West, and also a favorite of lawmen, who received special treatment. William Pinkerton of the Pinkerton National Detective Agency was known to have been a steady customer. Fannie, who had traveled to America with her family from England, had started her house at the age of twenty, when she herself quit walking the streets. She quickly became known for offering the most attractive girls, who ranged in age from eighteen to twenty-five, and made sure they practiced proper hygiene. In addition, this well-known madam gained a reputation for discretion, never turning in a wanted man, and would ban forever from her house anyone who abused one of her girls.[19]

The partnership—and close friendship—between Butch and Sundance had probably developed gradually during visits Sundance had made to the Park during the previous year to court Etta Place. The more time the two men had been around each other—especially socializing at the Bassett ranch—the more they would have discovered how much they had in common. The Bassett ranch was the social headquarters of the Park, and there was some sort of entertainment taking place almost every week to relieve the mundane routine of daily chores and the stress of isolation. Butch and Sundance also may have visited nearby saloons with bartenders and patrons whose minds would go blank if ever questioned by peace officers about the presence of known outlaws.

Butch and Sundance had many similar traits that would have formed a common bond between them. Both had been raised in strict religious households and valued their families but had become estranged due to their criminal ways. Each of them had gone to work away from home at a young age to help support their families—Sundance on the canal and horse farm, and Butch learning the cowboy trade. They had not only later worked as regular cowboys herding cattle but had specialized in wrangling horses, probably spending as much of their careers inside a corral, breaking, training, and caring for those animals, as they had pushing cows. They had each served an eighteen-month prison sentence for horse stealing. Both were well-read, as evidenced by Sundance's childhood affinity for books and Butch's regular use of the Bassett library when he worked at the ranch. They also shared a fondness for the proverbial nightlife of wine, women, song, and gambling, and could discuss larceny at length like others discussed sporting events. And they say that opposites attract—Butch was usually cheery, whereas Sundance was often moody—and each appreciated the other for the perspective provided by his individual outlook. And, unlike Harvey Logan or Swede Johnson, neither man believed in indiscriminately killing another human being.

Most of all, however, they were compatible in the roles they played within the structure of the Wild Bunch. This relationship decidedly was not a classic pairing of "brains and brawn." The crafty Butch saw in Sundance not only the tough gunslinger side, which he respected, but an insightful person who could serve as a trusted sounding board for his criminal planning. While other members would come and go, Butch and Sundance remained a steady force that held together the basic fibers of this fickle group of dangerous hooligans, and provided the necessary framework to avoid reckless slipups that could spell doom for the gang—and for themselves.

Butch and Sundance did not fit the mold of tyrannical leaders, but operated what could be called a loosely democratic organization. They would entertain opinions from the gang while formulating plans for a robbery. Although the final grand scheme would come from Butch, the two wanted their associates to feel comfortable with the details and thereby avoid any dissension or breakdowns in discipline during the execution stage. This practice of inviting input was unique among outlaw gangs, where a strong leader generally dictated plans.

To his credit, Butch also instituted a policy to discourage violence as much as possible during the execution of their robberies. He preferred to rely on intimidation and negotiation instead of gunplay—even though if any of them had been captured they would have likely faced the hangman. This policy was not always adhered to by the members, but was faithfully followed by Butch and Sundance.

It is probable that Butch and Sundance personally holed up for most of the winter of 1897–98. Butch may have thought about visiting his family, and Sundance may have rendezvoused with his seafaring brother in San Francisco, but neither man was up to any mischief. Nonetheless, a fair portion of the notorious criminal reputation of Butch and Sundance and their outlaw gang during this time and from heists in previous years was established without the two leaders having actively participated in the exploits.

Granted, Butch may have consulted with members in the planning of their own robberies now and then, but it seemed that every unsolved train, bank, store, stagecoach, or piggybank holdup occurring in the West was placed at the doorstep of the Wild Bunch. At least, that was the mind-set of the authorities in the Rocky Mountain region, and they intended to do something about it.

When spring arrived, the governors of Colorado, Utah, and Wyoming met in Salt Lake City to discuss eradicating the outlaw gangs—the Wild Bunch in particular—that had been terrorizing the tristate area. The governors thought that perhaps they could be successful by dispatching peace officers who could cross boundaries and be authorized to make arrests in all three states. Another plan called for such large bounties placed on the heads of gang members that every bounty hunter in the West would be on their trail.[20]

Nothing immediately came of this governors' conference due to an event that shook the nation—on April 24, 1898, the United States of America declared war on Spain. And the huge outpouring of jingoism—patriotic fever—generated by the impending conflict would be caught by even the Wild Bunch.

This war had been fueled by events in Cuba, ninety miles south of Florida, when the Cuban people had rebelled against Spanish rule and declared that Cuba was now an independent country. Spain had responded to the uprising by bringing in troops, declaring martial law, and mistreating and imprisoning Cuban civilians.

The United States was concerned about this growing conflict, mainly because American business had invested great sums of money in the Cuban economy, especially in sugar plantations. The insurrection in Cuba was not only bad for business, but had struck a chord with the American people with memories of 1776 who empathized with the Cuban people in their honorable quest for freedom, particularly after hearing stories of Spanish cruelty. The flames of the revolt were further fanned by yellow journalism—sensationalized and often false reporting—by newspapers owned by William Randolph Hearst and Joseph Pulitzer. The United States government soon became fearful for the safety of its citizens living in Cuba. With intentions of protecting Americans, the navy dispatched a battleship—the *Maine*—to anchor in the harbor of Havana as a show of force.

At nine forty on the evening of February 15, 1898, there were two distinct explosions on the *Maine*, with a brief interval between them. The first blast lifted the forward part of the ship, and the second, which was more prolonged and of greater volume, has been blamed on the partial explosion of at least two of the forward magazines. In this catastrophe, two officers and 264 of her crew were killed. Those sea-goers who were not immediately killed by the explosion were pinned between decks by the tangle of wreckage and were drowned as the *Maine* sank.

No one knew for certain the cause of the explosions that devastated the *Maine*, but outraged Americans blamed Spain for the disaster. There was no hard evidence, however, and thus President William McKinley refused to lead the country into war. Many believed that the president was weak, and that Spain should be taught a lesson. The rallying cry that rang from coast to coast was "Remember the *Maine!*"

Just a month later, on April 24, in the face of intense public pressure, McKinley asked Congress for a declaration of war. The United States commenced mobilizing for what Secretary of State John Hay called a "splendid little war."

Spain had about eight thousand troops in Cuba, and the United States had fewer than thirty thousand men in its ranks. The American navy, however, was powerful and highly trained for combat, whereas Spain's navy was weak and unprepared. The United States Navy immediately established a blockade of Cuba to prevent Spain from landing any additional troops and supplies.

The first major battle of the war took place thousands of miles from Cuba. Immediately after the declaration of war, Commodore George Dewey had set sail with several American warships from Hong Kong toward the Spanish fleet stationed in the Philippine Islands. On the morning of May 1, 1898, these American ships sailed into Manila Bay and attacked those Spanish vessels. Within a few hours' time, the ships from Spain had been defeated—without the loss of even one American life.

This victory cheered the country, but the conflict was far from over. Everyone understood that it would require ground troops in both the Philippines and Cuba to win the war. Volunteer units, including future president Theodore Roosevelt and his Rough Riders, formed across the country as patriots from all walks of life stepped forward to serve in this noble cause.[21]

An article in the *Cheyenne Sun Leader* urged Wyoming cowboys to volunteer for the service and "make the earth tremble and win glory in some of the greatest cavalry charges of modern times." Apparently a number of cowboys turned outlaw were also fired up by the prospect of serving their country and experiencing combat in Cuba.[22]

Butch Cassidy, the Sundance Kid, Elzy Lay, the two Logan brothers, and a handful of other desperadoes assembled that spring near Steamboat Springs, Colorado. This meeting had been called to discuss the prospects of forming a volunteer unit and offering their services to the United States Army. Critics have suggested that the true intention of the Wild Bunch members was not one of patriotism, but rather an effort to seek amnesty in trade for their honorable service.

Perhaps patriotism with ulterior motives was the real reason for this meeting, but then again there is the distinct possibility that the adrenaline of Butch, Sundance, and their cohorts actually pumped with the love of their country and the desire to serve in its time of need. Nothing exists, however, to document a formal request or any discussions with the military or government authorities about establishing an elite outlaw unit. Alas, these men returned to their hideouts, and the United States Army was denied an opportunity to possibly reform these dangerous misfits—as it has done for so many wayward young men over the centuries.[23]

There are accounts that a number of Wild Bunch members did serve with army outfits in the Philippines. One of these men, Dave Lant, had escaped from prison with Harry Tracy the previous year, and was present when Swede Johnson killed the teenager William Stang. Those three men were on the run in March 1898 for that crime when they heard that a posse led by Valentine Hoy was on their trail. They had crossed into Colorado, and were headed toward Douglas Mountain on a steep trail leading from Lodore Canyon when they were observed by the posse. Hoy came forward, and was shot through the heart by a bullet fired from Harry Tracy's six-shooter.

The outlaws fled, and the posse regrouped and gathered lawmen from Utah, Wyoming, and Colorado. Finally the posse surrounded the trio in a valley near Lookout Mountain, Colorado, where they had holed up among some rocks. Tracy dared them to come and get him, while Lant and Johnson, who were turning blue from the cold, begged Tracy to give up. Tracy refused, until finally the three of them could no longer endure the low temperature and crawled out from their hiding place into the hands of the law.

Johnson was turned over to Wyoming authorities and placed in jail in Green River on account of a lynch mob being formed in Rock Springs. Tracy and Lant were locked up in Hahn's Peak, Colorado. On March 24, the outlaws overpowered the sheriff and escaped. They made the mistake of hailing a stage outside of town, however, and were recaptured. Several months later, those same prisoners whittled a gun out of a bar of soap, covered it with tinfoil, and marched out of the jail in Aspen to freedom. Harry Tracy moved to Oregon and Washington to resume his outlaw career.

Dave Lant had become disenchanted with outlawry and a life on the run, and believed that the army, needing infantry, would not delve into his past—and that leaving the country would help him avoid arrest. Consequently, he enlisted in the army—likely under an alias—and was sent to the Philippines. Lant served with distinction and was highly decorated for bravery in action.[24]

Another story tells about how several unidentified Wild Bunch members served in the Philippines, assigned to a unit as mule skinners. Their mission was one of the most dangerous in the country. They would be responsible for moving supplies through an area that was the territory of the ferocious Moro tribesmen.

Moro was the term used for the diminutive but fanatical Muslims—they averaged slightly over five feet tall—who lived in the southern Philippines. There were about 265,000 Moros at the end of the nineteenth century. Stories circulated about Spanish soldiers who had been captured by the Moros and had disappeared into the jungle, subjected to unspeakable horrors until finally dying an agonizing death over a slow fire. Other Moro practices, such as slavery and the rape of infidels, added to the fear that American forces had for this tribe. No American soldier wanted to encounter these vicious warriors—until the Wild Bunch arrived.

After several bloody skirmishes with the American outlaws, the Moros realized that they had met their match in ferocity. Moro tribesmen sustained great casualties in these fights, and retreated into the jungle to lick their wounds. Consequently, the supply line remained open.[25]

Butch Cassidy did make an official offer to assist in another way with the war effort in early 1898. A great number of lawmen had volunteered to serve their country, which left a void in manpower to chase outlaws and guard valuable shipments by rail. Express companies demanded that states provide militiamen to guard their shipments, although those men were desperately needed elsewhere. Butch was said to have sent a message to Governor W. A. Richards, and magnanimously given his word that he would not rob any trains in the immediate future. The governor, if such an offer was made, ignored the gesture and dispatched what outlaw hunters were still available after the Wild Bunch.[26]

The "splendid little war" was little indeed—in duration. Soon after American forces landed in Cuba, Spain was looking for a way out of the conflict. After negotiations lasting two weeks, an armistice was signed on August 12, less than four months after the war's beginning, and was later formalized by the Treaty of Paris. Spain granted independence to Cuba, and gave to the United States possession of Puerto Rico, the island of Guam in the Pacific Ocean, and the Philippine Islands.[27]

The end of the Spanish-American War meant that returning lawmen could trade their uniforms and rifles for high-heeled boots, wide-brimmed hats, and six-shooters, and once again aim their weapons at outlaws instead of foreigners in an effort to try to rid the West of this dangerous element—and the Wild Bunch was dead center in the sights.

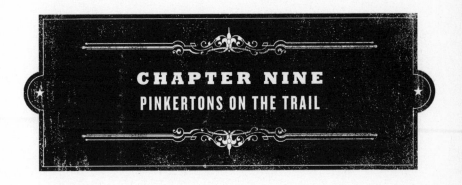

CHAPTER NINE
PINKERTONS ON THE TRAIL

With a watchful eye that never sleeps
The Pinkerton agent rides outlaw trails.
Within his sight he always keeps
The ones who rob the banks and rails.
And if there must be blood to shed
He'll have his six-gun in his hand,
And bring them in whether alive or dead
For the Pinkertons always get their man.

—"The Pinkerton Agent"

Perhaps the thought of actually going straight by serving in the United States Army struck a note within the hearts and minds of Butch Cassidy and the Sundance Kid. Consequently, they decided to temporarily abandon their criminal ways and return to work as ordinary cowboys again. They drifted south, along with Elzy Lay, but left their sweethearts behind at Brown's Park.

The three men eventually happened upon the WS Ranch, which was situated in a relatively lawless area of southwestern New Mexico. This spread rested within a valley along the San Francisco River near Alma, New Mexico, just across the Arizona border. The area had a reputation for providing a hideout for outlaws. Peace officers and posses were hesitant to enter this domain, where the populace was close-mouthed and the odds of capturing a fugitive or suspect were decidedly against them.[1]

William French, part owner of the WS and a former professional soldier in England, was not particularly interested in the past of any of his cowboys. He wanted to hire hardworking, loyal men who knew how to raise market beef without stirring up trouble in the process. Butch, Sundance, and Elzy certainly fit that description, and once again they went to work as cowhands. French became impressed with the skill and leadership ability of Butch Cassidy, who was going by the alias Jim Lowe. French was so impressed, in fact, that he made Butch trail boss of the spread. It appeared as if Butch had found himself a place to call home—at least until larceny beckoned.[2]

Humboldt, Nevada, was a former mining town that had fallen on hard times when the silver panic hit. But it did still boast a train depot that had regular service.

At one twenty-five a.m. on July 14, 1898, the Southern Pacific passenger train No. 1 chugged out of the depot at Humboldt. As the train slowly clicked along the tracks, two men surreptitiously hopped aboard the rear of the tender car and made their way up to the engine compartment. With six-shooters drawn, they surprised the engineer, Philip Wickland, and McDermott, the fireman. Wickland immediately stopped the train, but was ordered to pull it ahead to milepost number 3,784, where a third outlaw waited at a large pile of railroad ties holding the getaway horses.

Meanwhile, the rear brakeman had become suspicious when the train made the unexpected stop. He quickly realized what was happening and took off on foot back to Humboldt, where he telegraphed Winnemucca, the next stop on the line, to spread the alarm. Sheriff Charles McDeid responded by forming a posse and ordering that a special chase train car be readied.

The robbers made their way back to the express car, holding the train crew as hostages, and ordered the messenger, a man named Hughes, to open the door. Hughes refused. The outlaws had brought dynamite, and exploded a stick at the rear of the car as a warning. Wickland, afraid his train would be blown to pieces, pleaded with Hughes to open up. This time Hughes reluctantly complied.

The outlaws jumped aboard and set a second stick of dynamite on top of the safe. Everyone ran for cover as the explosive was detonated and discharged with a frightening thunderclap. When the smoke had cleared, it was found that the safe had been opened—and the roof of the express car had been blown off and the interior destroyed.

Sundance, Logan, and Currie cleaned out the safe, which reportedly held almost $26,000 in cash and pieces of jewelry. They covered their feet with empty money bags to disguise their boot prints, shook hands with the three railroad employees, mounted their horses, and raced away northward.

Its express car in tatters, the Southern Pacific train met Sheriff

McDeid's chase car about ten miles down the line toward Winnemucca, but by that time the outlaws had a two-hour head start. The posse would never have a chance to overtake them, but nonetheless stayed on the trail for some time. A $1,000 reward placed on the head of each train robber by the express company was a powerful motivator. Several men were later arrested for the crime, but the Pinkertons were convinced that the three kids—the Sundance Kid, Harvey Logan, and George "Flatnose" Currie—had been the actual culprits.[3]

After the robbery, while Butch remained working at the WS Ranch in New Mexico, the whereabouts of the Sundance Kid cannot be accurately determined. It can be speculated that Sundance and his accomplices made the rounds of friendly saloons and drank and gambled away much of the proceeds from the Humboldt robbery. Then again, Sundance could have returned to Brown's Park, or another hideout, and into the waiting arms of Etta Place, where he showered her with gifts purchased with the fruits of his criminal labors.

Sundance supposedly turned up again almost a year later in the town of Elko, Nevada. At midnight on April 3, 1899, Sundance, Harvey Logan, and George Currie, wearing masks, reportedly burst into the Club Saloon on Railroad Street while the bartender was counting the day's receipts. The owner yelled for the town constable, and received a clout along the side of his head with a revolver barrel for his impudence. One robber watched the door, another held the owner and bartender at gunpoint, while the third rifled the safe. The three masked men then raced out of the saloon with anywhere from $550 to $3,000, depending on whose story was to be believed.[4]

Although Sundance, Harvey, and George were accused of the crime—the same three who had robbed the Humboldt train, witnesses claimed—there is some doubt about whether they actually pulled off the heist. The Wild Bunch was known for stealing from rich, powerful corporations, such as express companies and banks, not small businesses. This saloon caper was highly out of character. Perhaps the three had been customers there, and thought that they had been cheated while gambling, or had received some other treatment that gave them a bad taste in their mouths, and sought revenge by robbing the place. Otherwise, there is no explanation for their involvement.

Back at the WS Ranch, Butch Cassidy and Elzy Lay continued to impress their boss, William French, with their steady work. The man known as Jim Lowe and his partner, called Mac McGinnis, were ideal employees. Butch handled the cowboys with such proficiency that even local merchants complimented French for the top-notch outfit he had put together. Surprisingly, the traditional end of the cattle roundup—carousing and random shooting—had been eliminated by Cassidy, which was what impressed the townspeople the most. Butch's strict rules led to a high turnover rate, but plenty of men were available to take the places of those who departed. Doubtless the cowboy crew at the WS was steadily bolstered by members of the Wild Bunch, who adhered to any rules set down by their leader.[5]

The WS cowboys enjoyed a relatively lively social life at the nearby town of Mogollon, where community dances and other activities were regularly held. Butch may have been romantically involved with a local lady named Agnes Meader Snider, of whom nothing is known.[6]

There was a distinct possibility, however, that Butch was about to take a leave of absence from his job at the WS Ranch to handle some important business in concert with a handful of trusted associates.

On a rainy Friday morning at two eighteen a.m. on June 2, 1899, the Union Pacific westbound No. 1 Overland Flyer Limited was flagged down by two men swinging emergency lanterns at milepost 609, just east of a bridge and siding known as Wilcox, Wyoming. The engineer, W. R. Jones, fearing that the bridge up ahead had washed out, brought the train to a screeching halt.

No sooner had the locomotive stopped than two masked men jumped into the engine compartment and ordered Jones and his fireman, Dietrick, to move the train up the tracks across the bridge. Jones at first refused, and was slugged over the head with the butt of a Colt revolver. He grudgingly pulled the train forward, and just as it had crossed the bridge the outlaws set off dynamite charges that had been placed earlier on the support beams. The explosion blew fiery pieces of the bridge high into the night sky.

The robbers uncoupled the passenger cars from the engine, baggage, express, and mail cars. The frightened conductor made his way through the passenger cars, warning everyone not to interfere with these dangerous outlaws. He needn't have worried—Butch had established a Wild Bunch policy of always assuring passengers that no harm would befall them if they behaved. The policy was in effect when he was present or had masterminded the robbery.

Engineer Jones was ordered to move up another two miles toward Medicine Bow, where four more bandits anxiously awaited. The outlaws' faces were blackened with burned cork and they wore masks made from white napkins possibly stolen from a Harvey House restaurant.

Jones and Dietrick were escorted to the mail car, and the clerks inside were ordered to open the door. The two clerks, Burt Bruce and Robert Lawson, hesitated too long—a stick of dynamite was exploded and the door was blown off its hinges. The mailbags offered nothing of value. The outlaws moved on to the express car, where waiting inside was a man who was destined to become a significant footnote in history.

Charles E. Woodcock, the express car messenger, was ordered to open the door. Woodcock defiantly refused. The robbers wasted no time placing a charge of dynamite under the door. The charge was touched off and, to everyone's surprise, the blast ripped out the entire side and roof of the car—illuminating the night for miles and sending debris rocketing in every direction.

Shards of wood rained down on the area surrounding the tracks. The bandits had measured out too much explosive for the task, and the car had been reduced to a twisted metal frame. Woodcock was dazed by the concussion, but otherwise uninjured.

The robbers ordered Woodcock to open the safe inside the express car, and once again he refused. This time the proper measurement of dynamite was used, and the two safes were blasted open. Inside, the robbers helped themselves to somewhere between $30,000 and $50,000 worth of cash, unsigned banknotes, gold, diamonds, fine watches, and other jewelry.

The train robbers then escaped on horseback in a northerly direction, once again taking advantage of relay stations where fresh mounts
waited.[7]

In all there were six members of the Wild Bunch involved in this
robbery—Will "News" Carver, Ben Kilpatrick, Harvey and Lonnie
Logan, George Currie, and the Sundance Kid. The man missing from
the scene of the crime was the one who had likely planned the heist,
Butch Cassidy. Had the gang leader been keeping his word to the governor about not robbing a train in person in Wyoming?

This possibility was confirmed by Will Simpson, the lawyer who
had prosecuted Butch in 1894 and had later arranged for his pardon.
Not long after the robbery, Simpson ran into Butch and chastised him
for breaking his word to the governor by taking part in the Wilcox
train robbery. Butch assured the lawyer that he had not participated
in the holdup and had not gone back on his word. Simpson was satisfied that Butch was telling the truth.

Whether or not Butch was telling the truth, the posse that trailed
several of the escaping train robbers noticed an extra set of tracks
eventually joining the others. In addition, several days after his meeting with Simpson, Butch visited Tom Skinner's saloon in Thermopolis,
Wyoming, where he traded in a "considerable volume of gold coin." It
can be safely assumed that even if Butch was not actually present during the robbery, he had certainly been the one who had planned it.[8]

After the robbery, the train robbers split up on the trail into two
bands of three each, one group heading north, the other south. The
diligent posse that tracked the northerly threesome soon met with some
success.

The trio of Sundance, Harvey Logan, and George Currie made a
brief stop at the CY Ranch near Horse Ranch, Wyoming. Their visit
was soon reported by ranch owner Al Hudspeth to Converse County
sheriff Josiah Hazen, who urged his fourteen-man posse to hurry
along the trail. On June 5, Hudspeth and his men jumped the three
outlaws while they rested under a rock ledge at Jumbo Water Hole.
Bullets filled the air, and in the gunfight Sheriff Hazen was shot and
killed, reportedly by Harvey Logan.

Sundance, Logan, and Currie had staked their horses in a box canyon, and were now cut off by the posse. At nightfall, they sneaked out of their hiding place on foot and dashed up the draw, losing a small portion of their loot while crossing two creeks that had swollen over their banks due to heavy rains.

The posse had been demoralized and frightened by the killing of the sheriff, and did not give chase. They chose instead to pack the sheriff's body back to town and not risk losing any more lives.[9]

The Sundance Kid was spotted a week later after he had patronized a store in Battle Creek, where he traded his played-out horse and $20 cash for a fresh mount. He was evidently on his way to the gang's hideout cabin at Brown's Park, where Etta Place may have been waiting.[10]

The Union Pacific Railroad immediately offered a $1,000 reward for the robbers—*dead or alive*. The Pacific Express Company, who employed brave messenger Woodcock, matched that amount, as did the United States government. The price on the heads of the six men who had robbed the westbound No. 1 Overland Flyer near Wilcox was now at $3,000 each, or $18,000 for the bunch—the Wild Bunch members who had perpetrated the crime.

The national press certainly believed that Butch Cassidy may have been involved with the Wilcox train robbery and the murder of Sheriff Josiah Hazen. On June 25, 1899, the mug shot taken of Butch when he had arrived at the Wyoming State Penitentiary was published in the *New York Herald* with an article about the Hole in the Wall gang. Butch—identified as Buck Cassiday—was now a national figure. Although he was not directly blamed for the crimes, the article made it clear that he was poised to become the leader of this band of dangerous desperadoes.[11]

The spectacular holdup of the Wilcox train compelled the Union Pacific to hire the Pinkerton National Detective Agency, which dispatched scores of agents—including Charles Siringo and W. O. Sayles, two of their most experienced men—after the criminals. Texan Siringo, a twelve-year veteran at hunting criminals, was an expert tracker who often worked undercover, and it has been said that he became a member of the outlaw gang while gathering evidence. He claimed he was friends with Billy the Kid and Pat Garrett, and had indeed listed Garrett as a reference when he joined the Pinkertons. Other lawmen were likely also on the trail, as were professional bounty hunters who hoped to cash in on the reward money and fame that could be theirs for subduing the notorious Wild Bunch.[12]

The Pinkertons, according to their creed, never slept while such dangerous men were terrorizing the territory. The chase by these zealous detectives would continue until their quarry was caught or killed, no matter how long it took. Siringo and his partner soon sniffed out the trail of the Wilcox train robbers by tracing the stolen unsigned banknotes, which began surfacing in such cities as Monticello, Utah; Cortez, Durango, and Mancos, Colorado; and Alma and Mogollon, New Mexico. Siringo was unable to identify who had laundered the banknotes, and eventually lost the trail completely—for the time being.

Other Pinkerton agents found success when they were informed that money from the robbery, identified by the torn corners, had been deposited in a bank in Harlem, Montana. The depositors were Lonnie Logan—Harvey's brother—and his cousin Bob Lee, who owned the Curry Brothers Saloon in town. The two were tipped off about their slipup and, fearing pursuit by Pinkertons, they immediately sold the saloon and vanished in the dead of night. Bob headed south and found a job dealing faro in Cripple Creek, Colorado. Lonnie decided to pay a social call on his aunt and uncle in Dodson, Missouri. Both men were soon paid a visit by Pinkerton agents. Bob Lee was taken into custody without a whimper in Cripple Creek; Lonnie Logan was shot to death by agents as he attempted to escape out the back door of his relatives' house.[13]

Butch Cassidy—a.k.a. foreman Jim Lowe—had returned to his duties at the WS Ranch at Alma just as if nothing had happened. He surrounded himself with trusted associates, and may have had a hand in planning robberies committed by other Wild Bunch members.

In late June of 1899, Elzy Lay, the man calling himself Mac McGinnis, decided to leave his wrangler job at the ranch. Likely with Butch's assistance and advice, Elzy joined up with Sam Ketchum,

Harvey Logan, and Will "News" Carver. On July 11, the four bandits held up the Colorado & Southern train near Folsom, New Mexico, and made away with an undetermined amount of cash.[14]

The train robbers fled the scene with a posse led by Huerfano County sheriff Edward Farr nipping at their heels. The lawmen managed to overtake them at Turkey Canyon, and the two sides clashed in a vicious firefight. During the course of this blistering exchange of bullets, Sheriff Farr was mortally wounded by a shot from the six-gun of Elzy Lay, who himself had been severely injured. Harvey Logan and Will Carver escaped, but both Ketchum, who had also been wounded, and Elzy Lay were arrested.[15]

On October 2, Elzy Lay stood trial for the murder of Sheriff Farr. Although the case against him was shaky—no direct evidence was presented that he had actually pulled the trigger of the pistol that had administered the fatal shot—the state wanted to send a message that killing a peace officer would not be tolerated. The jury convicted Elzy Lay of second-degree murder, and the judge sentenced him to life in prison. Inmate number 1,348 entered the New Mexico State Prison on October 10, 1899, to begin serving his sentence.[16]

Butch was of course greatly troubled by the incarceration of one of his best friends, but was relieved that Elzy had escaped a first-degree murder conviction that would have called for his execution. By this time, however, Butch had other concerns that threatened his own freedom.

William French was visited by Pinkerton agent Frank Murray, who showed the WS owner photographs of various men, asking whether he recognized any of them. Yes, French admitted, one was his foreman, Jim Lowe. Murray informed him that he had selected the photo of Butch Cassidy, leader of perhaps the most enterprising gang of outlaws the West had ever known. French now suspected that his ranch was harboring many members of the infamous Wild Bunch. The lone Pinkerton man did admit that he was not prepared to arrest Cassidy at the moment—he would need an army of men to accomplish that feat.[17]

Butch was away from the WS at the time, but French told him

about Murray's visit. The rancher was perhaps a bit surprised when Cassidy appeared unconcerned about being exposed as the famous outlaw—not that Butch confessed. He told French that he had bought Murray a drink at a saloon in Alma on the evening after his visit to the WS.

What he didn't tell French was that Butch had saved Murray's life in Alma that night by not allowing him to be harmed, which could have easily been the case with Wild Bunch members present who were at war with the Pinkertons. Butch had intimidated Murray enough to make him promise to remain silent about the true identity of Jim Lowe. Despite this intimidation of a Pinkerton man, Butch must have felt the hairs on the back of his neck rise with the thought that there would be more lawmen and bounty hunters making inquiries about him at the WS—and not all of them would cave like Murray. Not only that, but there was a clock ticking within him that had periodically led him across the West in search of greener pastures.[18]

Butch soon left the WS Ranch—but not before rustling a herd of horses that he and a partner calling himself Red Weaver drove into Arizona. The two men were arrested in Apache country by a suspicious sheriff when they stopped to buy supplies. They were released on bail, and the case was either closed or they never returned to stand trial.[19]

The parting of ways between Butch Cassidy and the WS Ranch—a place where he was appreciated and could have remained for the rest of his working life—likely had a deeper meaning than just the wanderlust that Butch had always embraced.

Cowboys often whiled away their days riding the range alone. Many tasks required only the strong back of a single cowboy. Windmills needed constant repairs in order to properly draw water. Weeds grew to impede natural waterways and had to be cut down to allow the water to freely flow. Cattle in distant pastures needed to be checked for losses from predators or rustlers, or from wandering too far away. Barbed-wire fencing had to be strung or tightened, and sagging posts had to be made sturdy or replaced. Ice that formed in water tanks had to be broken so cows could drink. Worn and damaged tack, such as bits, bridles, and halters, needed immediate attention. On a ranch, there was always some random chore that could be worked on by a cowboy all by himself. And during those times of aloneness, that cowboy had plenty of hours to simply think, plan, scheme, reminisce, or deal with troublesome thoughts.

Thirty-four-year-old Butch Cassidy had spent his share of time alone at the WS Ranch. And he possessed one of those minds that never stopped working or went on idle. Some people can flip a switch and place themselves in low gear, but not Butch. So it was that he began to have the kind of thoughts that he was not in the habit of entertaining. He was normally planning a heist or considering which part of the Western range might hold the best opportunity for him and his companions. But now his mind kept interfering with his usual thought process, and in its place he contemplated a provocative scenario that had been heretofore unthinkable. Butch Cassidy, the outlaw who had masterminded so many successful holdups, had made the decision that he wanted to reform and go straight.

Butch had evidently received a scare from the Pinkerton detective who had tracked him to his doorstep. If this man could accomplish that task, then so could other agents or peace officers. Butch wondered whether time was running out on him. Granted, he had not killed anyone—yet. Perhaps that evil deed was only a matter of time, when he would have to defend himself during a robbery and take a life, which was against his beliefs. Then there was the nagging fate of Elzy Lay. His friend would be hammering rocks for many years to come, possibly for the rest of his life, for killing that sheriff.

Butch considered what he had to offer in the workplace, and assured himself that he could make a go of it, possibly become well-to-do, just by using the skills and talents he had accumulated over the years. He could give up outlawry, settle down, and live the life of a common man. Contrary to what people may have thought, he had not amassed great wealth—much of the money from his holdups had been squandered. But he had enough tucked away, and was willing to work his way up. The idea of going straight must have been a difficult notion for Butch to digest, but he was nonetheless convinced that it was the right direction in which to steer his life.

Butch traveled to Salt Lake City—after all, he was a Utah Mormon—and visited the law offices of Orlando Powers. Under the veil of client-attorney privilege, Butch admitted that he had committed many crimes and that hefty rewards were offered on his head. Explaining that he wanted to reform, he asked the lawyer whether there was any way he could receive a pardon for those charges against him without going to prison. Powers did not beat around the bush. No, he emphatically stated, that would be impossible. Butch had robbed too many big corporations that would want retribution. The lawyer also was of the opinion that even if Butch were to receive amnesty or a pardon in Utah, other states and territories would continue to hound him.[20]

Butch was predictably disheartened, but not defeated. He sought the assistance of Parley P. Christensen, the former sheriff of Juab County, Utah. Christensen, an old friend of the Parker family, agreed to set up a meeting between Butch and Utah governor Heber M. Wells. This request to the governor by Christensen was a risky move that could have put his career and reputation on the line. Moreover, to accept the invitation for a face-to-face meeting with an outlaw wanted in at least four states was a political, if not legal, gamble by Wells. Surprisingly, Wells agreed to a meeting.[21]

The notorious outlaw pleaded his case, and the governor listened. Butch was heartened when he walked out of the governor's office. The governor had promised to look into the matter and get back to Butch as soon as possible.

Butch's high hopes were soon dashed when he was informed that the governor would have seriously considered amnesty except for the fact that he discovered that Cassidy was wanted for murder in Wyoming. Most crimes could be worthy of a pardon with extenuating circumstances, but rarely murder. Although Butch swore he had not committed that crime, the governor washed his hands of the situation. Butch was back to square one in his quest to go straight.[22]

Meanwhile, Orlando Powers had come up with a unique plan. Over the last decade, he pointed out, railroad companies had suffered 261 train robberies, with eighty-eight people killed. If Butch were to retire—taking his gang with him—it would be a decision well within the interests of the railroads. He could possibly even serve as a train guard to demonstrate his good intentions. Word of Butch Cassidy's affiliation with the railroads would certainly be a deterrent to the outlaw element, especially members of his own gang. Powers noted that the railroads were quite influential in Western legislatures, and could likely secure the amnesty Butch wanted in order to roam freely about the West.

Both sides were intrigued by the scheme. Union Pacific officials agreed to a parley with Cassidy at Lost Soldier Pass, near the Wyoming-Utah border, forty miles north of Lander. As desolate as anywhere in Wyoming, the area gave Butch comfort—if negotiations broke down, he could vanish into the rugged terrain. His old friend and lawyer Douglas Preston was chosen to escort the railroad men to the rendezvous by buckboard.

Unbeknownst to Butch, a terrible storm prevented Preston's party from leaving on time, and when they did get under way they became lost. There was no way to get word of the delay to Cassidy.

Butch hung around Lost Soldier Pass until finally he became angered at the apparent snub, and wary of being victimized by some trick. He rode away in disgust—but not before placing a note under a rock that read: "Damn you Preston, you have double-crossed me. I waited all day but you didn't show up. Tell the U. P. to go to hell. And you can go with them."[23]

During late August, four cowboys drifted into the small town of Tipton, Wyoming, which lay midway between Rawlins and Rock Springs. Butch Cassidy, Harvey Logan, the Sundance Kid, and an unidentified man—who may have been Ben Kilpatrick or Bill Cruzan—dined at a railroad company eating establishment, where they were served by waitress Lizzie Warren. Butch's gregarious personality likely helped them avoid suspicion as they cased the town. And if they were remembered by a waitress, it would be likely that some good-natured flirting, which was the specialty of the handsome Sundance Kid, followed by a generous tip had set everyone at ease. Apparently no one at the railway station seemed overly concerned, either, and all eastbound and westbound trains remained on schedule.

At two thirty a.m. on August 29, 1900, the Union Pacific passenger train No. 3 rolled out of Tipton after taking on water, and headed westward toward Table Rock up a grade a mile or so outside of town. It was not long before engineer Henry Wallenstein felt the hard metal barrel of a pistol stabbing into his ribs. He turned to observe a masked man who ordered him to stop the train up ahead at the bonfire next to the tracks at milepost number 740.4. Wallenstein grudgingly brought his train to a halt. Three more masked men armed with Winchester rifles were waiting at the fire. They ordered conductor E. J. Kerrigan to unhitch the engine and baggage and express cars from the passenger cars. The locomotive then pulled the attached cars up the track, leaving the passenger cars behind.

The messenger locked inside the express refused to open up when ordered. For encouragement, the robbers attached a charge of dynamite to the door and gave the man one last chance to obey. Finally, the express car door slid open—to everyone's surprise and amusement, out stepped Charles E. Woodcock, the man who had withstood the devastating dynamite blast during the Wilcox train robbery. Apparently he had learned his lesson and did not want to be at ground zero of another explosion. The robbers then proceeded to blow open the safe and remove bundles of cash and several packages of jewelry.

As has been the case with most robberies, the exact amount taken varies with each account. Railroad officials claimed that only about $50.40 had been stolen, but Charles Woodcock told the press by a slip of the tongue that the loss was actually closer to $55,000. He boasted that he had hidden several packages of money behind a trunk before the holdup or the take would have been even greater.[24]

While Butch, Sundance, and their associates were riding off to rob the Union Pacific, Orlando Powers in Salt Lake City had come up with another plan to present to the owners of the railroad. Evidently Butch had impressed the lawyer with his sincerity enough to compel him to go above and beyond the call of duty in an effort to salvage the idea of amnesty with help from railroad officials. The Union Pacific Railroad was of like mind, and still desperately wanted to put an end to Butch's string of robberies.

Powers and the railroad people asked former gang member Matt Warner, recently released from prison, to talk to Butch on their behalf. Explain the reason behind the Union Pacific officials' delay for their scheduled appointment at Lost Soldier Pass, they said. Warner, who would surely be trusted by Butch to be telling the truth, agreed to be the messenger.

Matt Warner, given $175 travel expenses, boarded a train for Rock Springs, thinking that Butch would be holed up at Brown's Park. When the train stopped at Bridger Station, just east of Evanston, Wyoming, Warner found a telegram waiting for him. Governor Wells wrote: "All agreements off. Cassidy just held up a train at Tipton."[25]

At about eleven p.m. on the day of the holdup, news of the Tipton robbery reached the Union Pacific offices in Omaha. The company had been notified of the robbery by the railway conductor calling from a pay telephone. Modern communications in the form of the telephone were extending out from Cheyenne, and long-distance service had begun connecting major towns in Wyoming.

Posses were immediately dispatched from Rock Springs and Rawlins. By sundown the following day, the posse from Rawlins guided by Deputy United States Marshal Joe LeFors had traveled almost 120 miles from the holdup site to the Colorado line. As luck would have it, LeFors observed three men and a packhorse climbing the north slope on the opposite side of the Little Snake River. The twelve-man posse had been in the saddle all day, however, and they were weary. Reluctantly, but out of necessity, they chose to make camp for the night and strike the trail of the fleeing bandits in the morning.[26]

The posse was in the saddle by dawn and was soon following distinct hoofprints. They had ridden about thirty-five miles when they observed indistinguishable movements within a thick grove of willows, a perfect ambush site for the outlaws to be waiting. LaFors was apprehensive, but knew he must investigate. The posse spread out and used extreme caution in approaching the willow stand on horseback. No gunshots rang out to deter their progress. As they came closer, the legs of shying horses could be made out. LaFors dismounted and led two other men forward, their six-shooters cocked and ready to fire. Another group of men was sent to circle around to the other side, prepared for battle.

The stealth was all for naught. The LaFors posse had been the victim of a tactic Butch had employed ever since his first robbery. The posse had stumbled upon one of Cassidy's relay stations, and the animals found were ones worn out and left behind. The robbers were long gone. LaFors was discouraged to realize that he had been tricked by the elusive Wild Bunch. There was no way they could overtake the fleeing bandits now. LaFors and his disgruntled posse wheeled their mounts and headed for home. The Wild Bunch boys had escaped again unscathed.[27]

Legend has it that the fleeing Tipton train robbers halted long enough to bury a portion of their loot somewhere in Uintah County, Utah, between Diamond Mountain and the Colorado border. Treasure hunters have searched the area to this day without success for this alleged cache of Wild Bunch stolen valuables.[28]

On the morning of Wednesday, September 19, 1900, Butch Cassidy, the Sundance Kid, and Will "News" Carver could be found seated in a saloon in Winnemucca, Nevada, enjoying a shot or two of whiskey. Carver had earlier had an encounter with a skunk and reeked with a terrible odor, a description the Pinkertons would later print on a wanted poster. The three men had tied their horses to a hitching post behind the F. C. Robbins Mercantile Store in an alley that ran behind the First National Bank of Winnemucca.

At noon, Butch, Sundance, and Carver pushed away from the bar. Moments later they strode through the front door of the First National

Bank at the corner of Bridge and Fourth streets. They had not bothered to conceal their faces with masks.

Butch held a Colt .45-caliber six-gun, while Sundance brandished a pair of Colt .45s. Carver carried a Winchester carbine. The robbers ordered the five people inside the bank to raise their hands. Carver moved to the door, and Sundance ordered the hostages to stand against the wall, where he guarded them.

The head cashier, George Nixon, was escorted by Butch to the closed vault and told to step inside and carry out all the bags of gold coins. Nixon explained that the time clock had been set and he was unable to open the vault door. His escort was in no mood for delays—banks did not time-lock vaults in the middle of business hours. Butch pulled out a knife, placed the blade against the terrified cashier's throat, and threatened to start cutting if the vault was not immediately opened. Nixon wisely chose to obey. Incidentally, George Nixon would later serve in both the Nevada state legislature and the United States Senate.

Within moments, Butch stashed the gold coins from the vault into ore sacks and grabbed all the loose currency from the drawers—$32,640 in total.

After less than five minutes, the robbers marched their five hostages out the back door of the bank into the fenced yard behind the building. Butch and Will Carver leaped over the fence into the alley while Sundance held his two six-guns on the hostages. With a warning not to move, Sundance vaulted the fence and joined his companions in the alley behind the Robbins store, where the horses had been tied.

The three mounted men raced their horses down Bridge Street, and dug their spurs into the animals' flanks. Cashier Nixon ran out into the street, firing a revolver in the air as a warning. One former hostage retrieved a shotgun, but did little more than blow out the window of the next-door saloon when he pulled the trigger.

The bank robbers were soon out of the town limits, kicking up dust in their wake as they rode parallel to the tracks of the Southern Pacific Railroad. Although the sheriff wisely fired up a switch engine and chased the outlaws, his calculations about where to stop were incorrect, and the robbers easily outdistanced the train.

True to form, Butch had planned his escape as efficiently as the robbery itself. About thirty-five miles east of town, a fresh set of horses waited in the corral at a ranch. From there they headed northeast, disappearing into "the Junipers," a wilderness area on the Nevada-Idaho border. Posses searched the vicinity for a week or two, but eventually realized that they had been outsmarted and quit the hunt.[29]

Historians debate whether or not Butch, Sundance, and News Carver actually robbed that bank in Winnemucca. The men who pulled off the holdup were known to have arrived in the Winnemucca area by September 9, and camped at the CS Ranch, fourteen miles outside of town. The distance between Tipton, Wyoming, to Winnemucca, Nevada, is six hundred miles; some have argued that the trio could not have traveled that far by horseback in ten days, which is likely true.

Perhaps these unconvinced historians, however, have not factored in the probability that the three bank robbers rode the train in disguise to reach their destination. The Sundance Kid later confirmed in a magazine article that the three had pulled off the holdup, although he did not mention their itinerary or a train ride before the heist.[30]

One interesting anecdote to the getaway of the bank robbers concerned a generous gesture on the part of Butch Cassidy. He had recently made the acquaintance of ten-year-old Vic Button, whose father managed the CS Ranch where Butch and the others had camped prior to the holdup. The boy described Butch as a friendly man with a ready grin, but what he liked most was Cassidy's white horse, the fastest animal Vic had seen. One day Butch told the boy, "You like that horse? Someday he will be yours."

True to his word, before disappearing into the Junipers, and with the hot breath of a posse down his neck, Butch instructed a cowpuncher at the ranch where they changed mounts to give the white horse to the kid at the CS Ranch. Vic Button would later write: "For a man, when he was crowded by a posse, to remember his promise to a kid—makes you think he could not have been all bad."[31]

The Winnemucca bank robbery could be counted as another remarkable criminal achievement by Butch and the boys. Considering the enormous risks in robbing a bank, they had once again defied all odds with this bold act. They had ridden into town and snatched away more than $30,000 from right under the noses of the townspeople. It was as if Butch had the desire to flaunt his abilities by successfully robbing both a train and a bank within a span of three weeks, showing the railroad and the Pinkertons that he could not be deterred.

The Union Pacific and Winnemucca heists brought the Wild Bunch such notoriety that special detectives and Pinkerton agents were exclusively assigned to stop them. Wells Fargo and Company, which had a network of express lines and banks across the country, tapped detective Fred Dodge to catch the outlaws at any cost. Rewards for the gang's capture had now grown to more than $10,000 a head—dead or alive.

The makeup of these man-hunters who chased Butch and Sundance at the turn of the century was decidedly different from that of the posses or lawmen who hunted the James-Younger Gang or Billy the Kid—or even Butch and Sundance in their early days as outlaws. The men now on their trail were not local sheriffs leading an untrained mob of merchants and saloon hangers-on with limited time and resources and questions about jurisdiction. Instead, they were determined professionals who were part of the changing world of law enforcement, and could utilize up-to-date technology to track their prey.

Butch and Sundance were no longer hunted by people alone, but by a system. Butch Cassidy may have been a master schemer, and Sundance may have had courage to spare, but both were wise enough to know that the odds had turned greatly against them. The cats in this deadly game of cat and mouse now held a decisive advantage over mice who craved the kind of cheese that banks and trains had to offer.

CHAPTER TEN
END OF THE AMERICAN TRAIL

The boys are comin' to town, whoop la!
What does the marshal do? He's gone
An' hid, that's what he did,
Fer he knows a thing or two—Fer he
    knows a thing or two, yip, yip!
Fer he knows a thing or two.
The boys are comin' to town, Oh, my!
What does the old town do? She goes to
    bed while they paint 'er red,
Fer she knows a thing or two—Fer she knows
    a thing or two, wow, wow!
Fer she knows a thing or two.

—"The Boys Are Comin' to Town"

The twentieth century dawned on a confident, optimistic America. Manifest Destiny had served its purpose for expansion—the West was occupied all the way to the Pacific Ocean. A technological revolution had transformed American society. A decided victory over Spain in Cuba confirmed the United States as a world power, and the country, under the presidency of William McKinley, was now seeking to establish its global identity.

America's coming of age was marked by great advances in electricity—compliments of Thomas Edison and Nikola Tesla—which brought forth such inventions as the incandescent lamp, the electric flatiron, electric welding, the cathode ray tube, the AC transformer, and the AC motor. New household and business gadgets included the telephone, the Kodak camera, the safety razor, the phonograph and wax cylinder record, the band saw, the electric fan, the stock ticker, a gasoline automobile, and even an experimental airplane.

The country enjoyed the establishment of symphony orchestras in every major city, art galleries the equal of many in Europe, opera companies, vaudeville, theaters, fine restaurants, spacious parks, and other civilized cultural amenities.

America was the third-largest producer of steel, the world's greatest exporter of agricultural produce, and one of the world's leading industrial powers. The country was well on its way to recovery from that bloody, violent conflict of brother against brother, and was for the most part a nation of families living in quiet, pleasant, safe small towns or on fruitful farms and ranches, with vast, untapped natural resources available to most of its citizens.

With the advent of the new century, outlaws who could rob a bank or a train and remain at large were becoming as rare as the buffalo. The robbers had to contend with growing armies of peace officers, professional man-hunters hired by the railroads and organizations like the Pinkertons, and human bloodhounds who sniffed out crooks for the bounty money. Perhaps more important, bad guys had to try to outwit an array of daunting technological crime-fighting forces as well.

Lawmen used the telegraph and telephone to disseminate descriptions of suspects and gather timely information about their movements. Wanted posters could be mass-produced and widely distributed by using an improved printing process, and in many cases would carry not only a description but a photograph of the criminal. Banks hired armed security guards to patrol the premises and protect their assets. The railroad organized its own gang of gunfighters, outfitting them with high-powered rifles, and sent them out in high-speed trains with horses in boxcars to use in the chase. No longer would a man like Charles Woodcock—brave but overmatched—be expected to ward off a gang of train robbers bent on stealing from express car safes.

Exorbitant rewards were placed on the heads of outlaws who refused to submit to civilization and quit their thieving or murderous ways. Even the venerable Hole in the Wall hideout itself was in jeopardy—raids by citizen armies with blazing six-guns and Winchesters resulted in the retrieval of stolen livestock, and a number of the disreputable inhabitants were sent running for their lives.

In the face of such crime-fighting advances and public outcry, ordinary desperadoes were doomed—and so possibly were the best in the business, Butch Cassidy and the Sundance Kid—if they continued to rob trains and banks.

The most dogged pursuer of the Wild Bunch was Pinkerton Charles Siringo, who possessed a bloodhoundlike ability to track desperadoes. Posing as an outlaw to obtain timely information about his quarry, Siringo received a tip that Harvey Logan had been spotted in the company of Ben "Tall Texan" Kilpatrick near Grand Junction,

Colorado, only a day's ride ahead of him. It was evident to Siringo that the two men were headed for sanctuary at Robbers Roost, and he planned to meet them there.[1]

Siringo rode into Hanksville, a town near Robbers Roost, where he entered the general store owned by Charlie Gibbons. Wild Bunch members were regular customers at Gibbons's store, and Siringo knew it. He intended to make the owner talk—one way or another.

Gibbons swore that he had not seen Logan or Kilpatrick. What about others, say Butch and Sundance? Siringo demanded. Eventually, Gibbons reluctantly admitted that Butch had left a bag full of twenty-dollar gold pieces at the store for safekeeping shortly after the Winnemucca robbery. But the outlaw had recently returned to retrieve the loot and ridden off to parts unknown.

Otherwise, Gibbons could not—or would not—provide information about any other member of the Wild Bunch. Siringo was aware that the man was lying and simply protecting his interests by not informing on his valued customers. Siringo was a Pinkerton, and the urge to pistol-whip the man to force him to talk must have been on his mind. Instead he rode off, not ready to totally alienate a potential future informant. The leads that had brought him to this domain of the desperado had gone stone-cold. But there would be another day.[2]

On orders from the Pinkerton home office, Siringo headed over to Circleville, Utah, Butch's childhood home. He nosed around the Parker homestead and spoke to neighbors, gaining such intimate knowledge as one of the nicknames Butch had received as a child—"Sallie." Other than that, the Pinkerton man drew a blank. Butch had purposely kept his activities away from the Circle Valley. He had not involved his family in his crimes or kept them informed about his exploits, and they could truthfully admit to that fact.

Siringo's presence must have been an especially distressing and painful time for Max and Ann Parker. They had never stopped loving their son or worrying about his health and welfare. To be confronted by questions that carried implications about Butch's character and accusations about his lawbreaking ways, especially to a devout Mormon family, was devastating. No doubt Ann's heart was further broken by the memories of her oldest son, and perhaps she had even questioned her faith over unanswered prayers for his deliverance. The Parkers would have been greatly relieved when the weeklong visit by Charles Siringo had come to an end.

One interesting—and perhaps surprising—aspect of the visit was that Siringo demonstrated an interest in one of Butch's sisters, though he did not reveal her name. "I had hard work to keep from falling in love with Miss Parker," he wrote, "the pretty younger sister of Butch Casiday [sic]." What would Butch have thought about one of his sisters being romanced by a Pinkerton? Worse yet, what if *she* had flirted with him?[3]

Perhaps the most relevant tidbit of information Siringo learned from his visit was the manner in which members of the Wild Bunch maintained contact. A series of "blind post-offices"—such as rock crevices and hollow trees—had been established all along the outlaw trail from Hole in the Wall in the southern Big Horn Mountains of Wyoming to Brown's Park in a desolate valley near the Utah-Colorado-Wyoming border to Robbers Roost in the desert of southern Utah. Members of the gang were the only ones who had been told the secluded locations and how the primitive but effective system operated.

In one case, a hollow tree stump in Linwood, Utah, had been used as the drop point. Butch's sister Lula explained how it worked: "Butch and others of the Wild Bunch used this tree as their post office, addressing a letter to a fellow gang member in care of Robbers Roost. The next member of the Bunch who came along delivered the letter. The tree had a hole in it, wrapped around by an iron band. Inside the hole was a bottle with a string attached. Notes were put into the bottle and let down into the tree, after which the hole was plugged and the iron band replaced to conceal the plug."[4]

Siringo departed the Circle Valley and wandered down to Alma, New Mexico, the area where Butch, Sundance, Harvey Logan, Elzy Lay, and perhaps other outlaws had worked for the WS Ranch. Once again, Siringo posed as a cowboy of questionable pedigree, engaging

A savage, parched wilderness of steep-walled canyons and hidden draws in the high desert of southern Utah, Robbers Roost was a favorite hideout for many men running from the law. Both Butch and Sundance would take refuge there over the span of their criminal careers.

The Great Blizzard of 1886–87 devastated herds throughout Wyoming and Montana, leaving many cowboys without a livelihood. Some turned to crime out of desperation. Cowboy artist Charles M. Russell, who observed the winter firsthand, depicted a dying steer in his early piece *Waiting for a Chinook (The Last of the 5000)*.

Butch Cassidy was sent to the Wyoming State Penitentiary for stealing a five-dollar horse in 1894. His mug shot would later appear in newspapers across the nation, heralding him as the leader of the Wild Bunch.

Ann Bassett was a prominent rancher in Utah who enjoyed an on-and-off relationship with Butch Cassidy.

The Ohio-born Ellsworth "Elzy" Lay was a flashy dresser and good with the ladies. After killing a man who had attempted to assault a woman, Elzy fell in with the Wild Bunch while hiding out in the Brown's Park area of Colorado.

Harvey Logan, also known as Kid Curry, was a cold-blooded killer. During his lifetime, he would be wanted on warrants for fifteen murders, but it was said that he had killed at least twice that number.

A drunken Tom O'Day participated in the Wild Bunch's robbery of the Butte County Bank in Belle Fourche, South Dakota, in 1897. His subsequent capture ruined a perfectly good holdup.

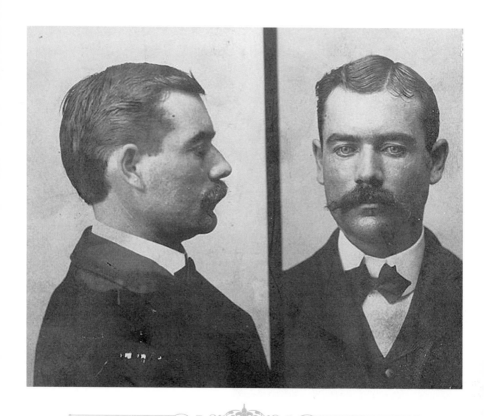

Ben "the Tall Texan" Kilpatrick was a dapper man who stood six feet, two inches. Born into an outlaw family of horse thieves and cattle rustlers, Kilpatrick met his end while robbing a train in Texas in 1912.

The Sundance Kid poses with the mysterious Etta Place, photographed together in New York City in 1901.

Laura Bullion first became the common-law wife of William Carver, but later took up with Ben Kilpatrick, who was said to have won her in a dice game. She has been called "the Rose of the Wild Bunch."

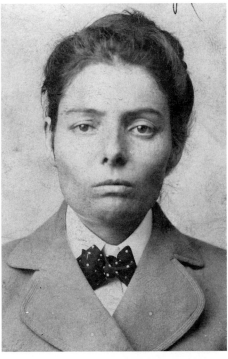

On June 2, 1899, the Wild Bunch robbed the westbound Union Pacific train near Wilcox, Wyoming. The gang was forced to blow up the express car after the messenger, Charles E. Woodcock, refused to open the door. The outlaws escaped with up to $50,000 in cash, plus other loot.

After the Wild Bunch pulled off the spectacular Wilcox train holdup, the Pinkerton Agency dispatched Charles Siringo, an expert tracker, to hunt down the outlaws.

While in Fort Worth, Texas, in 1900, members of the Wild Bunch sat for this photo, which was later distributed all over North and South America by the Pinkerton Agency: (*left to right*) the Sundance Kid, William "News" Carver, Ben "the Tall Texan" Kilpatrick, Harvey Logan, and Butch Cassidy.

William T. Phillips of Spokane, Washington, claimed until his death in 1937 that he was indeed Butch Cassidy. It would take more than seven decades for the myth to be disproven: Phillips's true identity was William T. Wilcox, a former fellow inmate of Butch's from the Wyoming pen.

saloon patrons in friendly conversation with ulterior motives. He was an excellent manipulator, and likely softened up his potential informants with free whiskey and cigars. He eventually was told about the night that the WS Ranch foreman, Jim Lowe, had saved the life of Pinkerton man Frank Murray in that very saloon. Siringo had read the report submitted by Murray, and the details matched with the story he now heard—except that he knew that Jim Lowe was actually Butch Cassidy.[5]

Siringo moved on to visit several mining camps around the Mogollon Mountains, where he heard more stories about Jim Lowe and received what he believed was a solid tip about the location of this enigmatic man. But when Siringo wired Denver for permission to check out the lead, he was told to forget about it, that Jim Lowe was not an outlaw. Instead, Siringo should leave the field and return to the home office in Denver for further instructions. The man who sent the wire ordering Siringo off the trail was none other than Frank Murray.[6]

Siringo could have poked around the area all he wanted without running into his main targets. At the time of his presence in outlaw country, Butch, Sundance, Harvey Logan, Will Carver, and Ben Kilpatrick arrived in Fort Worth, Texas, for a wedding celebration— as well as a farewell party for Butch and Sundance.[7]

At the turn of the century Fort Worth was a favorite destination of cowpunchers from all over the West. Boasting electric lights and streetcars, it was a modernized city. Some of the first automobiles manufactured by Henry Ford could be seen rolling down the streets. The city's stockyards were the end of the trail for cattle drives, and every necessity, delicacy, or vice a young man could dream of was waiting there for a price.

In 1876, the year of Custer's Last Stand on the Bighorn River, the Texas and Pacific Railway began servicing Fort Worth, which was situated on the Trinity River. Almost overnight, the increase in business at the city's stockyards transformed a sleepy little village into a boomtown. The wholesale cattle industry fueled a period of incredible growth and created well-paying jobs that lured migrants from the war-torn South who were seeking a fresh start. Fort Worth, now called the "Paris of the Plains," became the westernmost railhead for the shipment of cattle, and an important transportation center. The two most prominent cattle-slaughtering outfits of the time, Armour and Swift, both established their operations at the stockyards.

Although business was booming, prosperity came at a price. Merchants sold provisions to cattlemen soon departing civilization for the long, arduous drive up the 1,500-mile Chisholm Trail north to Dodge City, Kansas, and Miles City, Montana. With those cattle drives were cowboys, young men who were thirsty and love-starved, and wanted to enjoy one last fling before hitting the dusty, dangerous trail. Punchers were accommodated by a district of saloons, dance halls, gambling dens, pool parlors, girlie shows, and houses of ill repute where they could whoop it up to their hearts' delight—as long as their money lasted.

Naturally, boys will be boys, and incidents of shootings, knife fights, brawls, robberies, and muggings were commonplace. Wherever there were cowboys with money to spend, the most motley assortment of thieves, confidence men, ruffians, hell-raisers, outlaws on the run seeking a place to blend in with the scenery, and petty criminals of every description were quick to follow. Such Western luminaries as Sam Bass, Bat Masterson, Billy the Kid, Wyatt Earp, and Doc Holliday had at one time or another partaken of the pleasures at the Blue Light Saloon, or the Tivoli Hall Saloon, or the Theatre Comique, or the White Elephant, or the classy brothels run by Jessie Reeves, Josie Belmont, or Mary Porter. This part of town where no decent person would dare venture was soon bestowed with an appropriate name—Hell's Half Acre.

As Fort Worth's importance as a transportation hub and cow town expanded by leaps and bounds, so did its red-light district. Hell's Half Acre, located on the opposite end of town from the stockyards, had originally been limited to the lower end of Rusk Street. By 1881, "the Acre" covered more than two and a half acres, spreading across the city's main north–south thoroughfares. As the district grew, it became wilder and more lawless. City leaders and the good and decent citizens of Fort Worth were predictably concerned about the growth of this crime-infested part of their town. They elected a man named Timothy Courtright, known as Longhair Jim, to serve as city marshal, with instructions to put an end to the unbridled violence and debauchery.

Courtright proved himself to be an aggressive enforcer of the law who would fill the jail to beyond capacity on especially busy nights. In fact, Courtright was too effective. Cowboys started avoiding Hell's Half Acre, which caused many businesses to suffer. Consequently, Courtright was defeated in the next election with help from the area's commerce interests. The cardsharps, con men, shady ladies, and their ilk gladly returned to ply their illicit trades, and it was back to business as usual in Hell's Half Acre.

Another attempt to reform the district was soon to follow that temporary relapse of morals, ethics, and values. And ten years after he had been ostensibly fired for doing a good job, Jim Courtright was back, but this time his luck ran out. On February 8, 1887, the former city marshal engaged in a gunfight with former Dodge City saloon-keeper and known murderer Luke Short on Main Street. Courtright was shot dead, and Short went on to earn the nickname "the King of Fort Worth Gamblers."[8]

It was on that same Main Street in early November 1900 that Butch, Sundance, Harvey Logan, Will Carver, and Ben Kilpatrick took up residence in the Maddox Hotel, at 1014½ Main. Managed by Elizabeth "Lizzie" Maddox, who also operated a gaming room in the apartment she shared with her husband, Kendall, the hotel served as base camp for excursions by the outlaws into the depths of this district of sinful pleasures.[9]

Sundance may have been accompanied to Fort Worth by Etta Place. If so, his days and nights were likely spent in a more fashionable part of town, and carousing with his associates would have been kept to a minimum.

It is worth noting that there was a saloonkeeper in Hell's Half

Acre at that time by the name of Mike Cassidy, who had drifted into town in the 1880s. He was known as a shady operator, with minor criminal offenses, who was married and had a family. There are those historians who believe this Mike Cassidy is one and the same as the cowboy-rustler from Circle Valley whose name Butch adopted. No evidence exists, however, to prove or disprove this theory, or whether or not Butch may have run across "Mikey Mike," as he was known, while visiting Fort Worth.[10]

One reason the Wild Bunch made the sojourn to Fort Worth was to celebrate the nuptials of one of their own. Will "News" Carver was marrying Callie May Hunt, better known as Lillie Davis. Carver had met his intended at Fannie Porter's brothel in San Antonio, where the bride-to-be worked. The particulars of this wedding ceremony—said to have occurred on December 1, are unknown. One source claims the marriage certificate was signed by a Tarrant County justice of the peace, with Carver using the alias William Casey. Lillie Davis contended that she mailed the marriage certificate to her father in Palestine, Texas, as proof that she was leaving her profession and settling down to domestic life. No documentation has ever surfaced in either case.[11]

Regardless of legalities, the wedding reception was likely a rousing affair, possibly with the Wild Bunch boys dressed in unaccustomed formal attire. Casting aside faded jeans and soiled wide-brimmed cowboy hats, they donned fashionable new three-piece suits and matching derby hats.

A few blocks from the Maddox Hotel, at 705 Main Street, stood the Swartz View Company, the studio of photographer John Swartz. Inside the second-floor studio was taken the most notable and ill-conceived photograph of the Old West era. On November 21, Butch Cassidy, Harry Alonzo Longabaugh, Harvey Logan, Ben Kilpatrick, and Will Carver—dressed in their Sunday-go-to-meeting clothing—sat together for a portrait.

Butch's derby was tilted jauntily to the left, Carver's to the right. Logan pushed his hat back to expose his forehead and wore a nosegay in his buttonhole. Ben Kilpatrick's lanky frame dominated the center of the photo. Sundance appeared uncomfortable, uncertain about whether or not to smile. All the men wore white shirts with crisp, stiff collars and long ties, and exhibited shiny watch fobs. The well-dressed gentlemen in the photo might have been mistaken for a group of bankers or merchants.

The notion to record their visit to Fort Worth with a lasting souvenir such as a group photograph has been credited over time to both Butch and Sundance. It would be in keeping with Butch's personality to find amusement in joking around, perhaps even mocking—in a cowboy way—the well-to-do folks who wore such dude clothing every day. On the other hand, Sundance was known to have a propensity for dressing up in nice clothing and showing off whenever the occasion arose. Whatever the reason, this photograph would prove to be a foolhardy idea.[12]

Each member of the Wild Bunch ordered a six-and-a-half-by-eight-and-a-half-inch print, not on common tintype stock but made with the new, expensive dry-plate processing method. John Swartz was so proud of his work that he displayed a copy of the photo in the front window of his shop, where passersby could appreciate it.[13]

This error in judgment by the five outlaws who had found success through anonymity had now presented their likenesses for all the world to see, an act that would come back to haunt them. In fact, the moment the shutter of John Swartz's camera snapped could be regarded as the beginning of the end for the Wild Bunch.

Legend has it that Fred Dodge, a special agent for Wells Fargo, passed by Swartz's shop one day and recognized Will Carver in the photograph. He immediately ordered fifty prints of the photo, and set about identifying the other four men. Dodge never mentioned the historic discovery in his memoirs, which casts doubt upon the story. But someone did note the importance of the print in the window, and sent a copy to the authorities.[14]

Before long, every core member of the Wild Bunch had been identified. Wanted posters were updated with the photograph and distributed to seemingly every town and village in the West. Law enforcement's quest to put an end to the gang's career had been made much easier by one click of a camera shutter.

The Pinkertons sent a print of the photo to George Nixon, head cashier of the bank in Winnemucca, for identification. Stories circulated that Butch had actually mailed that copy to Nixon. Regardless, an enlargement of the "Fort Worth Five" photograph adorned the wall in the lobby of the Winnemucca bank for many years. Vic Button, the boy who was given Butch's white horse, was said to have received a print of the photo personally mailed to him by Cassidy, a story confirmed by Button's daughter.[15]

Within days, peace officers and private detectives from the Pinkertons and Wells Fargo swarmed all over Hell's Half Acre like hungry locusts, putting fear and trepidation into the hearts of every thimblerigger and painted woman as they combed the area for the Wild Bunch. By that time, however, the five outlaws had departed Fort Worth.[16]

It is unclear whether Butch, Sundance, and their associates understood that their group photograph had compromised their identities and brought more unwelcome attention from the law. Perhaps they did not care. In recent months Butch had experienced what he described as an unexplainable restlessness. It seemed that the West was closing in on him—becoming too small.

The nation was progressing into an era of rapidly growing technology, removing some of the wildness on which Butch thrived. Even his old stomping grounds of Grand County, Utah, with less than 750 inhabitants, had been linked to other towns by telephone lines. Places an outlaw could hide were becoming few and far between as more and more settlers established homesteads within or near traditional sanctuaries, bringing the law in tow.[17]

The gang had successfully robbed both a train and a bank recently, but most holdups these days ended in failure, especially train robberies. The railroads had installed express cars that were nearly impregnable, and had beefed up the number of security guards on runs that carried a large amount of valuables. Trained to shoot first and ask questions later, the guards were armed with the latest repeating shotguns loaded with buckshot. If that was not enough to deter potential robbers, an array of new and fearsome devices was being implemented or tested—Gatling guns, electrically charged car doors, hand grenades, and even burning oil or a shot of steam from the boiler that could be sprayed on anyone bold or foolish enough to demand that the express car door be opened. In addition, promotions, pay raises, and favorable assignments for train crews were now linked to their performance, and a robbery was counted as a black mark on their record. Engineers were not about to just hand over control of their trains as easily as they had in the past.[18]

Bandits were not up against random individuals any longer; they faced an organized system that connected various arms of the law that could throw a net over virtually the entire country. The sophistication of these innovative law enforcement practices, combined with the $10,000 bounties on their heads, had convinced Butch Cassidy that it would be only a matter of time before the Wild Bunch would be eliminated—either by a lengthy incarceration or, more than likely, death.

The Sundance Kid was in complete agreement with his partner. Both men had thus far made it through their outlaw careers without having to kill anyone. Although they shared most criminal traits with the other gang members, they were the only two who were not cold-blooded killers. Each of them had broken most of the other commandments, but the most sacred one of the Ten Commandments in Mormon or Baptist teachings was "Thou shalt not kill."

But if they continued robbing trains and banks, the time would come when they would be obliged to shoot their way out of a tight spot, killing an innocent employee or a bystander who challenged them or a peace officer who was just doing his job. Also, each of them had been locked up for a period of eighteen months, and if caught now they knew they would be imprisoned for the rest of their lives—if not executed for murders they had not committed but that had been blamed on them. It would not take much solid evidence to convict either one of these notorious criminals of a capital offense.

The two outlaws were not stupid or stubborn men. They were perceptive enough to know that the days of the Wild Bunch and the Wild West were gone forever. They could not run from modern technology and coordinated law enforcement efforts—the system—and hope to escape.

No doubt the two men discussed the proposition at length, debating the pros and cons, and had come to a mutual agreement. Butch Cassidy and the Sundance Kid would give up banditry—quit the Wild Bunch—and start anew as honest citizens in some distant place. Both had stashed away a fair amount of money from their recent heists, and could afford to establish a business or buy a ranch. Now the only question was: Where could they go where they would not be recognized and could live a normal life?

Nearby options were immediately dismissed. There was nowhere in the United States that they could settle down and not eventually be recognized. They would be poked and prodded around the county by law enforcement until finally being captured. Canada was not an option, either. Sundance had worked north of the border, and was aware that the Canadian Mounted Police was a top-notch outfit that "always got their man." Mexico did not appeal to them, either.

What about South America? Perhaps one of them had read an article in *National Geographic* magazine that had presented a glowing portrayal of Patagonia, a region in Argentina that stretched between the Andes Mountains and the Atlantic Ocean. The cattle business in Patagonia was on the verge of an economic boom. Great Britain had suffered an outbreak of hoof-and-mouth disease, and would now be required to import beef and mutton. And there were other nearby markets available, such as neighboring Chile, as well. From all indications, Patagonia would be the ideal place to raise cattle—and hide from the authorities.[19]

It was decided—Butch and Sundance would travel to this faraway region called Patagonia, establish a cattle ranch, and cash in on the flourishing market for beef and other livestock in Europe and South America. The journey would not only save them from the long arm of the U.S. law, but offer a brand of adventure and excitement that they had never before experienced.

Butch and Sundance may have traveled to San Antonio for a brief visit after they departed Fort Worth. By then they had agreed on this new direction to their partnership, and would now separate to settle their affairs and then rendezvous in New York City. From that city, they would board a steamship destined for South America and start their new life.

There was one last piece of personal business to address, however, and her name was Etta Place. At some point, Sundance informed Butch that his girlfriend would be accompanying them to South America. Butch's initial reaction is unknown. Perhaps Sundance threatened to pull out of the deal if he could not bring along the woman he loved. Or, more likely, Sundance may have convinced Butch that they would be hiring a cook and housekeeper anyway in South America. Why not Etta? Besides that, she could ride and shoot as well as any man, and those skills could be of use to them. So it was decided. The beautiful Etta Place would be making the overseas trip with them.[20]

While Butch headed for Wyoming, likely to dispose of the ranch he and Al Hainer had owned on Horse Creek, Sundance and Etta traveled to New Orleans, where they celebrated New Year's Eve in style. Calling themselves Mr. and Mrs. Harry Place, the couple boarded an eastbound train and journeyed to Pennsylvania. Their destination was Phoenixville and Mont Clare, Harry Longabaugh's childhood home—places he had not laid eyes on in almost twenty years. Harry's parents had passed away, and his brother Elwood was still based out of San Francisco in the whaling business, but his two sisters and brother Harvey remained in the vicinity.[21]

Sundance likely escorted Etta around town, showing her the Schuylkill Canal, where he had toiled for much of his youth. Then there was the school, which he had only sporadically attended. And the lending library where he had paid one dollar for a card to check out materials that had branded the code of the West in his heart. They may have ridden out to visit the nearby horse-raising operation that had instilled within him a lifelong love of horses.

Much had changed in these factory towns over the years, and it was a good bet that Harry looked over the brick-and-concrete metropolis of each and was thankful that he had chosen to escape to the boundless prairies and mountain vistas of the West. Finally, it was time to reacquaint himself with his sisters and brother.

Sundance introduced Etta to his family as his wife, although there is no evidence they ever legally married. Sister Samanna and her husband, Oliver Hallman, who lived in Mont Clare, were thrilled to see Harry and to meet Etta. There was one problem, however—the Pinkertons had, off and on, staked out Samanna's home, looking for her notorious brother. Sundance and Etta would have to practice discretion and deception. Regardless of possible peering eyes, the four enjoyed their clandestine time together. Samanna was especially happy to hear that her brother intended to become an honest citizen in South America. Sundance and Etta possibly visited with Harvey, but likely shied away from Emma, who had already changed the spelling of her name to Longabough so as not to hurt her seamstress business. Before leaving, the couple paid a solemn visit to Morris Cemetery in Phoenixville, where Sundance's parents had been buried.[22]

In mid-January, Sundance and Etta took a train to Buffalo, New York, and checked into Dr. Pierce's Surgical Institute, or Invalids Hotel, a holistic healing center located at 653 Main Street. The facility specialized in Turkish baths and remedies for "chronic diseases—specifically those of a delicate, obscure, complicated or obstinate character."[23]

Sundance had mentioned to his family that he had an old bullet wound in his left leg that required attention. No record of such an injury has been found. The alleged wound could have been simply a contrived story meant to impress his kin with his wild past and Western credentials. Pinkerton files list the reason for treatment as either a sinus condition or possibly even a social disease. No hospital records exist, and the exact reason for Sundance and Etta's visit cannot be determined. If his story was true, however, it would have been interesting to know when and where he had suffered the wound.[24]

After their discharge from the medical center, Sundance and Etta treated themselves to a honeymoon at Niagara Falls, the traditional destination of newlyweds. They then boarded a train and journeyed to New York City, arriving on February 1, 1901.

The couple—once again posing as Mr. and Mrs. Harry Place— checked into a second-floor luxury suite in Mrs. Catherine Taylor's boardinghouse at 234 West 12th Street. The rooming house contained twenty rooms, and could accommodate twenty-five boarders. The widow Taylor employed a chef and two servants, and was assisted by her thirteen-year-old son. Harry Place let it be known that he was a cattle buyer all the way from out West in Wyoming.

Before long, Etta's "brother," calling himself James Ryan, arrived and rented a room from Mrs. Taylor. Butch Cassidy had successfully rendezvoused with Sundance and Etta for their trip to South America. They were flush with money and the prospects of adventure and a new life. But first they were anxious to see all the wondrous sights this vibrant city of nearly three and a half million people had to offer.[25]

As tourists they explored the city for three weeks. Accustomed to saloons, snowcapped mountains, and desolate open spaces, the three Westerners must have marveled at the skyscrapers, automobiles, and bright streetlights that welcomed them.

These out-of-towners would have sat in the audience of all the popular vaudeville shows and performances at the various music halls— and sung along with popular songs: "When You Were Sweet Sixteen," "The Band Played On," and "On the Banks of the Wabash, Far Away." And they would have obtained tickets for the best seats at only the best plays that were running in Broadway theaters. Dining at five-star restaurants would have been a nightly affair, where they would sit among the city's upper crust and never once remark about how many primitive campfire meals of beans and more beans they had cooked and eaten at some desolate location while on the run.

The trio might have developed a special taste for the quaint taverns where they would frolic until well into the night, then return to their respectable boardinghouse perhaps a little too drunk and loud. There were several notable nightspots that may have become favorites—Connelly's Bar at 3rd Avenue and 23rd Street, Pete's Tavern at Irving Place and 18th Street, and Joe's Bar on Union Square.

They could have taken a ferry out to the Statue of Liberty, and looked back at the New York skyline, which the Brooklyn Bridge dominated almost as much as the buildings. Another sight to see was the towering Tower Building and the Flatiron Building, which was presently under construction. On an afternoon stroll, they may have stopped for a while to watch the workers building the city's first subway.

And, probably while Etta browsed and shopped at the fashionable ladies' shops, the two men sneaked over to the Dewey Theatre on East 14th to see a real, live big-city burlesque show. In quieter moments, while Butch spread good cheer among tavern patrons and made new friends, Sundance and Etta could have snuggled together for an intimate nighttime horse-drawn carriage ride under the warm glow of the city's bright lights.[26]

On February 3, Sundance and Etta posed for a formal portrait at the DeYoung Photography Studio, at 826 Broadway, one of the top studios of the day. Sundance mailed a print to David Gillespie in Little Snake River Valley, who made the notation: ". . . from New York City, with a picture of him and his wife, saying he had married a Texas lady he had known previously." That print or another copy of the photo that may have been intended as a wedding portrait found its way into the hands of Pinkerton agents. Perhaps Sundance had sent the photo as a memento to his sister Samanna that was never delivered due to a local postal clerk who was paid by the agents to check for contact between brother and sister. The photo would subsequently be reproduced on wanted posters of the Sundance Kid.[27]

The three tourists were tossing around cash like millionaires—and one place that was a must-see on any visit to New York was the famous Tiffany & Co., then located at the corner of 15th Street at Union

Square. A unique store long renowned for its luxury goods, especially jewelry, Tiffany promoted itself as an arbiter of taste and style.

Tiffany also promoted itself with its own outlandish purchases, such as some of the crown jewels and a bejeweled corset said to belong to Marie Antoinette when the monarchy was overthrown in 1792. Tiffany also partnered with P. T. Barnum, the master promoter, for the presentation of a gem-studded miniature silver-filigree horse and carriage as a wedding present to Tom Thumb and his bride. The company, which had won a gold medal for jewelry and the grand prize for silverware at the Paris Exposition of 1878, set aside its prestige and produced a solid-gold chamber pot—with an eye peering up at the center of the bottom—as a gift that Gilded Age philanthropist Diamond Jim Brady, the first person in New York to own an automobile, gave to actress and singer Lillian Russell. By 1887, Tiffany's vaults held $40 million in precious stones, among them the largest flawless and perfectly colored canary diamond ever mined—the 128.5-carat "Tiffany Diamond" that remains to this day in the New York store.

The normal clientele at Tiffany had always been America's wealthy or those high-rollers who sought a high-priced souvenir. No matter how ostentatious or whimsical their desires, there was always some unique product that carried the Tiffany name inside the display cases that would satisfy every taste. Tourists flocked to this famous landmark, and would purchase some item, any item, just to say they had shopped at Tiffany.

And speaking of big spenders at Tiffany & Co. in New York—Butch Cassidy bought a $40.10 gold watch—serial number 68210-1685—while Sundance purchased a $150 gold lapel watch for Etta and a diamond stickpin for himself.[28]

Sundance reportedly paid a visit to Dr. Isaac Weinstein at 174 Second Avenue in Manhattan. He may have been referred to Weinstein for further treatment by Dr. Pierce in Buffalo—one of Weinstein's partners who had trained at the University of Buffalo. Once again, the nature of his ailment is unknown, but could have been a chronic sinus infection.[29]

The weather had been cooperative when the three tourists had arrived in town, but by February 10 the temperature dropped into the teens and a major snowstorm struck the East Coast. Butch and Sundance had endured blizzards of monstrous proportions in their roles as cowhands, especially the Great Blizzard of 1886–87, but neither had witnessed an event the likes of which this storm produced.

On February 13, thousands of New Yorkers and tourists gathered at the Battery to witness a spectacle of nature's fury. A warm front upstate had caused gigantic blocks of ice to float down the Hudson River to the harbor. When these massive chunks rounded the Battery, they encountered huge blocks of ice flowing from the East River. The two ice floes converged, trapping as many as one hundred vessels of various sizes, from tugboats to ocean liners.[30]

A week later, on February 20, 1901—the weather having warmed and the ice having been cleared from the East River—Butch, Sundance, and Etta checked out of Mrs. Taylor's boardinghouse and took a hack to Pier 32, where they booked passage on the ship SS *Herminius*. In those days passports, although they had been around since 1791, were optional and not required by law.[31]

The following morning, the freighter cast away bound for Buenos Aires, Argentina, by way of Montevideo, Uruguay. Mr. and Mrs. Harry Place and James Ryan waved good-bye to New York City, and—unbeknownst to Pinkerton or Wells Fargo agents or sheriffs or posses across the West—steamed away to what they hoped would be freedom and a fresh start in the promised land of faraway Patagonia.

CHAPTER ELEVEN
PATAGONIA

I am a vaquero by trade;
To handle my rope I'm not afraid.
I lass' an otero by the two horns
Throw down the biggest that ever was born.
Whoa! Whoa! Whoa! Pinto, whoa!

My name to you I will not tell;
For what's the use, you know me so well.
The girls all love me, and cry
When I leave them to join the rodero.
Whoa! Whoa! Whoa! Pinto, whoa!

—"Pinto"

The SS *Herminius* (originally known as the SS *Spyridon*) was a British passenger/cargo steamer weighing 3,548 tons that was built in 1898 by Russell & Company for the British & South American Steam Navigation Company, Liverpool.

The crew, which was composed of officers, seamen, stewards, and the engine-room force, existed solely to please the whims of the passengers. The captain was the supreme ruler of the ship, and in emergencies could exercise his command over every department, but would usually confine his attention to operating the craft and leave the two other divisions of the ship's labor to their heads. Closely connected with sailing was engineering, which the passengers would recognize only as the throb of the engines and the churning of the screws in the water. The third department of the ship was housekeeping, which was under the control of the chief steward.

Long before the sleeping passengers would arise in the morning, a large army of workers had been toiling all night to remove all traces of disorder from the day before and make certain that the public parts of the ship had been put in order. When the passengers began to appear on deck, all cleaning of the ship would end or be kept at a minimum, and a new line of duties commenced—attending to the passengers' wants and needs, which were apt to be numerous and varied while at sea.

The primary want and need of the passengers was without question food and the eating thereof. Hungry stomachs in dining salons required feeding not merely three regular meals a day but must be constantly provided with sustenance every hour of the day and night, from the time the moorings were cast off at one port until the vessel arrived at its destination. The feeding of the passengers and crew required an enormous amount of supplies, all of which must be in the correct amounts and kept fresh.

How were supplies stored to fill the elaborate bills of fare in this floating hotel? The public markets that supplied daily provisions to hotels on land were far away across the water. But down in the bottom of the ship the chief steward had a market of his own, one that he had stocked to his satisfaction while the ship was docked. A series of narrow corridors lined with doors led the stewards through their private marketplace.

One door might open to a fair-size room as cold as winter, with sides of beef, veal, and mutton hung about. Every pound of meat inside this room was the responsibility of a specific steward. Down the corridor another door opened, and hanging from hooks along the walls and ceiling were bunches of birds—chickens, ducks, turkeys, pigeons, squabs, and other small birds. Another room was reserved especially for salt meats—hams, bacon, and tongues. There were certain items of food that must be alive when cooked, such as oysters, clams, and lobsters, which were kept in their own room. One refrigerator room held tubs of butter on shelves, along with that other popular product of the farm—fresh eggs. Sterilized milk and cream were stored in a separate cold room. This market also contained a great supply of ripe fruits and green vegetables. Perishable supplies were stocked in proportion to the number of passengers booked and no more, to ensure freshness. Needless to say, refrigeration required a supply of tons of ice.

There was also a gigantic stock of nonperishable goods that were kept and restocked from one voyage to another until eventually used. Water was stored in great tanks that were located in out-of-the-way places. Tea and coffee were used in large amounts—more tea than coffee on English ships. Coffee was generally made in two enormous urns holding about ten gallons each. These beverages were supplemented by wine and liquors, beer in kegs, and bottles of beer.

Cooking for the passengers would begin early in the morning and continue all day and into the evening. One meal was being prepared while another was being served. The head chef of the galley was the lord of his department. His numerous assistants would relieve him of any work that did not require a master's hand and a gourmet's taste.

Grand staterooms were provided for first-class passengers, and small cabins near the stern for steerage-class passengers. Steamers contained adequate space for recreation, with the promenade deck and boat decks above the main deck. Most people took advantage of warm weather outside by sitting around in deck chairs, walking the deck watching the ocean, and playing deck games. Indoor cricket, badminton, table tennis, shuffleboard, and quoits—a game of throwing disks over a stake—were all played to pass the time and for exercise.

Perhaps Butch and Sundance at some point tossed around a baseball, or a bicycle was on board and Butch could show off his expertise. Other indoor activities included playing cards, chess, dominoes, or cribbage. Gambling was generally discouraged, likely much to the chagrin of Sundance. But there was always the possibility that a private game of poker might have been arranged between consenting adults in a cabin away from public view. Areas were also set aside for quiet reading or working on hobbies, as well as rooms for playing or practicing musical instruments.

The men were permitted to smoke on the top decks, and in those days smoking was even allowed in the dining rooms. On most voyages, there were concerts, entertainers, and bands and dances, which would allow single male and female passengers to mingle. These shipboard activities that gave passengers the opportunity to get to know one another, however, would adhere strictly to the social distinctions of the "Old World," and each social class was usually kept apart. No doubt the fun-loving Butch Cassidy thrived in this atmosphere if there were any single ladies aboard.[1]

Butch, Sundance, and Etta arrived in the port of Buenos Aires, Argentina, on March 23, 1901. As Mr. and Mrs. Harry Place and James Ryan, they checked into the fashionable and expensive Hotel Europa in the center of the city. Soon after settling into their quarters, Sundance visited the London and River Platte Bank and deposited about $12,000—two thousand pounds in gold notes. At the same time, he reportedly inquired about the bank's security, giving the impression that he was worried about robbers. Apparently he could not refrain from casing the bank.[2]

Patagonia was located at the southern end of South America in territory shared by Argentina and Chile. Locating the perfect piece of land on which to establish a working ranch in an unfamiliar continent was a formidable proposition that Butch and Sundance did not leave to chance. They contacted the United States vice consul, a Buenos Aires dentist by the name of Dr. George Newbery, asking him for suggestions for possible ranch sites in Patagonia.

To their delight, the doctor knew of an ideal location for raising livestock. He told them of a secluded area in Patagonia that featured lush pastureland, unspoiled since the day Magellan discovered it. The region was located in western Chubut Territory, in the valley of Cholila at the foot of the Andes Mountains near the Chilean border. About 750 miles by steamer and overland from Buenos Aires, the territory was more than four hundred miles from the nearest railroad. Telegraph wires had not yet been strung, and villages or neighbors were few and far between. What could be better for outlaws seeking seclusion?

Butch, Sundance, and Etta took Newbery's advice and traveled to Cholila. They found the land to be reminiscent of western Montana, with plentiful grasslands dotted with lakes, and snow-covered mountains looming on the distant horizon. Like the areas where Butch and Sundance had retreated in the American West, this land was peaceful and isolated. It was an ideal place to raise cattle and other livestock, and indeed a place to vanish from civilization—and the Pinkertons. They could drive their herds of cattle and sheep over into Chile and sell them for an excellent profit until markets in Europe were established. The three emigrants decided to look no further.[3]

In June of 1901, Butch and Sundance purchased sixteen colts from an estancia near Cholila for the price of $855. The two men registered their brands in October at Rawson, the capital of Chubut—Butch choose an R under his alias Santiago Ryan, while Sundance took O< under his alias, Enrique Place. They registered a joint brand, a reversed P superimposed with an R, which stood for Place and Ryan.[4]

While Butch, Sundance, and Etta settled in South America, back in northern Montana a train robbery was pulled off in the early afternoon of July 3. The Great Northern Railroad's westbound Express No. 3, the Coast Flyer, was stopped by outlaws in a remote area outside of Wagner, Montana.[5]

A bandit, probably Harvey Logan, climbed over the tender, took control of the locomotive, and ordered the engineer to stop the train. The baggage-express car was then separated from the passenger cars, and the train was pulled forward. Everything was going according to the same ingenious plan that had made Butch Cassidy a criminal mastermind.

Yet in this instance, there was bloodshed. Two trainmen, running along the tracks to put out warning flares to prevent a collision with an oncoming train, were shot down by the robbers. One later died of his wounds. An eighteen-year-old girl made the mistake of leaning out the window of the passenger car to see what was going on, and received a bullet in the shoulder, which was bloody but not life-threatening.

Using four separate charges of dynamite, the bandits blew up the safe in the express car and emptied the contents, possibly totaling as much as $40,000. The robbers then jumped down from the car, mounted their horses, and tore off south toward the Milk River. The innocent passengers, already terrified, were peppered with another volley of pistol fire as the robbers escaped. Fortunately, no one was hurt by this malicious act. Posses were dispatched, but the trail soon went cold. The notorious Wild Bunch had committed their final train robbery as a gang, and split up to ride in every direction.[6]

Reports claimed the Coast Flyer was held up by anywhere between four and six members of the Wild Bunch. Harvey Logan, Ben

Kilpatrick, and Camilla Hanks were said to have been present—and according to some, even Butch Cassidy and the Sundance Kid.

On November 5, 1901, Ben "the Tall Texan" Kilpatrick, who had been staying in a St. Louis hotel with his companion Laura Bullion, was arrested for passing stolen banknotes. Laura was taken into custody the next morning when forged banknotes were discovered in the satchel she was carrying. Among Laura's possessions were notes that described Harry Longabaugh, and a pocket dictionary with his name written on the flyleaf. The couple remained silent, which led the St. Louis police and the Pinkertons to believe they were holding Harry Longabaugh, the Sundance Kid, in their jail. Ten days later, the mistake was revealed when Kilpatrick was properly identified.[7]

This case of mistaken identity does not by any means exonerate Sundance or afford him a rock-solid alibi, but it does cast doubts about his participation. There was always the chance that he was present, but more than likely he was living a peaceful life with Etta Place in Argentina at the time of the robbery.

What about Butch Cassidy? There are several questions that must be asked to determine the possibility that he may have accompanied the other gang members that day. Did Butch need more money than the amount he had taken to South America? Would he have gone through the time-consuming journey—more than two months' turnaround time in addition to overland travel in America—between the continents by steamer and then the long trip in-country back home to Cholila, when there was plenty of work to do to settle in his new country? Most of all, would Butch have allowed the gunplay—probably initiated by trigger-happy Harvey Logan—during and after the robbery?

Probably not is the answer to all three questions, although Butch's sister Lula believed that Butch was involved in the train robbery. It would be more likely that Butch had set to work on the homestead, which would have to have been carved from the wilderness, as well as daily chores associated with building a livestock business. And from all indications, that was exactly what occupied the three of them from the moment they had arrived in Cholila.[8]

• • •

On March 3, 1902, after a year in country, Sundance and Etta boarded the luxury liner SS *Soldier Prince* and returned in style to the United States. Apparently Sundance was suffering from his recurring illness or injury, and had decided to seek medical attention.

The couple arrived in New York City on April 3, and took a room at Mrs. Thompson's rooming house at 325 East 14th Street. Sundance and Etta found time to visit Coney Island, the popular beach and amusement park in Brooklyn. They also traveled by train to visit Samanna in Mont Clare, where Sundance graciously invited his two nephews to visit him in Cholila. The family was told that the reason for Sundance's trip was once again treatment for an old gunshot wound.

Sundance and Etta returned to New York City in June, perhaps by way of Chicago for additional medical treatment. On June 25, they returned to Tiffany & Co., where Sundance picked out a watch that cost $15.35.

On July 10, they boarded the steamer *Honorius*, which was not a passenger ship but a freighter—Harry Place was listed as purser, and Ethel as a steward. The ship arrived in Buenos Aires on August 9. Four days later, Sundance closed out his account with a remaining balance of $1,105.50 at the London and River Platte Bank. He and Etta then boarded the SS *Chubut* and traveled up the Nuevo Gulf, headed back to the homestead, which would also require their going overland by mule train and by horseback.[9]

Meanwhile, on April 2, 1902, while Sundance and Etta were stateside, Butch filed the necessary documents to petition the Registry of the Colonial Land Department in Buenos Aires for the purchase of four leagues—over 25,000 acres—of government land in the territory of Chubut, Argentina, in the names of James Ryan and Harry A. Place. Submitted as proof of their intention to improve this land, Butch attested to the fact that they were presently grazing thirteen hundred sheep, five hundred head of cattle, and thirty-five horses on the land. With the paperwork filed, Butch Cassidy and the Sundance Kid were now property holders in this faraway land, where they were faithfully fulfilling their intention to go straight and make a new life for themselves.[10]

During the six months that Sundance and Etta were away, Butch Cassidy grew lonely. Little entertainment could be found in the isolated area other than perhaps a fiesta in the nearby small village of Esquel or some cow talk with ranchers at the Lands of the South Company, where livestock was bought and sold. But Butch did not have a real grasp of the native language, which limited his communication ability with natives and deprived him of his well-known glibness. Most likely, Butch spent many hours reading books in the quiet of his cabin—when he was not working from dawn to dark on improving the homestead and caring for the stock.[11]

To combat his loneliness, Butch wrote a long letter to Mathilda Davis, the mother of Maude Davis and mother-in-law of Elzy Lay. He revealed much about the life that the three expatriates had created for themselves in Patagonia.

> *Cholila, Ten. (Ter.) Chubut*
> *Argentina Republic S. Am.*
> *August 10, 1902*
> *Mrs. Davis*
> *Ashley, Utah*
>
> *My Dear Friend.*
>   *I suppose you have thought long before this that I had forgotten you (or was dead) but my Dear friend I am still alive. And when I think of my Old friends you are always the first to come to mind. It will probably surprise you to hear from me away down in this country but U.S. was too small for me the last two years I was there. I was restless. I wanted to see more of the world. I had seen all of the U.S. that I thought was good. And a few months after I sent A—— over to see you, and get the photo of the rope jumping of which I have got here and often look at and wish I*

*could see the originals, and I think I could liven some of
the characters up a little for Maude looks very sad to me.*

*Another of my Uncles died and left $30,000, Thirty
Thousand to our little family of 3 so I took my $10,000
and started to see a little more of the world. I visited the
best Cities and best parts of the countrys of South A. till I
got here. And this part of the country looked so good that I
located, and I think for good, for I like the place better
every day. I have 300 cattle, 1500 sheep, and 28 good
saddle horses, 2 men to do my work, also good 4 room
house, wearhouse, stable, chicken house and some chickens.
The only thing lacking is a cook, for I am still living in
Single Cussidness and I sometimes feel very lonely for I am
alone all day, and my neighbors don't amount to anything,
besides the only language spoken in this country is Spanish,
and I don't speak it well enough to converse on the latest
scandals so dear to (?) hearts of all nations, and without
which conversations are very stale. But the country is first
class. The only industry at present is stock raising (that is
in this part) and it cant be beat for that purpose. For I have
never seen a finer grass country, and lots of it hundreds
and hundreds of miles that is unsettled and comparatively
unknown, and where I am it is good agricultural country,
all kind of small grain and vegetables grow without
Irrigation but I am at the foot of the Andes Mountains.
And all the land east of here is prarie and deserts, very
good for stock, but for farming it would have to be irri-
gated, but there is plenty of good land along the mountains
for all the people that will be here in the next hundred
years, for I am a long way from civilization. It is 16 hundred miles to Buenos Aires the Capitol of the Argentine,
and over 400 miles to the nearest RailRoad or Sea Port in
the Argentine Republic but only about 150 miles to the
Pacific Coast to Chile but to get there we have to cross the*

mountains which was thought impossible last summer when it was found that the Chilean Gov. had cut a road almost across so that next summer we will be able to go to Port Mont, Chile in about 4 days, where it used to take 2 months around the old trail and it will be a great benefit to us for Chile is our Beef market and we can get our cattle there in 1/10 the time and have them fat. And we can also [illegible] supplies in Chile for one third what they cost here. The climate here is a great deal milder than Ashley Valley. The summers are beautiful, never as warm as there. And grass knee high every where and lots of good cold mountain water. But the winters are very wet and disagreeable, for it rains most of the time, but sometimes we have lots of snow, but it don't last long, for it never gets cold enough to freeze much. I have never seen Ice one inch thick.[12]

The letter ends with those words—Mrs. Davis likely tore off the signature so law enforcement authorities could not identify the author should they come snooping. Butch was careless when he noted his specific whereabouts at the top of the first page. The $30,000 he mentioned was probably his share from the Winnemucca heist in 1900.

In spite of the language barrier, the three Americans quickly endeared themselves to the community. Butch and Sundance went out of their way to curry favor with the locals, generously handing out candy to children and, at times, gold to poor peasants. The local people had never heard of Robin Hood, but Butch and Sundance were certainly playing the role in an effort to fit in. Yet they never felt entirely comfortable—saddled horses were usually tied up behind their cabin, just in case the outlaws needed to make a hasty escape.

Etta Place, in her role as hostess of the ranchero, certainly made an impression on the members of the immigrant population that comprised their social life. Welshman Milton Roberts described Etta as "good-looking, a good rider, and an expert with a revolver." Another visitor said that she "never wore dresses, just pants and boots," and she was "free, forward, and very playful."[13]

Etta, usually described as beautiful or elegant, was said to have stolen more than one male heart, including that of a Scottish immigrant named John Gardner. A neighboring sheep rancher, Gardner called Etta "his first and his only love." He claimed that he was drawn to her by the scholarly interests they shared, loaning her magazines and books he regularly received from back home. He held a dim view of Sundance, calling him "a mean, low cur," which could be dismissed as simply jealousy. In view of Sundance's temperament, it is doubtful that this relationship became intimate.[14]

Sundance was also described by Gardner as "not so much a bad character as a cold-blooded one" who was proficient in the use of the revolver, and "a genuine cowboy, very capable with animals."[15]

It was inevitable that the three fugitives could not escape the long arm of the Pinkertons for long. Sundance and Samanna regularly exchanged letters, which she duly noted in her business accounting book. Some or all of those letters were not delivered unopened from Cholila, but had been resealed. The Pinkertons had persuaded Mont Clare postal employees to open mail sent by Sundance to his sister and soon learned that the two outlaws were ranching in South America.

In early 1903, veteran agent Frank Dimaio was dispatched to Buenos Aires. He knew that the three were using the aliases Harry and Ethel Place and James Ryan. Dimaio visited the U.S. vice consul, Dr. George Newbery, who freely admitted that the Americans were ranching in Cholila. He did, however, advise the agent to wait until after the rainy season to investigate, or risk his safety on dangerous or washed-out roads. Dimaio reluctantly took the doctor's advice. But before returning to the United States, he distributed wanted posters of his quarry written in Spanish to steamship companies and law enforcement agencies across the country, and set up a code to be used when communicating with Pinkerton officials.[16]

Robert Pinkerton, president of the company, planned to trick Butch and Sundance into traveling to Buenos Aires, where they could be taken into custody and returned to the United States to stand trial for their crimes. There was only one problem—money to pay for the expedition. The Pinkertons set about soliciting cash from former victims of the Wild Bunch, including railroad and express companies, to finance the operation to arrest the two fugitives. Although it was estimated that the cost would be only $5,000, none of the victim companies were willing to donate to the fund. Perhaps they worried that if Butch and Sundance were brought back to the States they would escape and seek revenge. Better to have them far away in South America.

The Pinkertons were always conscious of the bottom line, and refused to use their own resources to fund the expedition. William Pinkerton offered a lame excuse for their reluctance in a speech to a convention of police chiefs, when he said that "being expert ranch men [Butch and Sundance] engaged in cattle raising on a ranch they had acquired, located on a piece of high table land from which they commanded a view of 25 miles in various directions, making their capture practically impossible." Regardless of lame excuses, the American banditos had received a reprieve until appropriate arrangements could be made.[17]

Incidentally, in November of 1903, famed regulator Tom Horn was awaiting hanging for the murder of fourteen-year-old Willie Nickel. Days before his execution was scheduled to take place in Cheyenne, Wyoming, Horn was secretly informed that preparations were under way to bust him out of jail, and the men who had been hired to do it were none other than Butch Cassidy, the Sundance Kid, and the rest of the Wild Bunch.

Rumors of this impending jailbreak reached the ears of authorities, and security was beefed up, with army troops patrolling the vicinity of the jailhouse. Horn received a second message two days before his hanging, telling him to be ready the next day. That night, gamblers in every Cheyenne saloon were setting and changing odds that the attempted breakout would or would not happen, and, if so, whether it would be successful.

At eleven-oh-eight a.m. on November 20, however, Tom Horn realized that Butch, Sundance, and the boys were not coming to his rescue. At that time, he was hanged by his neck until he was dead with a rope he had personally woven.[18]

In Cholila, Butch, Sundance, and Etta had settled into a peaceful life of raising livestock. They had built a comfortable four-room cabin constructed of cypress logs—with four-pane double-hung glass windows imported from the United States—that differed from the neighboring stone ranch houses. Perhaps the cabin, resembling a frontier structure from the American West, made them feel more at home. They added a stable, a chicken coop, a bunkhouse for their cowhands, and a number of corrals. Butch may have built himself a smaller separate cabin, while Sundance and Etta lived in the main house. They built a compact cellar under the main house that could double as a hiding place, if necessary.[19]

Primo Caprara, a guest in the home of Butch, Sundance, and Etta, wrote: "The house was simply furnished and exhibited a certain painstaking tidiness, a geometric arrangement of things, pictures with cane frames, wallpaper made of clippings from North American magazines . . . many beautiful weapons and lassos braided from horsehair. . . . The lady, who was reading, was well-dressed. I had a friendly dinner . . . she kept perfumed water in the house's wash basins, spoke some Spanish."[20]

The three strangers eventually made a favorable impression on their neighbors by attending local fiestas, welcoming visitors into their home, and frequently inviting guests for dinner parties. Etta gained a reputation as an excellent cook, especially with Mexican cuisine. "The only white woman in the province," she raised eyebrows by dancing with territorial governor Lezana at his inaugural ball. In fact, that dance may have compelled the governor to pay them a visit, during which "Place played the samba on his guitar and Ryan danced with the daughter of Don Venutra Sol." Evidently, the Sundance Kid was a guitar picker.[21]

Local historian Raul Cea, whose father, Pedro, was a teenager who lived near the three Americans, said: "Senora Place had a dog—a spaniel, I think—that went with her everywhere. She was devoted to it. Ryan was more gregarious than his companions. He also loved to read and frequently borrowed books from English-speaking neighbors." He went on to describe the three as well-to-do and very cultured. "They set a table with a certain etiquette—napkins, china plates. Their windows went up and down."[22]

Butch became known as a real gentleman, and Sundance impressed everyone with his fast draw and expert marksmanship. But when it came to cowboying, the gauchos around Cholila, wearing their low-crowned, wide-brimmed hats, baggy pants, and high boots, were skeptical about the skills of these foreign newcomers. Cea explained: "At first, the local gauchos thought the North Americans were too refined for ranch work. In those days, they didn't have fences and the cattle were all mixed together. The gauchos chortled at the prospect of watching the gringos try to separate their cattle from the herd, but they proved to be very good cowboys, handy with lassos, and the gauchos came away from the roundup with a new opinion."

At some point, perhaps when the governor visited the ranch, two photographs that were likely by professional photographer Carlos Foresti were taken. The first photo, *The Tea Party*, depicts the three Americans in front of their cabin, with Butch and Sundance seated, and Etta wearing an apron and holding a teakettle. Two dogs—one of them likely Etta's favorite spaniel—sit at their feet. The second photo shows nine people lined up in front of the ranch house. Butch stands on the far left beside three horses, Sundance and Etta to the far right, each holding a single horse by its reins. In between stand four unidentified men and two unidentified women. Etta's ever-present spaniel sits at her feet. Butch and Sundance are dressed in distinctly Western attire, with white shirts, vests, gun belts hanging low on their hips, and cowboy hats creased in Montana Peak style.

Sundance mailed copies of the photographs to Samanna back in Mont Clare, where apparently they eluded interception by the Pinkertons. The photos remained in private hands during the lifetime of the outlaws.[23]

Butch, a former jockey, was likely fascinated and perhaps mildly shocked by the manner in which the gauchos conducted horse races. The Argentine riders were known for their cruelty to the animals, and in one type of contest, called *cinchada*, two horses were tied tail-to-tail with lassos attached to the saddles. The rider who pulled his opponent backward across a line in the dirt would win. In another match, called *pechando*, two riders faced each other at a predetermined distance and raced at top speed until crashing headlong. The charges were repeated until one of the animals could no longer continue. In addition to distance races, one variation called "crowding horses" had two riders galloping as fast as possible while trying to prod the other rider and his horse off the track.[24]

The Sundance Kid, a frequent gambler, likely discovered that card playing was a popular pastime in Patagonia, where a native game called *truco*, played with a forty-card deck, was common. The game required quite a bit of conversation and signaling between the players. The two Americans probably stayed away from this game due to their problems understanding the language. Sundance, on the other hand, may have shown the locals a few card tricks of his own and taught them the game of poker to even the score. Another game of chance, called *taba*, resembled dice in a certain respect. Players tossed the anklebone of a cow or a horse after placing bets on whether it would land on heads or tails.

Both men likely attended cockfights, the most popular betting game in the region. Each town had its own cockfighting arena, and authorities made money from licensing bird owners and taxing a portion of the handle. It is doubtful whether Etta ever accompanied them to watch the brutal blood sport.[25]

In late 1903, Sundance and Etta once again boarded a steamship and returned to the United States. The Pinkertons believed that the couple visited Fort Worth and, judging from an unsigned postcard sent to Sundance's sister Emma, attended the 1904 World's Fair and Exposition in St. Louis. The Fort Worth trip suggests that Etta, whom Sundance had once called a Texas girl, was spending time with her family. By February 1904, however, Sundance was back in Cholila buying bulls for the ranch.[26]

It seemed as if the three expatriates had settled into a pleasant life in Patagonia. They had a wonderfully furnished and constructed cabin and necessary outbuildings, their livestock had brought them a profit, and they were liked and respected by their neighbors.

What then could have compelled Butch, Sundance, and Etta to abandon all their hard work and peaceful, law-abiding existence for a return to a life of crime?

CHAPTER TWELVE
THE *BANDITOS AMERICANOS*

Sam made it back to Texas all right side up with care;
Rode into the town of Denton with all his friends to share.
Sam's life was short in Texas; three robberies did he do:
He robbed all the passenger, mail, and express cars too.

Sam met his fate at Round Rock, July the twenty-first,
They pierced poor Sam with rifle balls and emptied out
    his purse,
Poor Sam he is a corpse and six foot under clay,
And Jackson's in the bushes trying to get away.

                    —"Sam Bass"

In February 1905, two distinguished-looking Americans calling themselves Brady and Linden checked into the Hotel Argentina in the town of Rio Gallegos, on the southern tip of Argentina. One account reports that there were not two but three of them, perhaps including a lady, and they rented a house outside of town. They caught the attention of the locals by galloping their horses at breakneck speed to and from town when they purchased supplies, which earned them the nickname "those crazy Yankees."[1]

These strangers said they were representatives of a livestock company in Rio Negro province, and were shopping for land to purchase. The two gentlemen made a small deposit with the Banco de Londres y Tarapaca, and then circulated around town, dining in style, tipping well, and even buying a surveyor's telescope and a compass to help them in their quest to find local real estate.[2]

On February 14, Brady and Linden proceeded into the bank in Rio Gallegos just before closing time. They pulled Colt .45 revolvers on bank manager Arturo Bishop and cashier Alexander Mackerrow, both of whom had been distracted by paperwork. Forcing Bishop to open the safe, the armed banditos stuffed $100,000 worth of cash and silver into a canvas bag, then ran outside with their loot, jumped on their horses, and galloped out of town. They made their escape in the direction of the Gallegos River, about fifteen miles away.[3]

The robbery was a vintage Wild Bunch caper, and blame has traditionally been placed on the shoulders of Butch and Sundance. Yet careful research casts doubt on their involvement. In 1997, a symposium of scholars and outlaw enthusiasts was held in the town of Esquel, Chubut province, in southern Argentina to determine guilt for the unsolved crime. Evidence was presented that concluded that Butch and Sundance could not have possibly committed the robbery.

First, the descriptions of the robbers did not sufficiently match Butch and Sundance, though they did resemble the two American outlaws in some respects. The shorter bandit had green eyes, a sunburned complexion, and a trimmed chestnut or black beard, which could have been dyed. The taller man—about five feet, ten inches tall—had green eyes, a light complexion, and blond hair. But the Rio Gallegos robbers were said to have been twenty-five and thirty years old. In 1905, Butch was pushing forty and Sundance was nearly thirty-nine—quite a disparity from the description of the men who committed the holdup.[4]

Second, Butch's alias—Santiago Ryan—can be found on a purchase order from a store near Cholila at about the time of the heist. Neighbors also testified that the two men were at home at the time. Finally, a government agricultural census survey taken during February 1905 indicates that Butch and Sundance were present at their ranch. Rio Gallegos was 750 miles away from Cholila, ruling out a quick trip back and forth.[5]

From all indications, on the day of the bank robbery the three transplanted Americans were living as law-abiding citizens, raising livestock, and making the best of their opportunity to go straight. But, as fate would have it, the Rio Gallegos holdup was about to turn the lives of Butch, Sundance, and Etta upside down.

The police chief in Buenos Aires was in possession of a Pinkerton wanted poster, and decided that he need look no further for the bank robbers. He contacted Eduardo Humphries, the sheriff of Esquel, and ordered him to arrest Butch and Sundance for questioning in the Rio Gallegos bank robbery. The police chief reasoned: "As their specialty is armed robbery of banks, trains and public buildings in broad daylight, and they were in the country it is presumed they are the perpetrators."[6]

Sheriff Eduardo Humphries was friends with Butch and Sundance, and was known to have a romantic interest in Etta. He was not about to hand them over to the authorities, and therefore chose not to act on the warrant. Instead, he warned his friends about their looming arrest, a move for which he was later fired.

The happy existence of the three homesteaders had come to an end. Other law enforcement officers would surely be dispatched, perhaps even an army of officers, who would execute the arrest warrant with bullets. Butch, Sundance and Etta would need to take immediate and desperate action to stay out of custody.[7]

Butch and Sundance must have questioned their decision to become law-abiding citizens. They had departed the land they loved for a foreign country with unfamiliar customs and culture, yet had earned friends, a thriving business, and the respect of the community. Now all the work they had done for themselves would go for naught. Butch, Sundance, and Etta had no other choice but to flee.

On April 19, 1905, Butch wrote to Richard Clarke, from whom he had ordered supplies, that the trio was leaving Cholila and that their merchandise should be delivered to Daniel Gibbon, a neighbor and friend. On May 1, Butch wrote another letter to neighbor John C. Perry, a fellow immigrant who had been the first sheriff in Crockett County, Texas. He informed Perry that he, along with Sundance and Etta, were leaving Cholila that very day. Perry, who was retired, was aware of the two men's outlaw past, but had overlooked it. Butch and Sundance had proven themselves as men of character, and he was likely disappointed but not surprised by their hasty departure.[8]

On the day Cassidy wrote to Perry, Annie Gillies Parker, Butch's mother, passed away at the age of fifty-eight with her family at her bedside. Her heart, broken ever since the sunny day in June 1884 when her son rode away from home, had finally given out. She had not seen Butch in nearly twenty-one years.[9]

On May 9, the three fugitives, carrying little more than cash and their necessities packed in satchels, boarded a steamer on Lake Nahuel Huapi and sailed to Chile. Wenceslao Solis, one of their gauchos, accompanied them, and then returned to Cholila with their saddles and instructions about how to liquidate the ranch and their possessions.[10]

The ranchland could not be sold because it was homesteaded

property and not deeded to them, but the ranch buildings and provisions were purchased by Thomas T. Austin, the manager of a Chilean land and cattle company, for eighteen thousand pesos. The livestock were sold at a later date, and the money held for them by neighbor Dan Gibbon. The personal possessions they had left behind, such as furniture and dishes, were split up among Gibbon, Wenceslao Solis, John Perry, and other friends.[11]

On June 28, 1905, the Sundance Kid wrote a letter to Dan Gibbon from Valparaiso, Chile:

> *Dear Friend:*
>
> *We are writing to you to let you know that our business went well and we received our money. We arrived here today, and the day after tomorrow my wife and I leave for San Francisco. I'm very sorry, Dan, that we could not bring the brand R with us, but I hope that you will be able to fetch enough to pay you for the inconveniences.*
>
> *We want you to take care of Davy and his wife and see that they don't suffer in any way. And be kind to the old Spaniel and give him pieces of meat once in a while and get rid of the black mutt.*
>
> *I don't want to see Cholila ever again, but I will think of you and of all our friends often, and we want to assure you of our good wishes.*
>
> *Attached you will find the song "Sam Bass," which I promised to write down for you. As I have no more news, I will end by begging that you remember us to all our friends, without forgetting Juan and Vencylow [sic], giving them our regards and good wishes, keeping a large portion for yourself and family.*
>
> *Remaining as always your*
> *true friend,*
> *H. A. Place*[12]

Both apologetic and wistful, Sundance's sadness at leaving the friends he had made in Chubut province was genuine, but he may also have been glad to shake the dust off his boots and embark upon another adventure. Life had been quite tame for the two former outlaws, and perhaps they were ready to make a change.

The robbery of the Banco de Londres y Tarapaca in Rio Gallegos was never solved. Authorities, having made up their minds that Butch Cassidy and the Sundance Kid were the perpetrators, likely never investigated any further. Several former members of the Wild Bunch had been rumored to have moved to South America, and it is possible they had robbed the bank with tactics learned from Butch Cassidy. Nevertheless, Butch, Sundance, and Etta were uprooted and on the run once again. The same system that had chased them out of the United States was after them on this continent as well.

The whereabouts of Butch in the following months cannot be accurately determined; Sundance and Etta likely returned to the United States, likely traveling from Valparaiso, Chile, to Buenos Aires by the trans-Andean train, then boarding a steamship to Colón, Panama, a common transfer point for passengers heading for New York City. The manifest of the SS *Seguranca*, which departed Colón on July 22, 1905, and arrived in New York on July 29 with 105 passengers, lists a Mrs. E. Place, an American citizen born in 1879, and a Mr. R. Scott, a married American merchant born in 1867—the year Harry Longabaugh was born.

Why the two had changed plans from Sundance's letter to Dan Gibbon and traveled to New York City is unknown. They may have been unwilling to wait for a ship heading to San Francisco and boarded immediate transport. The SS *Seguranca*, with a capacity for five hundred passengers, regularly shuttled workers between the yet-to-be-completed Panama Canal and New York City. On the voyage departing July 22, seventeen passengers and crew members came down with yellow fever and were quarantined at their destination. It is not known whether Sundance or Etta was among those who contracted the illness.[13]

Etta may have traveled alone to New York, and the Mr. R. Scott listed on the manifest was unrelated to Sundance. Another story suggests that Sundance was detained in Chile by authorities while Etta departed solo. This theory was based on a Pinkerton memo issued on January 26, 1906, from the company's Philadelphia office, which had intercepted a letter from Sundance to his sister Samanna at the Mont Clare post office.

Although no official Chilean documents have surfaced to support the notion, historian James D. Horan interviewed Percy Seibert, a friend of Butch and Sundance from their future Bolivian mining days. Horan's notes of the interview were written in a personal shorthand that may be accurately interpreted only by Horan himself.

> Sundance, going back, 1905, woman . . . restaurant posters, depicting 75000, 10,000 joked with constable if found, split . . . got stouter . . . woman started to go out. Number of deputies, to pick up—as was custom, no single action .45—use blackjack or billy, cock it faster ordinary man . . . Smith a Wesson lawmen . . . covered man, chief of police shot, no intention, accident, showed cops gun, held week, had lawyer . . . sent message to Butch, who had 1000 English, gave bill, northern Argentina—1906 . . . picked up Sundance to help him.[14]

As best as can be interpreted, Horan wrote in his notes that Sundance and Etta were eating dinner in a Chilean restaurant when a local constable approached them. This man apparently joked that Sundance resembled the man on a wanted poster who had a reward of $10,000 on his head. Etta decided to excuse herself and leave when additional constables or deputies carrying nightsticks entered. Sundance became concerned about the situation and drew his Colt .45 revolver. A scuffle ensued, and Sundance's six-gun accidentally discharged, the bullet wounding the chief of police. Sundance was hauled off to jail, and held behind bars for a week until he could post the $1,500 bail—$1,000 of which supposedly came from Butch, who arrived to help his partner. In which case, Etta may have left the country without Sundance.[15]

By December 1905, however, Butch, Sundance, and Etta reunited in the town of Villa Mercedes in San Luis, Argentina. Located four hundred miles west of Buenos Aires, Villa Mercedes was a bustling commercial center for daily shipments of cattle by rail.

On Tuesday, December 19, the vault at the Banco de la Nación on the corner of Belgrano and Riobamba streets was bulging with the proceeds of the town's monthly cattle sale. That afternoon, four "well-mounted horsemen" rode up to the bank and tied their animals to the hitching post. While one man waited outside with the horses, the other three burst through the front door with six-shooters drawn. They loudly demanded that the contents of the safe be handed over. Señor Harleb, the bank manager, apparently did not move quickly enough or protested the intrusion and was whacked over the head with the butt of a revolver. The robbers then rifled the safe, and stuffed into sacks as much as fourteen thousand pesos—perhaps $90,000. The three banditos were out the door within four minutes of entering, and leaped onto their waiting chargers with the loot in hand. The foursome galloped in a southerly direction out of town.

A man named Garcia, the treasurer of the bank, ran outside with a gun in his hand and squeezed off a volley of shots at the fleeing robbers, but failed to hit any of them. Several others on the street also fired at the mounted men but missed. A posse was immediately assembled by the police, and gave chase.

Just north of Buena Esperanza, the banditos inexplicably reined up and exchanged heavy fire with their pursuers. According to one account, a bullet wounded one of the outlaws, and the others paused for a moment to care for this person. In spite of the brief delay, the robbers had prepared well for their getaway. Fresh horses and supplies waited at relay points along the way toward the Chilean border.

The posse, with horses lathered and laboring, was no match for the well-mounted horsemen. Worse yet, they were eventually deterred by torrential rains that swelled the rivers and streams. Reluctantly they turned back to Villa Mercedes.[16]

Within five days of the robbery, the Pinkerton National Detective Agency provided information to Buenos Aires newspapers that accused James Ryan, Harry Longabaugh, Miss H. A. Place, and Harvey Logan of committing the crime. These four outlaws, authorities and the public were informed, were members of a North American gang that had been hiding out in Chubut province.

Miss Place, who was identified as Longabaugh's wife, was described as "an interesting woman, very masculine, who wears male clothing with total correctness, and who is dedicated more to the occupations of men than those of women." It was also noted that this lady was a "fine rider, handles with precision all classes of firearms, and has an admirable male temperament."[17]

The police in Villa Mercedes began gathering as much information about the bank robbers as they could find. They interviewed patrons at a bar located two blocks from the bank who swore that the suspects had been drinking whiskey there prior to the holdup. The witnesses were shown photographs of Butch, Sundance, Etta, and Harvey Logan, and could positively identify the first three as customers, though not Logan. In addition, a ranch foreman outside of town pointed out Butch, Sundance, and Etta in the photos as the three North Americans who had been staying at the ranch until just hours before the armed robbery. The authorities may have now known who had committed the crime, but catching them would be a more difficult proposition. The trail of the bank robbers had gone cold.[18]

Butch Cassidy, the Sundance Kid, and possibly Etta Place, the three escaping outlaws—the fourth apparently went his own way—floated off the pages of history for a while after crossing the Salado River on a raft and heading for the port city of Antofagasta, Chile. Butch and Sundance would eventually resurface, but Etta simply vanished forever without a trace—in the same cloud of mystery as her sudden appearance.

Countless theories have been formed about the origin of Etta

Place, and just as many have sought the reason she left Sundance after the Villa Mercedes bank robbery. One report, allegedly originating with Butch, claims that she was taken by Sundance to the United States, possibly to Denver, for treatment while suffering from chronic appendicitis. Sundance then left her there and returned to South America. Yet this theory is implausible from the standpoint that a person with an attack of appendicitis, which would require immediate surgery, would seek treatment at the nearest medical facility and not endure a long seagoing trip to find relief.[19]

More likely Etta had tired of her lifestyle in South America and took her share of the Villa Mercedes robbery back to the States for a fresh start. Perhaps Sundance had refused to accompany her, fearing that he would be recognized and arrested wherever they might settle. She may have outgrown her youthful adventurism and risk taking, and wanted to settle down and have children before she became too old, and Sundance chose not to be part of that picture. Or possibly the two of them were simply sick and tired of each other and decided to "divorce."

One provocative theory must be considered. Reports surfaced that one of the banditos who held up the bank in Villa Mercedes was wounded by a posse member during the chase. Could it have been Etta Place who had been shot, possibly by a fatal bullet? For Butch or Sundance to admit that she had been killed during the course of a robbery would be to incriminate themselves, and it was unlikely they would be so foolish. As far as can be determined, neither man ever mentioned her name again to anyone who recorded the fact.

Etta as easily as any of them could have been on the receiving end of that random bullet from a posse member that struck one of the fleeing outlaws—and there is a probability that the person wounded was not Butch or Sundance. Her limp body could have been taken from her saddle onto Sundance's horse so as not impede the getaway, or supported aboard her own horse until the outlaws had eluded the pursuit and arrived at a safe place to dismount and tend to her wounds.

By time, she could have lost too much blood to save her or

make it worthwhile to carry her to a doctor. In a scenario that would be preferred by romantics, she could have died in the arms of her long-time lover, Harry Longabaugh. In that event, the body of the beautiful Etta Place could even now be buried in an unmarked grave beneath the South American soil at a location known only to Butch Cassidy and the Sundance Kid.

The search for a clear vision of Etta has frustrated historians for over a century. What is known, however, is that Etta Place, the enigmatic girlfriend-mistress-wife and accomplice, would not be present for the final chapter in the lives of Butch Cassidy and the Sundance Kid. On January 10, 1906, three North American men were arrested in Neuquén Territory—between Villa Mercedes and Cholila, Chubut province—for the robbery of the bank in Villa Mercedes. Three days later, the authorities realized they had the wrong men and they were released from custody. The three victims would later file claims against the government for their wrongful detention.[20]

After the Spanish conquest of Bolivia in 1532, silver deposits were discovered at Potosí, transforming the region into one of the wealthiest in the Spanish Empire. By the end of the eighteenth century, however, the silver had been depleted and the country fell on hard times. But the loss of silver mining would soon be replaced by a new mineral—tin.

Workers descended into the underground tin mines with hammers and pickaxes to extract the exposed minerals. This raw mineral would then be hauled to the surface and crushed under a primitive mill composed of an indented flat stone on which an enormous round boulder was rocked back and forth by means of long poles inserted into holes in its side to provide leverage. It was backbreaking work—both underground and aboveground—for which the native people of the lowest classes were compelled to labor.

By the beginning of the twentieth century, the invention of the vacuum-packed tin can and the assembly of the automobile raised the demand for tin. In addition, the industry benefited from the new rail access that linked the major tin mines to the Pacific Ocean, opening up a worldwide market. Bolivia became prosperous again, this time as an independent country.

In spite of the booming industry, the men, women, and children who extracted the tin faced appalling conditions in the mines, with low pay and no access to education or political representation to help them escape or improve their lot. The majority of the indigenous population lived their daily lives under the most primitive conditions in deplorable poverty—all for the benefit of a small elite who became incredibly wealthy.

In 1906, an American was hired by Clement Rolla Glass to buy and handle livestock that would haul supplies for the Concordia Tin Mines at Tres Cruces, Bolivia, seventy miles southeast of La Paz. The mine was located sixteen thousand feet up in the Santa Vela Cruz Mountains, part of the Bolivian Andes. Using the alias Santiago Maxwell, Butch Cassidy was hired at $150 a month plus room and board.

Glass was impressed with his new employee right from the start. At one point, Butch was handed $200 to buy a string of mules. He returned with excellent animals and, much to Glass's surprise, $50 left over. Butch was soon promoted to escort the Concordia Mine payroll to the workers, which was often in excess of $100,000. Glass would comment that Butch was "an excellent and trustworthy employee . . . a good bargainer and always rendered a strict account of funds turned over to him."[21]

Meanwhile, the Sundance Kid had found a job working for Roy Letson, a railroad construction contractor. Sundance broke mules and drove them from northern Argentina to a camp near La Paz. Letson remembered Sundance as a shy but rather likable man. "Longabaugh kept very much to himself most of the time," Letson recalled. "I told him my destination was Bolivia and he said that he would be glad to go along. We were several weeks on the trip. He was employed by our company to break the mules to harness and saddle and done a very good job . . . well dressed . . . did have a very fine Tiffany gold watch . . . it was not long before he was on the go again."[22]

Sundance—calling himself Enrique or Harry Brown—was on the go to the Concordia Mine, where Butch Cassidy was employed. Butch vouched for this stranger, and Rolla Glass was happy to hire him as a payroll guard.[23]

Butch and Sundance were soon introduced to North American mining engineer Percy Seibert, who was Glass's assistant. Siebert never became close to Sundance, but was impressed with the outlaw's shooting prowess. "Sundance was inclined to be distant, even sullen, and it was difficult to strike up a friendship with him." Perhaps Sundance's sullen behavior had something to do with the missing Etta Place. He could have been grieving her death or the fact that she had left him, or vice versa. From all indications, Sundance was drinking heavily, perhaps to drown his sorrow. He had never been that happy-go-lucky person that described Butch, but Sundance had now retreated further into himself and did not seek a shoulder to cry on.[24]

On the other hand, Percy Seibert said of Butch: "Butch Cassidy was an exceptionally pleasant, cultured and charming man. He took well with the ladies and as soon as he arrived in a village he made friends with the little urchins and usually had some candy to give them."[25]

Seibert and the two outlaws became fast friends, and often ate Sunday dinner together with Seibert's family. Seibert owned a windup gramophone and had a huge record collection, which served as entertainment. Their host did notice that Butch would always sit in a chair at the dinner table that was near the window that overlooked the valley, or would choose a seat on a small sofa that gave him a clear view of the three doors that led to the outside of the house.[26]

Seibert told of the day when Butch had engaged in a lively debate with Rolla Glass about which was the superior weapon, the Winchester rifle or the six-shooter. "At last Butch turned to Longabaugh. 'Let's show him, Kid.' Longabaugh jumped up, spun the chamber of his six-shooter and said, 'Let's go, Butch.' Cassidy looked around and selected four empty bottles. He tossed two to Longabaugh and kept the other two.

"Outside, both outlaws settled into a semi-crouch, then threw the bottles high in the air. I never saw anything like it. I never saw two guns drawn faster and I was with men skilled in firearms all my life. Before I knew it the Colts were in their hands and they were shooting. The four bottles crashed in splinters. They repeated this trick several times. Sometimes Butch missed but the Kid always hit the falling targets. However, against Mr. Glass, they weren't too good in firing at fixed targets. As Butch said, 'I guess we're better when our targets are moving.'"[27]

Butch took his job as security guard seriously, as evidenced by the day that two dangerous local outlaws named Nation and Clifford decided to rob the mining company. Butch caught wind of this possible holdup and confronted the two would-be robbers. They claimed they were broke, and stealing the payroll was the only way they had to get some money. Butch gave them $50 and ordered them out of the mining camp, an act that greatly impressed Percy Seibert, who had taken over as manager of the mine when Glass departed. Butch would usually accommodate transient outlaws with a meal or allow them to shoe a horse, but would never allow them to stay for any length of time, for which Seibert was also pleased. Seibert did not want his camp to gain a reputation as a hangout for bandits.[28]

Butch and Sundance were loyal and dependable employees, but would occasionally leave the camp for personal business. In April 1906, Sundance returned to Cholila to oversee the sale of two hundred sheep and thirty mares that Dan Gibbon had been caring for. In other instances, the two friends would disappear for purposes known only to themselves, but it was said that they would always return with money jingling in their pockets. Both were known gamblers, especially Sundance, but they were more than likely committing minor robberies across the country and bringing home loot rather than winnings from the tables.[29]

Although they had been situated in South America for more than five years, Butch and Sundance had not been forgotten back in the United States. The criminal adventures of the two outlaws in their new home country were splashed across the pages in the magazine section of the *New York Herald* on September 23, 1906.

Under the headline "Yankee Desperadoes Hold Up the Argentine Republic," the article presented a mostly fictional account of the Villa Mercedes bank robbery, falsely accusing Butch and Sundance of shooting the bank manager in the head, which never happened. Even more fascinating was the fabrication about Butch and Harvey Logan riding through the mountains together in a stagecoach. Apparently one of the passengers had a trunk filled with gold, which was the target of the two bad guys. When the coach arrived at a place where the road ran adjacent to a deep ravine, Butch and Harvey tossed the passenger and the driver "headlong into the abyss below." Then the two outlaws made off with the gold on the backs of two horses they unhitched from the coach and rode bareback, "escaping unmolested to their distant plateau."[30]

Harvey Logan would have had difficulty participating in that robbery—he was dead. On June 7, 1904, Harvey and several accomplices robbed a train outside of Parachute, Colorado. To their disappointment, the safe was empty and they made off with around $50 and a posse hot on their trail.

The bandits managed to elude the posse for a couple of days, but finally on June 9 the pursuers caught up with the outlaws in a gully near Rifle, Colorado, and a serious gun battle ensued. Supposedly more than two hundred rounds of ammo were fired from both sides. During the fusillade, Harvey Logan was hit three times—in the arm and both lungs. Knowing he was puffing his last labored breaths, Logan held off the posse while his partners escaped. Then the killer known as Kid Curry killed himself with a bullet through his brain.

His corpse was identified as Tap Duncan, an alias Logan was using at the time. The railroads, loath to admit that the dead outlaw was Logan and be forced to pay the $30,000 reward on his head, wanted the body buried as Duncan. The Pinkertons, determined to know the true identity of the dead man, had a coroner in Glenwood Springs, Colorado, examine the body. The doctor confirmed by known scars and marks that the body was that of Harvey Logan. On July 12, 1904, the *Saint Paul Pioneer Press* published four photographs of the corpse, and there could be no mistaking that the body was that of Logan.

Harvey had once told his jailers and defense attorney in Knoxville, where he broke from jail in 1903, that he would rather die than do a long stretch in the pen. Still, rumors soon began to circulate that Logan had somehow escaped the shoot-out and made it safely to South America. As the legend grew, he was said to have lived peacefully on a ranch in Patagonia, married a native girl who bore him eight children, and died there in 1941 at the age of seventy-six. Yet Butch Cassidy, who regarded Harvey as one of the two bravest men he had ever known, had tried to talk Logan into joining them in Argentina. Harvey adamantly refused.[31]

And the other bravest man Butch had ever known? An easy choice—Charles Woodcock, the messenger in the railroad express car that had been blown sky-high near Wilcox, Wyoming.

Harvey Logan was never heard from again after the suicide. Consequently, it would be a safe bet that he took his own life in that gully because he either knew he was dying or did not want to spend the remainder of his life in prison or stand on the gallows.[32]

In November of 1907, Butch and Sundance took a leave of absence from the Concordia Mine and traveled to Santa Cruz, three hundred miles to the east, searching for land to buy. The idea of settling down on their own ranch remained alive within them. They were duly impressed with the area. It was off the beaten path at the time, but that isolation would be changing. Santa Cruz was scheduled to be connected with towns in southwestern Brazil by a soon-to-be-built railroad, which would make it easier to receive goods and to ship livestock to markets.

Butch wrote to his friends at the mine: "We arrived here about 3 weeks ago after a very pleasant journey and found just the place I have been looking for 20 years and [Sundance] likes it better than I do. He says he wont try to live any where else. This is a town of 18,000 and 14,000 are females and some of them are birds. This is the only place for old fellows like myself, one never gets too old if he has blue eyes and a red face and looks capable of making a blue eyed baby boy."

Butch had wasted no time finding himself a new romantic interest, about whom he wrote: "The lady feeds me on fine wines and she is the prettiest little thing I ever seen but I am afraid Papa is going to tear my playhouse down for he is getting nasty." No mention was made about Sundance, the ladies' man, showing any interest in any of the 14,000 females residing in that city, another indication of his lingering attachment to Etta Place.

Butch continued with an overview of the area: "This place isn't what we expected at all. There isn't any cattle here all the beef that is killed comes here from Mojo. The grass is good but water is scarce. Land is cheap here and everything grows good that is planted. But there is damd little planted. It is pretty warm and some fever but the fever is caused by the food they eat. At least I am willing to chance it. We expect to be back at Concordia in about 1 month. Good luck to all you fellows. J. P. Maxwell."[33]

Evidently the dream of settling in Santa Cruz was simply a passing fancy. Butch and Sundance soon went back to work at the Concordia Mine, and no evidence exists that they ever returned to the frontier town in Bolivia's eastern savanna, or even mentioned the place again. At the Concordia Mine, they felt welcome and comfortable—at least for the time being.

Yet eventually, possibly due to the Pinkertons' wanted posters, the true identities of Santiago Maxwell and Enrique Brown were revealed to one and all at the Concordia. Not only that, but the two men—for unknown reasons—freely admitted to being the outlaws on that wanted poster.

Percy Seibert may have been concerned at first that Butch and Sundance had designs on robbing the Concordia, but they assured him that they would never rob anyone for whom they worked. Seibert apparently took them at their word. Not only did they promise not to harm anyone at the mine, but Butch was not averse to discussing his criminal activities privately with Seibert, who was an avid listener.[34]

Butch explained that he and Sundance had fled America due to the pressure put on them by having the Pinkertons, railroad detectives, and even the U.S. Cavalry constantly on their trail. He admitted that the closest call they had ever experienced in a getaway had been in South America, when they were escaping from the posse after the Villa Mercedes bank holdup. He did not explain why that particular getaway was so dangerous, but it could have been because of a death in the family during the flight.

Seibert asked Butch why the two men had returned to banditry in South America after settling down and going straight. "There's always an informer around to bring the law on you," Butch replied. "After you've started, you have to keep going, that's all. The safest way is to keep moving all the time and spring a holdup in some new place. In that way you keep the other fellows guessing."[35]

Now that their secret had been exposed, both outlaws knew their days at the mine were coming to an end. Their departure was hastened when Sundance got drunk one night at a café in the town of Uyuni and began bragging about the holdups he and Butch had committed in South America. Although word had probably already leaked to the community that the mine was harboring two notorious North American outlaws, this was the final straw. Soon after that night Butch and Sundance settled up their accounts at the mine's company store, drew their final pay, and rode away from the Concordia forever.

Percy Seibert speculated that the two men had departed because they did not wish to bring disgrace to the company if the word got out that outlaws were welcome there. It would seem that the consciences of Butch and Sundance were at work again. They had been estranged for the most part from their families and homes over the years so as not to bring shame upon those people, and now they were leaving another place they loved. In all fairness, it also may have just been that they were following their own philosophy of keeping on the move so that the law was kept guessing.[36]

Butch and Sundance knew there were many more places in South America just waiting for them to rob, but what they could not know was that they were presently riding toward the end of their mortal trail.

CHAPTER THIRTEEN
SHOOT-OUT AT SAN VICENTE

There's a race of men that don't fit in,
  A race that can't stay still;
So they break the hearts of kith and kin,
  And they roam the world at will.

If they just went straight they might go far;
  They are strong and brave and true;
But they're always tired of the things that are,
  And they want the strange and new.

And each forgets that his youth has fled,
  Forgets that his prime is past,
Till he stands one day, with a hope that's dead,
  In the glare of the truth at last.

—"The Men That Don't Fit In"

Butch Cassidy and the Sundance Kid—posing as the Lowe brothers—soon found honest labor as mule skinners for a transportation company in southern Bolivia. They drove mule-drawn coaches and wagons hauling both passengers and freight, and tended to the animals and the stables. But the mundane job did not last for long, and they drifted across the border to Peru.[1]

At that time, the two men returned to their profession as outlaws. They stopped a stagecoach at gunpoint on a remote mountainous road as it traveled from the Santo Domingo Mine. The robbers were under the impression that the stage was carrying a large amount of money from the mine, but they searched the vehicle and found nothing. As was Butch's policy, the passengers were neither robbed nor molested, and the coach was sent on its way.

But where was the money? The wary officials at the mine were one step ahead of the bandits, sending this coach ahead as a diversion while the next one held thousands in gold. Butch and Sundance departed empty-handed, unaware that another coach would be coming.

With no roots to hold them, the two banditos rode off in search of an honest job or criminal heist, whichever came first, wandering around the countryside like roaming cowboys would do back home in the American West. Perhaps both dreamed of once again riding the purple sage country they had left behind. But they were older now, middle-aged men, and it was past time for them to settle down. Most cowboys their age were not living by shank's mare any longer but had found a lady to marry and had children to rear and a place to call home. The adventure and romance of the outlaw life may have been appealing to them in their youth. Now it was a burden. Perhaps they could commit that one glorious heist of enough money to have the stake they needed to buy that ranch and settle down for good.

In his memoirs, Percy Seibert attributed the May 1908 holdup of a Bolivian pay train near the town of Eucalyptus to Butch and Sundance. Two North Americans, said to be onetime workers for the railroad that ran between Eucalyptus and La Paz, robbed a railway paymaster of a construction payroll estimated at what would today be about $90,000. The two bandits escaped to the eastern slope of the Andes Mountains to Sacambaya, an abandoned Jesuit mission, where authorities considered it too risky to follow them. The robbery was followed by a second heist on August 19, another payroll taken at gunpoint. Law enforcement believed that both holdups were the work of the same two English-speaking men.[2]

It has been reported that by August, Butch and Sundance—using the aliases George Lowe and Frank Smith—were working or had been permitted to stay at the camp of a gold ore dredging operation near Esmoraca, which casts some doubt over whether or not they actually committed those two payroll robberies. Seibert could have been simply following the accepted practice from the American West of blaming every unsolved holdup on Butch and Sundance.[3]

The residential arrangement with A. G. Francis, who was supervising the gold dredging on the San Juan del Oro River at Verdugo, near Esmoraca, permitted Butch access to the town of Tupiza, fifteen miles north of their work site. While Sundance remained in camp, Butch visited the mining town and cased the bank for any vulnerability they could exploit in a robbery. He scouted potential escape routes, determining where he could post relay stations with fresh horses. Perhaps Butch and Sundance intended for this one last robbery to finance their retirement to Santa Cruz, the place where both of them had dreamed about living.[4]

The bank in Tupiza looked to be an excellent target, except for one problem—the Abaroa Regiment, a Bolivian cavalry unit, rode into town one day and established their base of operations in the hotel situated right next door to the bank. Butch prudently decided that it would be too risky to hold up the bank under those circumstances—although he was likely tempted—and abandoned his plans.

Another option existed for the two patient but willing outlaws, however. Butch's surveillance in Tupiza paid off with the information that a payroll of eighty thousand bolivianos—about half a million dollars—was about to be shipped by the Aramayo, Francke & Cia Silver Mine, which had an office in town. The Aramayo family lived in Tupiza in a mansion, but the tin mine operation itself was located at Quechisla, three days' ride away. All finances originated from Tupiza, and had to be transported to the mine.

This stimulating news called for serious up-close-and-personal spy work. Both Butch and Sundance checked into the Hotel Terminus and kept a vigilant twenty-four-hour watch on the company office for any sign of a huge payroll being readied for shipment.

On November 3, Carlos Pero, his son Mariano, and another man departed the Aramayo office leading two pack mules heavily laden with saddlebags. Butch and Sundance followed at a safe distance, and it soon became apparent that Pero was headed in the direction of the mines at Quechisla. They were aware that it would take three days of travel to the mine, crossing over oftentimes treacherous terrain with excellent sites where they could set up an ambush.

Carlos Pero and his entourage halted the first night at the village of Cotani, which gave Butch and Sundance the opportunity to ride ahead and locate an ambush site. The ideal spot for a holdup was found at the base of a mountain called Huaca Huanusca—roughly translated meaning "Dead Cow Hill."

On November 4, at nine thirty a.m., Butch and Sundance, armed with new Mauser carbines, Colt revolvers, Browning pistols, and plenty of ammunition in their cartridge belts, waited anxiously in that remote stretch of the primitive trail for the appearance of the mule train. When Carlos Pero and the other two men with their two pack mules came into sight around a bend on the cactus-studded hill, the two robbers stepped out to reveal themselves and brandish their weapons. Butch did all the talking while Sundance covered Pero and his companions from a distance.[5]

Carlos Pero reported: "We encountered two well-armed Yankees, who awaited us with their faces covered by bandannas and their rifles ready, and made us dismount and open the baggage, from which they took only the cash shipment. They also took from us a dark brown mule ('Aramayo'), which is known to the stable hands in Tupiza, with a new hemp rope.

"The two Yankees are tall; one thin and the other—who carried a good pair of Hertz binoculars—heavyset.

"They clearly came from Tupiza, where they must have been waiting for my departure to make their strike, because from the beginning they did not ask me for anything but the cash shipment."[6]

Pero went on to say that they both wore "new, dark-red, thin wale corduroy suits with narrow, soft-brimmed hats" so that only their eyes were visible. These courteous bandits ordered the mine employees off their mules "in a very pleasant manner." They knew exactly what they were looking for, Pero stated, and picked out the package wrapped in homespun cloth that contained the cash from the saddlebag without even checking anywhere else. They also did not ask for Pero and his companions to turn over any personal possessions, which was normal for a Butch Cassidy–Sundance Kid robbery.

The robbers were stunned, however, when they discovered that Pero was carrying only fifteen thousand bolivianos—$90,000—when they were expecting eighty thousand. Pero explained to them that the larger payroll was scheduled for the following week. Butch and Sundance grudgingly packed away their stolen loot on Aramayo, the stolen mule, and headed south in the direction of Tupiza.[7]

The two bandits had robbed this mule train in a polite and gentlemanly way, and in typical fashion had avoided bloodshed. Yet they did make one major mistake. Although he was masked, Butch's accent gave him away as a North American, which would considerably narrow the search. Whether Sundance spoke is not known.

Pero was permitted by the payroll thieves to resume his journey with the other mule toward the village of Guadalupe. The Pero caravan soon encountered a muleteer named Andrew Gutierrez on the trail. Pero wrote a note that Gutierrez carried to Aramayo headquarters at Salo. From there, a messenger hurried the message to Charjrahusai, where the telegraph wires virtually burned up with the news of the robbery by the two gringos. Every town in the area, including border towns in Argentina and Chile, were notified and given descriptions of the perpetrators.

Almost immediately, military patrols and bands of armed miners were turning the territory upside down as they combed every road, ravine, train station, mine, ranch, or settlement, no matter how small, in southern Bolivia. Stealing their pay was a good way to raise the ire of the mining community. Once again, the system, although not as sophisticated as that in America, had been activated to spread a wide net over every escape route. Butch and Sundance could run, but it was doubtful they could hide for long, especially in a foreign country where they could not blend in with the populace.

Carlos Pero was thankful to be alive, a thought that he contemplated that night while staying once again at a mining camp one day's ride from his destination of Quechisla. He composed a letter to the mine officials that detailed the events of the day, and speculated that the bandits had "undoubtedly planned their retreat carefully; otherwise, they would not have left us with our animals or they would have killed us in order to avoid leaving witnesses or to gain time."

It would have been quite simple for Butch and Sundance to guarantee their safe escape by killing the three men out there on that lonesome stretch of trail. Most robbers who had identified themselves by their accent would not have hesitated to act. But Butch and Sundance had a moral conscience about taking a life, and continued to practice what had been preached to them as children.[8]

Meanwhile, Butch and Sundance made their way through the treacherous Bolivian wilderness under the cover of darkness, eventually moving past Tupiza as stealthily as conditions warranted. They finally arrived sometime after midnight at Tomahuaico, where dredging engineer A. G. Francis had moved his operations.

Francis welcomed them to the camp despite the late hour. Butch had fallen ill, and took to his bed as soon as they arrived. Sundance stayed awake and, while cooking and eating a meal, told Francis all about the heist of the Aramayo mine payroll.

Not by any means did Francis approve of their criminal act, but, according to him, he would not entertain notifying the authorities, a fact that Sundance must have known. Francis admitted that he had been charmed by the outlaws, whom he called "very pleasant and amusing companions."[9]

In the morning, a mutual acquaintance of Francis and the outlaws burst into camp to warn them that there was a military patrol from Tupiza on its way to Tomahuaico. Butch and Sundance accepted the news with a nonchalance that surprised Francis, and finished their breakfasts before calmly saddling and packing their mules.

Much to the chagrin of A. G. Francis, the two outlaws insisted that he accompany them as a guide. Francis, who felt more like a hostage, said, "Needless to say, that was the last thing I wished to do, but argument was useless. Reflecting upon my position, I felt it to be a very unenviable one. However, no other course being open to me, I decided to put as good a face on the matter as possible."[10]

The two bandits and their guide traveled south and west along the San Juan del Oro River, and then turned north to traverse a winding ravine that led them to the Indian pueblo of Estarca. Francis was known at this pueblo, and arranged for them to spend the night at a private home. The dredging engineer had expected the robbers to flee south toward Argentina, and was surprised when they said they were going to "Uyuni and the north." He admitted that he feared for his life during every minute of this tense journey—thinking that he would be killed by soldiers who would ride down the outlaws—but he made no move to escape or try to send a message to the authorities.

In the morning, much to the relief of A. G. Francis, he was thanked for his services and told that he could return to his dredging operation.

He was asked to tell any soldiers he met along the trail that the outlaws were riding hell-for-leather for the Argentine border. Francis now believed that the two men were heading for Oruro, which had been a recent mailing address for Sundance at the American Hotel.[11]

Butch and Sundance were on the move again, and after ten miles came upon the town of Cucho, where they paused to ask directions. They headed out along a rugged trail that led them to San Vicente, a mining town situated 14,500 feet up in the Cordillera Occidental mountains—some thirty miles from the site of their robbery.

The weather in this windswept, barren town above the tree line was anything but accommodating, especially if an outdoor camp was contemplated. With that in mind, Butch and Sundance sought to escape the cold by inquiring about overnight lodgings at the home of Bonifacio Casasola. This resident referred the two travelers to Cleto Bellot, who was the *corregidor*, the mayor or chief administrator for the town.

Bellot told them there was no inn or hotel, but that Bonifacio Casasola, whom they had already met, would provide them his spare room and take care of their other needs. Butch and Sundance were pleased with that arrangement, and asked Casasola to buy them some sardines and beer. Sundance gave the man more than enough pesos to cover their bill. They unsaddled their mules and fed them, and then returned to their room to change clothes and relax. Oddly enough, they left their saddles and weapons outside their door on the patio.

Back in the room, the two robbers told Mayor Bellot that they had come from La Quiaca and inquired about the road leading to Santa Catalina, which was south of the border in Argentina, and also about Uyuni, seventy-five miles north of San Vicente. Bellot was gracious in every way, but he entertained ulterior motives throughout the conversation. He did not want the strangers to become suspicious, but he had already been warned to watch out for two Yankees and a brown Aramayo mule. The strangers had arrived with one black mule and one brown mule that plainly wore the Aramayo brand.

Eventually, Bellot was able to depart Casasola's hacienda, and hurried to seek out an army patrol that had arrived in town several hours earlier from Uyuni. This four-man patrol led by Captain Justo P. Concha included Uyuni police inspector Timoteo Rios, soldier Victor Torres, and another unnamed soldier. They had been out searching for the bandits who had robbed the Aramayo payroll, and had stopped for the night.

Captain Concha was inexplicably absent when the mayor arrived with the news, but Torres took it upon himself to go ahead on his own in command of the other two. The detail marched down the street toward Casasola's hacienda, while Bellot rounded up several "commissioners," members of what could be called a town council, who armed themselves and joined the military procession.

Victor Torres stepped onto the patio of the Casasola home with his gun drawn and cautiously moved toward the door of the room where the two strangers were staying. Butch Cassidy caught a glimpse of the soldier and snapped off a shot from his six-shooter that struck Torres in the neck. Torres was mortally wounded, but continued to fire shots at the unseen outlaws as he backed away before finally collapsing. The other soldiers and townspeople also retreated, all the while furiously pulling the triggers of their weapons. Butch and Sundance returned fire. The sporadic firefight could have lasted as long as a half hour, as the townspeople spread out and were joined by others to form a perimeter around the hacienda.[12]

After the initial shots were fired, Bellot immediately raced away from the scene and encountered Captain Justo Concha. The captain listened to the mayor's story, and then asked him to round up additional armed villagers. Bellot reported that while he was going door to door to raise the alarm he heard "three screams of desperation," but he failed to mention whether the sounds had originated from the house or from those who were surrounding it.

More and more villagers with weapons in hand arrived to assume positions around the house. Butch and Sundance were holed up inside the room in the Casasola hacienda, and there was no way they could break through that ring of firepower. Their rifles, a much more effective weapon when firing at a distant target, remained outside the room, and it was too dangerous to try to retrieve them.

No more shots were fired by either side until about midnight, when a local policeman named Rios split the silence with a single round. The robbers remained inside the house, and the armed soldiers and villagers waited patiently throughout a windy, bitterly cold night.

It was about six o'clock the following morning when Captain Concha and the soldiers, trailed by the others, decided they had waited long enough and approached the room. Inside, they found the bodies of two dead men—"one was in the doorway and the other behind the door on a bench."

Remigio Sanchez, a local miner, described the scene: "The captain entered with a soldier, and then all of us entered and found the smaller gringo [Butch] stretched out on the floor, dead, with one bullet wound in the temple and another in the arm. The taller one [Sundance] was hugging a large ceramic jug that was in the room. He was dead, also, with a bullet wound in the forehead and several in his arm."[13]

Three men in total had been killed in the action—soldier Victor Torres, Robert Leroy Parker, and Harry Alonzo Longabaugh. Torres was shot by Butch in the initial moments, and, according to reports, Butch had shot Sundance and then turned the revolver on himself—a murder-suicide. Both outlaws had been wounded, but with medical attention those bullet holes would not have been life-threatening. Whether they had feared incarceration in a Bolivian prison or believed they were trapped and would surely die, they had dictated the manner in which they arrived at the end of their mortal lives.

The two men who died in San Vicente were never officially identified to the public, except to state that they were one and the same as the robbers of the Aramayo payroll. The testimony of Carlos Pero verified this fact: "Despite having seen no more than the robbers' eyes and the corresponding parts of their faces at the time of the robbery, I recognized both of them, without any sort of doubt, as well as the hats they wore, with the exception of their clothing, which is different from what they wore at Huaca Huanusca." Pero also confirmed that one of the mules was indeed the Aramayo mule that was stolen during the holdup.[14]

An inquest was held in Tupiza, but no record of the proceedings exists. There are documents and reports, dated November 20, 1908, however, that include depositions that verify the murder-suicide—or assisted suicide and suicide—of the two Aramayo mine robbers.

Local magistrate Aristides Daza viewed the bodies before they had been moved, and also assisted with the inventory of personal effects found on the dead men. Butch had in his possession typical items such as a comb, a pocket mirror, cash, and seven business cards inscribed with the name "Enrique B. Hutcheon." Sundance carried an eighteen-carat gold watch, serial number 93220, which was missing a crystal; an English dictionary; a supply of antiseptic drugs, possibly for a sinus condition; and 93.50 in bolivianos.

In the pair's luggage, authorities discovered 14,400 bolivianos, a pair of binoculars, and an arsenal of weapons and ammunition. In addition, Captain Concha found a map of Bolivia with a route drawn on it, indicating that they had intended to go to Santa Catalina from San Vicente and then on to La Quiaca.[15]

On the afternoon of November 7, 1908, the remains of Butch Cassidy and the Sundance Kid were buried in unmarked graves—as *desconocidos*, or unknowns—in the Indian cemetery at San Vicente, Bolivia. Butch was forty-two years old, Sundance forty-one.

Legend has it that their neighbors in the graveyard were a German prospector who had the bright idea that he would thaw out a stick of dynamite on his stove and blew himself to kingdom come, and a Swedish prospector who accidentally fatally shot himself while dismounting from his mule.[16]

The story of the demise of the famous outlaws is based mainly on exhaustive research in San Vicente by author Anne Meadows. It certainly lacks the drama and unbridled firepower of the account popularized in the 1969 motion picture but, alas, is more than likely the true story.

For those who are disappointed by the climax, there is another version—generously embellished to the max but more in line with the celluloid depiction. This story was provided by New York journalist Arthur Chapman using the remembrances of Percy Seibert, who was not an eyewitness, and does not list sources, but is assuredly more dramatic.

In Chapman's account, Butch and Sundance were enjoying their sardines and beer in the room at the Casasola hacienda when a local constable recognized the Aramayo brand on the brown mule tethered outside. The constable dispatched an Indian messenger to inform the captain of a regiment of Bolivian cavalry that was bivouacked outside of town about his discovery. It was noted that the rifles belonging to the two men were stacked outside in the courtyard with their saddles.

Arthur Chapman wrote in part: "On receipt of the message, the Bolivian captain brought up his command and quietly surrounded the station. Then the captain himself walked into the room where Cassidy and Longabaugh were eating and drinking. 'Surrender, señors,' came the demand from the brave captain. The outlaws leaped to their feet. Longabaugh was drunk, but Cassidy, always a canny drinker, was in complete command of his senses.

"The captain had drawn his revolver when he entered the room. Before he could fire, Cassidy had shot from the hip. The captain fell dead and Cassidy and Longabaugh stationed themselves where they could command a view of the patio.

"A sergeant and a picked body of cavalrymen rushed through the gate, calling upon the outlaws to surrender. Revolvers blazed from door and window, and men began to stagger and fall in the courtyard. The first to die was the sergeant who had sought to rescue his captain.

"Cassidy and Longabaugh were firing rapidly, and with deadly effect. Those of the detachment who remained on their feet were firing in return. Bullets sank into the thick adobe walls or whistled through the window and door. Other soldiers began firing from behind the shelter of the courtyard wall. 'Keep me covered, Butch,' called Longabaugh. 'I'll get our rifles.'

"Shooting as he went, Longabaugh lurched into the courtyard. If he could only reach the rifles and ammunition which they had so thoughtlessly laid aside, the fight would be something which the outlaws would welcome.

"Blood was settling in little pools about the courtyard. The sergeant and most of his file of soldiers were stretched out dead. A few wounded were trying to crawl to safety. The mules had broken their halters and galloped out of the yard, among them the animal which had been the indirect cause of the battle.

"Soldiers were firing through the open gate and from all other vantage points outside the wall. Longabaugh got halfway across the courtyard and fell, desperately wounded, but not before he had effectively emptied his six-shooter.

"When Cassidy saw his partner fall, he rushed into the courtyard. Bullets rained about him as he ran to Longabaugh's side. Some of the shots found their mark, but Cassidy, though wounded, managed to pick up Longabaugh and stagger back to the house with his heavy burden.

"Cassidy saw that Longabaugh was mortally wounded. Furthermore, it was going to be impossible to carry on the battle much longer unless the rifles and ammunition could be reached. Cassidy made several attempts to cross the courtyard. At each attempt he was wounded and driven back.

"The battle now settled into a siege. Night came on, and men fired at red flashes from weapons. There were spaces of increasing length between Cassidy's shots. He had only a few cartridges left. Longabaugh's cartridge belt was empty.

"The soldiers, about 9 or 10 o'clock in the evening heard two shots fired in the bullet-ridden station. Then no more shots came. Perhaps it was a ruse to lure them into the patio within range of those deadly revolvers. The soldiers kept firing all through the night and during the next morning.

"At about noon an officer and a detachment of soldiers rushed through the patio and into the station. They found Longabaugh and Cassidy dead. Cassidy had fired a bullet into Longabaugh's head, and had used his last cartridge to kill himself."[17]

Strikingly different particulars yet similar stories—with the same end result. Butch Cassidy and the Sundance Kid had ridden to the end of the outlaw trail high up in the Andes peaks, six thousand miles from home.

End of the story. End of the legend.

Or was it really the end?

Were those actually the bodies of Butch and Sundance that were found by the soldiers inside that hacienda in San Vicente? Could anyone truly identify the remains of these foreigners who were not known in the region?

In fact, no one had been informed until well *after* their deaths that it was the famous Butch Cassidy and the Sundance Kid who had taken refuge in that hacienda. No doubt the two dead men were one and the same as those from the Aramayo payroll ambush, but could they be connected to Robert Leroy Parker and Harry Alonzo Longabaugh?

When word of the demise of Butch and Sundance reached members of the Wild Bunch and relatives back in America, most were skeptical. This was not the first time that rumors of their deaths had reached the States. Butch had admitted in one letter that things were "getting a little hot" in South America, which could hasten his return to the United States or move to another country or continent. Then again, something about these latest reports alarmed several of their friends.

After the shoot-out in San Vicente there was no further correspondence between either Butch or Sundance with their friends or relatives. The entries in Sundance's sister Samanna's business journal ended with her last letter to him, which was dated April 22, 1905. Members of neither family were ever officially notified of their loved one's death.[18]

Matt Warner contended that he, Elzy Lay, and several others, including Hanksville, Utah, shopkeeper Charlie Gibbons, were so concerned that they financed a trip for a man named Walker to South America in order to confirm or dispel this latest rumor. Walker returned to report that Butch and Sundance had indeed died in the shoot-out. He had talked to soldiers involved in the gun battle, and had even stood by the men's graves. No evidence exists to verify this story, and the identity and particulars of this man called Walker have never been revealed. In addition, no corroborating evidence can be found to verify Warner's claim that an expedition to South America was ever undertaken. Although various versions of this story have circulated over the years, Warner could have manufactured the event as a manner in which to communicate his own opinion on the matter.[19]

Matt Warner and Elzy Lay accepted these findings by Walker—if that story was to be believed—and never pursued another venture to confirm the deaths of Butch and Sundance, although rumors would persist for the rest of their lives. Warner wrote a 1937 letter to author Charles Kelly that stated: "[Butch] went to South America and part-nered with Harry Longabaugh. The two of 'em ranched and robbed in Bolivia and Argentina and was finally killed in a fight with soldiers that had been chasing 'em."[20]

Warner also addressed those rumors in his 1939 autobiography, when he wrote that Butch and Sundance had apparently stolen an army mule, and the soldiers "got on their trail and one night found a mule near their hideout in some deserted army barracks. Butch and Harry held the whole company off for hours and killed a lot of 'em. But their ammunition gave out, and they was killed. Some say Longabaugh was killed first and that Butch kept his last shot for himself." Warner did not believe, however, that Butch would shoot himself, but would have instead saved his last bullet for his enemy. His conclusion about whether one or both of them might have escaped and returned to the States: "It's all poppycock."[21]

While on the subject of Matt Warner, it should be noted that his wife passed away while he was serving that five-year sentence for his 1896 conviction of involuntary manslaughter. In 1900, he was released early from prison for good behavior, and settled in Carbon County, Utah, where he remarried and became the father of three children. He ran for public office under his real name, Willard Erastus Christiansen, and lost. Warner then decided to have his name legally changed to

Matt Warner, the name most people knew him by, and subsequently was elected justice of the peace and then served as a deputy sheriff. In later years, he worked as a night guard and detective in Price, Utah—all the while running a bootlegging operation on the side. Matt Warner died peacefully in 1938 at the age of seventy-four.[22]

As for Elzy Lay, he had spent seven years in the New Mexico State Penitentiary on his life sentence, and had become a trustee to the warden. At that time, he was said to have accompanied the warden to Santa Fe, and upon their return found that some inmates had taken the warden's wife and daughter hostage. Elzy took it upon himself to persuade the prisoners to release the two women, and for this act of bravery was given a pardon by Governor Miguel Antonio Otero on January 10, 1906.

Elzy settled in the small ranching town of Baggs, Wyoming, just north of the Colorado border, where he met and married Mary Calverta, a rancher's daughter. The couple, who would have a son and a daughter, soon moved to Southern California, where Elzy became a mining and oil geologist and supervised the building of the Colorado River Aqueduct system in Riverside and Imperial Valley, just north of the Mexican border. Elzy had kept in contact with Matt Warner, and on and off over a twenty-year period the two of them searched together without success for the lost Rhoades mine. Elzy Lay passed away on November 10, 1934, in Los Angeles, and was buried at Forest Lawn Cemetery in Glendale, California.[23]

Matt Warner and Elzy Lay managed to accomplish what Butch and Sundance could not do—stay out of trouble after being released from prison.

Among those contemporaries who believed that Butch and Sundance had perished in that mining town was A. G. Francis, who was the last person who knew them by any name to see them alive. The day after the two outlaws had died, he happened upon an Indian who told him about the white men who had been killed in San Vicente. He recognized their identities immediately after hearing the descriptions of them. Francis, however, knew them under their aliases of Smith and

Lowe, which caused confusion when he wrote about his relationship with them in 1913.[24]

Correspondence written in July and September 1909 that was uncovered by researchers Anne Meadows and Dan Buck revealed that the American consulate in Antofagasta, Chile, was trying to obtain from the American Legation in La Paz, Bolivia, a death certificate for a man named Frank Boyd or H. A. Brown, who had been living in Chile, in order to settle his estate. The man had been killed by "natives and police" along with a man named Maxwell at San Vicente.

The Sundance Kid was known to have used the alias Frank Boyd in Chile, and, according to Percy Seibert, at the Concordia mine Sundance was known as Brown and Butch as Maxwell. This situation would appear to open up another can of worms. Who would want to settle Sundance's estate in Chile? Etta Place? Had she been living in that country or had she journeyed there upon hearing of the death of her "husband"?[25]

Of course, there was also the possibility that Sundance, under one of his aliases, had been arrested in Chile for some crime, and had either skipped out on his bail or a fine, or they simply wanted to clear the books on his offense if he was indeed dead.

The Bolivian authorities responded to this request from Antofagasta, Chile, by submitting death certificates for two people whose identifications were unknown. This inadequate reply was followed up in January 1911 with a letter that stated that the Bolivians were "pleased to enclose herewith a complete record of the case of Maxwell and Brown, drawn up by the authorities of the district where they were killed, and which I hope will be of some use to you."[26]

The criminal exploits of Butch and Sundance did not cease to gain publicity after their alleged deaths. In February 1910, it was reported that the state department in Washington had been notified by authorities in Argentina that Butch and Sundance, and possibly Harvey Logan, had formed a gang that was so feared that the government was obliged to pay them to keep them from terrorizing the country.[27]

That same year, the Pinkertons were informed that a train robber arrested in St. Louis was identified as Jim Lowe, another of Butch's aliases. An agent hurried to the scene, only to find that this Jim Lowe was merely a small-time criminal from Kansas City.[28]

The Pinkerton National Detective Agency, incidentally, did not succumb to the rumors and kept the file of Butch and Sundance open throughout the early 1900s. To this day, the agency, now known as Pinkerton Government Services, has not officially declared Butch or Sundance dead.[29]

In May 1913, another Jim Lowe, a carpenter from Missouri, ran into problems while traveling through South America. Arrested on suspicion of actually being George Parker, who was wanted in North America, Lowe requested assistance from the American Legation in La Paz, which asserted that George Parker had been killed in one of the provinces several years past. Lowe was set free.[30]

The Parker family in Utah eventually learned of Butch's fate. Sister Lula wrote: "Word reached us that Butch Cassidy and the Sundance Kid had been killed in a gun battle in South America. We were shocked and sickened. I am glad mother was not alive to endure the hurt. Townspeople in Circleville were very kind and never mentioned it once to any of us. I never heard of one of our family that was twitted about Butch during all the long, sad years.

"We doubted the stories; yet we feared they might have some foundation, and we were sick that Butch had supposedly added murder to his list of crimes. But what could we do but try to live normally?"[31]

In 1939, Will Simpson, the lawyer who successfully prosecuted Butch and sent him to prison in 1894, was practicing law in Jackson, Wyoming. At that time, he claimed to have received evidence from two men who had traveled to South America to seek the truth that Butch and Sundance had indeed met their end there. This story was told by Simpson to his grandson, Alan Simpson, the Republican senator from Wyoming.[32]

In the early 1990s, Anne Meadows and Dan Buck teamed up with Clyde Snow, the famed forensic anthropologist, who had worked on investigations ranging from the Kennedy assassination and Custer's

Last Stand to the Nazi war criminal Josef Mengele. If anyone could identify the remains of Butch Cassidy and the Sundance Kid, it would be Clyde Snow. The trio and their crew journeyed to San Vicente, Bolivia. After receiving permission from Bolivian officials and soothing opposition to their digging in the graveyard from local townspeople, they began work on graves believed to be those of Butch and Sundance.[33]

Snow soon struck pay dirt when the crew unearthed the entire skeleton of a man who stood between five feet, eight inches to six feet, two inches tall, wearing a pair of decaying boots, size small. It was determined that this man was Caucasian, but it was difficult to check for bullet holes due to decomposition. Although there did not appear to be any distinct bullet holes in the skull, there was one hole in the frontal sinus area of the skull that could have been caused by a bullet. Also, copper stains near an eye socket and near the elbows on the skeleton could indicate metal fragments. There was also a thickening around the left tibia, which could have been the effects of an old bullet wound in the leg—Sundance had told his family about this alleged injury. Furthermore, the size of the boots was indicative of the small feet that Sundance was known to have had. It would seem that they had found the remains of Harry Alonzo Longabaugh, the Sundance Kid.[34]

No other adult bones were located nearby, and the expedition wrapped up with the hope that they had at least found the remains of one of the outlaws. Clyde Snow obtained permission to take some of the bones back to his laboratory at the Oklahoma medical examiner's office for further testing. His X-ray studies confirmed that the skeleton had metal fragments embedded in the skull and also the possibility of a gunshot wound in the lower left leg. Snow was able to use a DNA testing process that permitted a maternal descendant to be matched.[35]

Unfortunately, no match could be found, which excluded the possibility that the skeleton was that of the Sundance Kid. Just in case, the bones were also tested against Butch's descendants with the same results. It was later determined that the grave where they had been digging likely belonged to Gustav Zimmer, the German miner who blew himself up, hence the metal fragments.[36]

Although there has never been a "smoking gun" piece of evidence yet found that could verify or debunk the true identities and provide positive identification of the payroll thieves who were killed in the shoot-out at San Vicente, circumstantial evidence points to Butch and Sundance being the victims who died that day—the physical descriptions that matched Butch and Sundance with known aliases, the methods of their robberies in South America, and the fact that they vanished after leaving A. G. Francis on the trail to San Vicente.

Every indication from a logical perspective points to the violent death and subsequent burial of those two former Wild Bunch leaders in that forlorn cemetery high in the Bolivian Andes, except . . .

It seems that some notable figures in American history have refused to stay dead—and Butch Cassidy and the Sundance Kid can be counted among that number.

CHAPTER FOURTEEN
LIFE AND DEATH MYSTERIES

When I think of the last great roundup,
On the eve of Eternity's dawn;
I think of the past of the cowboys,
Who have been with us here and are gone.

I often look upward and wonder,
If the green fields will seem half so fair;
If any the wrong trail have taken,
And will fail to be in over there.

—"The Great Round Up"

No matter how deeply they may be buried, it seems that certain icons in American history have had a hard time staying dead. Conspiracy theorists usually lead the charge to keep a historical figure among the living, or at least put up enough of an argument to not allow them to rest in peace. Then there are those who just cannot let go of a famous or infamous person, and cling to the hope that the deceased has not died but has simply vanished of his or her own volition and will one day step forward and reveal that the demise was a hoax.

Almost immediately after the death of the two outlaws at San Vicente, people wanted proof of their true identities, which was only circumstantial and less than satisfactory, especially when the information originated in a foreign country. Following that phase of doubt and distrust, sightings of Butch and Sundance became commonplace and widely reported. And then there were the impostors—both Butch Cassidy and the Sundance Kid have had their share of people claiming to be them, or descendants who have tried to cash in by alleging that a relative was one outlaw or the other.

The most widely publicized and enduring of these fakes has been William T. Phillips of Spokane, Washington. Rumors had persisted for years, beginning with author Charles Kelly in 1937, that a man living in Spokane was really Butch Cassidy, who had escaped Bolivia alive. William Phillips had died in 1937, and his widow told Kelly that her late husband was not Cassidy but "knew Cassidy very, very well." Phillips's adopted son, however, believed that his father was actually Butch Cassidy. And so did some historians.

Various authors and researchers, including Jim Dullenty, looked into this possibility over the years. Dullenty wrote a series of articles in the *Spokane Daily Chronicle* in the fall of 1973 that proposed the idea of Phillips and Cassidy being one and the same. The stories jogged the memory of a local woman named Blanche Glasgow, who stated that William T. Phillips had written a story about Butch in 1934 after a trip to Wyoming, and that she had typed the manuscript for him.

This was big news. The manuscript, titled "Bandit Invincible: The Story of Butch Cassidy," was soon located and caused quite a stir when made public. The narrative was written in an amateurish style, and portrayed Butch as a turn-of-the-century Robin Hood, but there it was in black and white—the true story of Butch Cassidy. Or so many people thought.

In the 1970s, author Larry Pointer was greatly intrigued by this ninety-six-page manuscript. He noted that it contained many obscure and unusual details that only Cassidy himself would know. Pointer even believed that when comparing photographs, Phillips in his old age resembled the younger Cassidy. Pointer concluded that the Phillips biography was really an autobiography, and wrote the book *In Search of Butch Cassidy* that outlined his case and presented Phillips's story of Butch.

Pointer apparently was blind to the numerous discrepancies in the Phillips manuscript that have been the reason most historians over the years have dismissed the belief that Phillips was Butch Cassidy. For example, according to the manuscript, Phillips was known to be living in America at the same time that Cassidy was living in Bolivia. Phillips wrote that he escaped from Bolivia, went to Paris for plastic surgery, and got married in Michigan. A check of the official records, however, revealed that his marriage happened in May 1908—the shoot-out at San Vicente was not until November of that year. Additionally, he wrote about holding up trains that had not yet been invented, and even situated Butch's ranch in the wrong part of Patagonia. In spite of these errors, many people remained convinced— or at least entertained the possibility—that the manuscript was the autobiography of Butch Cassidy.[1]

Then, in August 2011, another bombshell was dropped. An Associated Press article trumpeted the fact that author Larry Pointer and Brent Ashworth, a history buff and the owner of B. Ashworth's Rare Books and Collectibles in Provo, Utah, had discovered another manuscript—a longer version of the original—that backed up the claim that William T. Phillips was actually Butch Cassidy. Ashworth supposedly paid $12,000 for the privilege of owning this piece of history.

This story went global faster than a prairie wildfire, and by day's end had burned across more than five hundred online news sites and blogs, followed by practically every other media outlet in the country. Every Wild Bunch buff and historian was assailed by associates to comment on this incredible find that confirmed Butch's identity—again. But before anyone could open their mouths about it, there was another explosion that rocked history.[2]

One day later, an article was published in the *Deseret News* that retracted the original allegation by Pointer and Ashworth. Further research had concluded that Phillips was not Cassidy and that the manuscript was indeed a fake. The real name of William T. Phillips was found to be William T. Wilcox, a man who had been in the Wyoming pen at the same time as Butch Cassidy. Wilcox was Wyoming State Penitentiary inmate number 134 and 324, and upon his release assumed the surname Phillips. His prison mug shot certainly portrays a younger version of Phillips. He had known enough about Cassidy from their prison days together to fake the manuscript.

Pointer and Ashworth had more than a smattering of egg on their faces, but at least they stepped forward to admit their mistake. Perhaps now that the truth has been told, this story will be put out to pasture—at least until the next manuscript is found.[3]

One of the more hilarious impostors to be taken seriously by anyone was Hiram Bebee, a supposed alias of the Sundance Kid. Author Ed Kirby believed that Sundance, using another alias, George Hanlon, had made his way back to the United States, and was arrested in 1919 for grand larceny and spent ten years in San Quentin. Upon his release, he settled in southern Utah, under the name Hiram Bebee. In 1945, Bebee was involved in an altercation with an off-duty town marshal in a saloon in Provo. Bebee pulled out his six-shooter and shot the marshal dead. For this crime he was sentenced to life in prison, where he died in 1955.

Bebee had boasted that he was indeed the Sundance Kid, and had his share of believers. What makes the comparison humorous is that Sundance was a handsome man known to stand anywhere between five feet, nine inches and six feet tall. Hiram Bebee was a gnomish-looking character who stood five-foot-two-and-three-quarters, according to prison records.[+]

A more recent case involved a decades-long debate concerning a man named William Henry Long. Numerous historians and researchers over the years have entertained the possibility that he was the Sundance Kid on the basis of circumstantial evidence. Long, who died in 1936, was a Utah rancher with a questionable reputation and a mysterious past. Family members presumed that he had been an outlaw in his younger days.

Jerry Nickle viewed the possible match of his step-great-grandfather and Sundance as a moneymaking opportunity for the family. In 2008, he established the Sundance Kid Project, and set out to prove that Long was actually Longabaugh. Most research was kept secret, except for occasional teasers, because a television production company was filming the process every step of the way. The shocking results revealing that Sundance had escaped Bolivia and assumed life as rancher William Henry Long would create a bidding war for the documentary and make the family rich—and notable in American history.

Everything appeared to be going along smoothly. A comparison of portraits of Longabaugh and Long by University of Utah anthropologist John McCullough was said to have revealed several identical traits in both men, including a notch in an ear, a broken nose, a cleft chin, and close matches in height, hair color, and eye color. This photo analysis helped secure a court order to exhume Long's remains from the Duchesne, Utah City, cemetery for further study.

William Long's body was exhumed on December 12, 2008, by the Salt Lake City–based Sorenson Forensics. DNA samples were collected and analyzed against those of known family members.

The results were not exactly what had been anticipated by Long's relatives. Modern science shot holes in the plans for a documentary and a place in history. It was leaked in December 2009 that the DNA findings from Long's badly decayed skeleton did not support the premise that William Long and Harry Longabaugh were one and the same person.

Long documentary producer Marilyn Grace began exploring alternative theories to explain the disappointing DNA results, such as the presence of underground water in the cemetery and the resultant disintegration of Long's wooden casket, which may have contaminated his bones. The documentary has been put on hold until Grace can raise the more than one million dollars needed to complete her production.[5]

The only manner available in which to be certain that Butch and Sundance did not escape and were buried in Bolivia in 1908—without matching DNA from their remains—would be to follow trails that were said to have been made by the outlaws themselves and those who knew them or supposedly saw them. Living ghosts generally do not leave fingerprints or other impressions to examine, and the remembrances of older people can be questionable, but there are those who would swear on a stack of Bibles that they were visited by Butch Cassidy long after his alleged demise.

One of the more intriguing—and perplexing—stories of Butch Cassidy's surviving Bolivia and returning to America came from none other than Lula Parker Betenson, Butch's sister. She had been a baby when Butch left home for good, and had never met nor seen her brother—that was, according to her, until 1925. Lula wrote:

"One day in 1925 (I know it was in the fall just before school started) some of my brothers were out on the range with the stock. My brother Mark was fixing the fence at the ranch when a new black Ford drove up—the kind with the old isinglass shades that you snapped on in a rainstorm. Mark looked up and surmised it was a cousin, Fred Levi. The Levi boys were cattle buyers, and Mark supposed he was coming for that purpose. The man walked across the field toward Mark. As he came near, his face broke into a characteristic Parker grin. At first Mark was puzzled. He studied the face and suddenly realized it could be but one person—Bob Parker. After a few moments' visiting, the two climbed into the shiny car and drove to the brick house in town. Bob didn't know the family had moved into town; so naturally he had gone straight to the ranch. That was home to him.

"Dad, eighty-one, was sitting on the step by the kitchen door of the brick house, enjoying the shade and the late afternoon calm. The flashy car drove into the yard, and Mark stepped out. Rather slowly the driver slipped out the left side of the car and straightened up. At first Dad wondered who it was.

"Bob's face for once was solemn; perhaps he wondered how he would be accepted. The screen door to the kitchen was open behind Dad's back. Bob took off his hat and twirled it through the door. It landed squarely on the post of the rocking chair inside. Then he grinned that unmistakable grin. Dad knew him. No one could describe that meeting after all the years of uncertainty and separation—forty-one years. That reunion proved the strength of Dad's heart; he survived it."[6]

Lula was called and asked to leave her family home to prepare supper for a guest at her father's house, which she agreed to do. She arrived, stepped into the room, and came face-to-face with a stranger who looked vaguely familiar. Her father announced with a smile, "Lula, this is Leroy!"[7]

Lula was predictably shocked, and lost any resentment she may have had toward her outlaw brother who had abandoned the family so long ago. The prodigal had returned. The family visited well into the night, with Bob wanting to hear everything they could remember about his late mother, whom he had not seen since that day he rode out in 1884.

Bob remained in the area for about a week, during which he told them about his exploits, about how he had traveled through Europe and had trapped, prospected, and lived with the Eskimos in Alaska for a short time. Bob also swore that Sundance and Etta had survived Bolivia—he had spent time with his two friends in Mexico City, including seeing a bullfight, which did not sit well with him. He admitted that he had never married or had children, and had been living under the name Roberts.

Bob departed Circleville for good, but not before asking the family not to mention that he had been there. For years the secret was kept. After Bob left town, Lula said he would occasionally write to his father, who would destroy the letters to protect Bob. It is not known whether or not she actually saw or read any of these letters.[8]

Lula claimed that Robert Leroy Parker "died in the Northwest in the fall of 1937, a year before Dad died. He was not the man who was known as William Phillips, reported to be Butch Cassidy." She eulogized: "All his life he was chased. Now he has a chance to rest in peace, and that's the way it must be." She never revealed where the alleged Butch had been buried, if indeed she knew the location.

Maximillian Parker, the English boy who had pushed and pulled a handcart across thirteen hundred miles of plains and mountains to settle in Utah, died in 1938 at the age of ninety-four.[9]

In the late 1960s, while the hit movie *Butch Cassidy and the Sundance Kid* was being filmed, Lula Betenson announced that she was writing a book about her famous brother. During this process, she was subjected to a barrage of letters from historians and pseudo-historians, which she politely answered, until, she claimed, they were leaking information misquoting her or inaccurately reporting what she planned to write about. When the book was published in 1975, it sold remarkably well. But some of her stories, especially about Butch's survival and visit, were met with skepticism from historians who had studied and researched the subject and wanted corroborating sources. Those sources were never provided by Lula.

Historian Jim Dullenty decided that the only way to confirm or debunk this impromptu family reunion would be to seek out information from other family members who might have witnessed or heard about the visit. He contacted Max and Ellnor Parker, the son and daughter-in-law of Butch's brother Dan. They confirmed Lula's story, but corrected the date of Butch's return to 1930 rather than 1925. Later, the couple related the same account to author Larry Pointer, adding such details as Butch sitting and rocking their young son, and revealed that Butch was living in Spokane, Washington, under the name William Phillips.

Lula had supposedly warned her kin about telling anyone else about Butch using the alias William Phillips. Was this the reason none of the other Parker siblings, who must have been present during this week-long visit, stepped forward to corroborate Lula's version of the story? Or were they unaware of Butch's presence in Circleville until after the fact? Or were they simply honoring the agreement made between Butch and the family to never reveal his visit?[10]

Lula's grandson, Bill Betenson, was not pleased that historians did not believe some of his grandmother's stories, saying, "Lula did not lie." He also stated that certain members of the family did not want her to write the book, citing the promise they had made to Butch when he visited. Bill Betenson said that Lula's son Mark had confirmed Butch's visit to Circleville in 1925 to him.[11]

This scenario presents a problem for researchers who cannot definitively confirm or debunk Lula's story. Her denials that William T. Phillips was Butch's alias could point to a cover-up on her part. If that was the case, it would open up the possibility that if someone claiming to be Butch actually visited the family, perhaps it was William T. Phillips of Spokane, Washington. If Phillips was contemplating writing a manuscript about Butch Cassidy at some future date, what better way to gain information and inspiration than by visiting the Parker family? After all, they had not laid eyes on Butch for more than forty years, and would not expect him to look the same, especially given the desperate trails he had ridden. According to photographs, Phillips did seem to resemble an older Butch.

If Phillips could pull off his ruse with the Parkers, he could have pulled it off with anyone, anywhere—even with a manuscript. The Parkers could never know whether or not the travels and exploits he related to them were true, and would have accepted them at face value. Phillips likely heard all about Butch's childhood in the Circle Valley from their days together in prison. But if he had made a blunder over something about the Parker family or his childhood, it could be dismissed as merely a faulty memory after all those years. He was able to deceive many historians with his manuscript for decades—perhaps he deceived the Parker family for a week.

One other note about Lula's stated date of Butch's death as 1937. According to researcher Jim Dullenty, Jose Betenson, Lula's husband, filled out a genealogy form from the Mormon Church for deceased members, and had put down 1909 as Butch's date of death, which she believed was the year of the Bolivian shoot-out. Later, sometime after 1950, a new form was submitted that corrected the date to 1937. Was this change made with the release of her book in mind?

The Parkers were not the only ones who claimed to have seen Butch alive and well long after the shoot-out. In the 1950s, Josie Bassett, who had called Butch her "Brown's Park beau," recalled visits with Cassidy in Nevada in 1928 and in Baggs, Wyoming, in 1930. Elzy Lay was said to have accompanied him on the Baggs visit, which could have been geographically possible, since Elzy was visiting his mother's ranch near Baggs around that time. Harv Murdock, Elzy Lay's grandson, reminded Josie that Butch had been killed in South America and could not have possibly been in America in the 1920s or 1930s. Josie Bassett told him: "I know Butch Cassidy a hell of a lot better than I know you. He was here in Baggs in about 1930." Considering the Brown's Park rumors that Butch had known Josie intimately, it would have been difficult for an impostor to trick her in later years.[12]

Josie, the older of the two Bassett girls, was married five times and had numerous lovers, including Butch, Will "News" Carver, and Elzy Lay. It was rumored that she had poisoned to death one of her husbands, but actually she had only bought a cure for alcoholism for him and the concoction proved fatal. She lived most of her life on her father's ranch at Brown's Park, but in 1913 moved to a homestead near Vernal, Utah, where she continued ranching. At the age of sixty-two, she was tried on the charge of cattle rustling, but was acquitted by using the defense that she had been framed by people wanting to steal her ranch. In 1945, she lost most of her land to a real estate scheme, and became known as an eccentric who would corner neighbors and tell them stories about her days with the Wild Bunch. In 1963, she broke her hip when a horse knocked her down, and died a few months later of heart failure at age ninety.[13]

There were a number of others who knew Butch from bygone days, and told of encountering him—John Taylor of Rock Springs, Wyoming, said Butch drove into his shop to have his Model T worked on in 1922; Tom Welch alleged that Butch, driving a Model T, visited him in Green River, Wyoming; Tom Vernon hosted Butch for two days in the 1920s at his home in Baggs; Boyd Charter said that Butch camped on their ranch near Jackson, Wyoming, during the summer of 1925, a fact his father mentioned to Will Simpson; Edith McKnight Jensen, Josie Bassett's daughter-in-law, remembered Butch visiting with her relatives at a cabin in Pahrump Valley, Nevada, in 1928; Mary Agnes Haymes of Silver City, New Mexico, said that when she was a child in 1936 or 1937, Butch came to their home to visit her grandmother; and Matt Warner's daughter, Joyce, believed that a man who visited her in Price, Utah, looking for her father in November 1939—eleven months after Matt's death—was Butch. And when she asked him point-blank whether he was Butch Cassidy, he admitted that they were one and the same and told her stories about the old days.[14]

If Butch had escaped the shoot-out at San Vicente, or had not been involved at all, why would he have waited to return to America until at least the mid-1920s? At that time, it appears that he became quite sociable and unconcerned about losing his freedom; although, curiously, any of those people who saw him could have, but did not, inform the Pinkertons about his presence. Not everyone with whom he came in contact would have been supportive of him or his past deeds. It would stand to reason that there would have been a "dirty little coward" like Bob Ford who would have wanted to make a name for himself by betraying Butch Cassidy. The fact that he seemed to move about freely would mean that if Butch had come home to visit and lived in the area, or even as far away as Washington State, he must have been regarded as untouchable by one and all, which is hardly likely.

According to known documents, neither Butch nor Sundance fathered any children. How then do we explain Sundance Jr.?

In 1970, the year after *Butch Cassidy and the Sundance Kid* was released, a drifter emerged from the shadows of history to proclaim that he was Harry Longabaugh Jr., son of the famous outlaw. Wandering around the West giving lectures and interviews about the Wild Bunch to whoever would listen, he explained that he was the son of Harry Longabaugh and Anna Marie Thayne of Carbon County, Utah—Etta's "half sister." Etta, he said, had been a housewife from Castle Gate, Utah, who abandoned her husband and two children to accompany Sundance to South America, leaving behind an expectant Anna.

Harry Jr., who apparently surfaced in California, where he had been riding the rails in empty boxcars, went by several names— Robert Harvey Longabaugh, Harry Thayne Longabaugh, and Harry Longabaugh II. He claimed he had been born in Cimarron, New Mexico, or Cimarron, Texas, or perhaps Conconully, Washington, on either January 4 or February 2, 1901. He could not produce a birth certificate to make a place or a date official.

But this Sundance Jr. did know his Wild Bunch history. Not only that, he was tall, with features that definitely resembled those of a Longabaugh family member. Various historians attempted to verify his lineage and the stories he told, but obvious fabrications were interwoven with the provocative bits and pieces of information that could be known only to Wild Bunch confidants, making it difficult to accept anything he said as truth.

On December 18, 1982, Sundance Jr. died in Missoula, Montana, while trying to escape a fire at the Priess Hotel. Sundance scholar and in-law Donna Ernst does not believe that this man was truly the son of Sundance, but she does not rule out that he could have been a family member, mainly due to the striking resemblance to a Longabaugh. Why then did he wait until the movie was released to make his presence known? No one will ever know.[15]

The fate of Butch and Sundance in Bolivia may have been subject to speculation and controversy, but the lives and demises of most of the other Wild Bunch members have been well documented.

Ben "Tall Texan" Kilpatrick, one of the Fort Worth Five, was arrested in St. Louis in 1901 for passing money traced back to that Wagner, Montana, train robbery. Convicted and sentenced to fifteen years in prison, Kilpatrick was released in June 1911, and immediately returned to his criminal ways. On March 12, 1912, he and an associate robbed a train in Dryden, Texas, and found only $37 in the safe. Ben began looting the car under the watchful eye of David Trousdale, the express messenger. Trousdale pointed out a package to Kilpatrick that he said held valuables. When Ben stooped down to pick up the package, Trousdale removed an ice mallet from underneath his coat and struck three vicious blows to Kilpatrick's head, breaking his neck, crushing his skull, and splattering his brains onto the express car wall.[16]

William "News" Carver, another of the Fort Worth Five—the one who celebrated his wedding in that town—had participated along with Butch, Sundance, and other members of the Wild Bunch in the robberies of the Tipton train and the Winnemucca bank. He also was part of the gang that held up the Wagner, Montana, train. After that heist, he returned to Texas. On the night of April 2, 1901, Carver found himself in a bakery in Sonora when Sheriff E. S. Briant and his deputies came to arrest him on suspicion of a murder in Concho County. Carver went for his six-shooter, but was shot six times before he could clear leather, and died of his wounds.[17]

In late 1901, Harry Tracy was captured, convicted, and incarcerated at the Oregon State Penitentiary for the killing of peace officer Valentine Hoy. On June 9, 1902, Tracy and another convict escaped, shooting and killing two corrections officers and three civilians in the process. An enormous manhunt ensued, and Tracy evaded capture for a month, mostly taking refuge in the Seattle, Washington, area. On June 28, 1902, he shot and killed his partner Merrill, whom he thought was becoming weak willed. Five days later, he set up an ambush, where he killed a detective and deputy. Tracy fled, and took several hostages at a residence, where he engaged law enforcement officers in another shoot-out. During that firefight, he killed two posse members before escaping. On August 6, 1902, in Creston, Washington, Tracy was cornered and badly wounded by a bullet to the leg during an ambush by a posse from Lincoln County. Harry Tracy crawled into a field to escape, and was soon surrounded. He committed suicide to avoid capture and incarceration. The *Seattle Daily Times* wrote of Tracy: "In all the criminal lore of the country there is no record equal to that of Harry Tracy for cold-blooded nerve, desperation and thirst for crime. Jesse James, compared with Tracy, is a Sunday school teacher."[18]

In June 1897, George "Big Nose" Currie, along with the Sundance Kid, Harvey Logan, and Tom O'Day, held up the bank at Belle Fourche, South Dakota, and then split up. Later, Currie and Logan were holed up in Fergus County, Montana, when a posse caught up with them and brought them back to Deadwood, South Dakota, where they were tossed in jail. In November, the two outlaws overpowered the jailer and escaped. Currie and his fellow gang members resumed their robberies of post offices and trains. On April 17, 1900, the Kid was caught rustling cattle in Moab County, Utah, by lawmen Jesse M. Tyler and Thomas Preece. A shoot-out ensued, and Currie was shot and killed. Harvey Logan was so enraged over the death of his mentor that he traveled to Utah and killed both Tyler and his deputy in a gunfight.[19]

Bob, or Bub, Meeks was involved in the Wild Bunch's 1896 robbery of the Montpelier bank. Arrested in June 1897, less than a year after the robbery, he was tried, convicted, and sentenced to thirty-five years in the Idaho State Penitentiary in Boise. On Christmas Eve, 1901, Bob attempted to escape, and was shot in the leg so seriously that amputation was necessary. Two years later, he scaled the prison wall and dived off after shouting, "Hurrah for hell!" He was not badly injured, but was committed to an insane asylum, where he escaped, but was recaptured. Bob Meeks served out his time and was released in 1912.[20]

Safecracker and poker player Tom "Peep" O'Day had joined Sundance, Harvey Logan, and George Currie to rob the bank in Belle Fourche, South Dakota. His drunken shooting that day and subsequent capture sabotaged a perfectly good holdup. O'Day managed to escape punishment for the crime when charges against him were eventually dropped. On November 23, 1903, however, he again found himself in trouble when he was arrested with a herd of stolen horses near Casper, Wyoming. He was convicted and sent to prison, and was released on June 1, 1908. After his stretch in the pen, O'Day went straight. He settled down, got married, and served as a celebrity greeter at a saloon in Deadwood, South Dakota, until his death in 1930.[21]

Josie Bassett's younger sister, Ann, who was also romantically linked to Butch Cassidy, became known as "Queen of the Rustlers" after taking over her mother's feud against the big ranchers. In 1903, Ann married rancher Henry Bernard, and shortly after the wedding was arrested for cattle rustling. She stood trial, but was acquitted and released. Her marriage to Bernard ended in divorce after six years. By that time, most of the Wild Bunch were either dead or had been captured and put in prison—she never saw Butch Cassidy again after he departed for South America. Outlaws from lesser-known gangs would drift in and out of the Bassett ranch, usually visiting only to obtain supplies or fresh horses, or to rest up for a few days. Ann Bassett remarried in 1928 to Utah cattleman Frank Willis, and they worked a ranch until she died on May 10, 1956, at the age of seventy-eight.[22]

Tom McCarty, Butch's first partner in crime along with Matt Warner, held up a bank in Roslyn, Washington, in 1892 with Matt and his brother Bill McCarty as accomplices. When approached by towns-people, Tom opened fire and wounded two men. The following year, he teamed up with his brother again and a nephew, Fred McCarty, to rob a bank in Delta, Colorado. During the course of the holdup, Tom ruth-lessly killed a cashier. The gunfire attracted nearby citizens, and a shoot-out ensued in which Bill and Fred McCarty were both killed. Tom fled to Montana, where he remarried and worked as a sheepherder. Around 1900, he was shot and killed in a gunfight.[23]

Few outlaws have been more popular over the years with both scholars and the general public than Butch Cassidy and the Sundance Kid, which is why they have been immortalized in books, movies, television shows, songs, and other pop-culture venues.

Butch and Sundance were legendary even while they were alive. In 1903—five years before their presumed deaths—their daring exploits inspired *The Great Train Robbery*, widely considered the first modern film. Almost seventy years later audiences flocked to theaters to see the film *Butch Cassidy and the Sundance Kid* starring Paul Newman and Robert Redford, which was nominated for seven Academy Awards and won four.

In between those movies were several cinematic portrayals, includ-ing the 1951 film *The Texas Rangers*, with Butch being played by John Doucette and Sundance by Ian MacDonald—and the Wild Bunch boasted John Wesley Hardin and Sam Bass. Five years later, *The Three Outlaws* featured Neville Brand as Butch and Alan Hale Jr. as Sundance. Butch also appeared in the popular 1965 comedy-Western film *Cat Ballou*, with Butch, played by Arthur Hunnicutt, as an over-the-hill outlaw tending bar at the Hole in the Wall.

The popular 1969 film inspired a 1970s television series, *Alias Smith and Jones*, about two outlaws trying to earn amnesty. *Butch and Sundance: The Early Days* was a 1979 prequel film that starred Tom Berenger as Butch Cassidy and William Katt as the Sundance Kid. In the 2000 movie *The Way of the Gun*, one character is called "Mr. Parker" and another "Mr. Longabaugh." A 2006 film set in modern times entitled *Outlaw Trail: The Treasure of Butch Cassidy* showed Butch's relatives searching for stolen loot that Butch and Sundance had allegedly stashed around the West. That year also saw the release of a TV movie called *The Legend of Butch & Sundance*, with David Clayton Rogers playing Butch, Ryan Browning as Sundance, and Rachelle Lefevre as Etta Place. *Blackthorn*, a film released in 2011, stars Sam Shepard as Butch, who survived the shoot-out and is living out his years as James Blackthorn.

In addition to motion pictures, recent television documentaries (PBS, History Channel, truTV) have portrayed various aspects of the Butch and Sundance legend—occasionally touching on fact as well as fiction. Even an episode of *The Simpsons* featured the "Hole-in-the-Ground gang," with the Sundance Kid, who, when asked by Comic Book Guy what happened to Butch Cassidy, answered, "We ain't joined at the hip." In the place name category, Sundance Square in downtown Fort Worth, Texas, was named after the Kid. And Swedish rock band Kent released a song titled "Sundance Kid" on their album *Vapen & Ammunition.*

The two-room cabin built in 1883 on Buffalo Creek in Hole in the Wall country has been preserved and moved to Trail Town, a tourist attraction in Cody, Wyoming. Other sites, such as Butch's childhood home in Utah, remain accessible, as do the various famous hideouts located along the outlaw trail. San Vicente, Bolivia, also welcomes tourists, but travelers to that remote, windswept mountain region should exercise caution.

After his success in *Butch Cassidy and the Sundance Kid*, actor-director Robert Redford bought an entire ski area on the east side of Mount Timpanogos northeast of Provo, Utah, which he named Sundance in honor of the character he played. After that, he founded the Sundance Film Festival, Sundance Institute, Sundance Cinemas, Sundance Catalog, and the Sundance cable television channel. Needless to say, he was enamored of the Sundance Kid.

The legend lives on in popular culture for these two men who left a lasting mark on the history of the American West. Some might say that the Old West died when they stepped aboard that ship headed for South America. One thing is certain, however: Butch Cassidy and the Sundance Kid have gained immortality and will always stand as a symbol of the final days of that romantic era as the last outlaws of the American frontier.

BIBLIOGRAPHY

MANUSCRIPTS

Greene, A. F. C. "Butch Cassidy in Fremont County." Unpublished manuscript. MS 1451, 1940. Wyoming State Archives.

Phillips, William T. "The Bandit Invincible." Utah Historical Society.

Wells, Governor Heber M. Correspondence Files, Utah State Archives, Salt Lake City.

COURT RECORDS

Alden, H. A. *Request for Pardon for Harry Longabaugh.* January 22, 1889. Penitentiary Commission, General Correspondence, Wyoming State Archives.

Document No. 124, Volume I, *Record of Pardons of the Secretary of the Territory of Wyoming.* Wyoming State Archives.

Moonlight, Governor Thomas. *Two Letters of Pardon for Harry Longabaugh.* 4 February 1889. Wyoming State Archives.

Records of the U.S. District Court, Wyoming. Case No. 30, *U.S. vs. William Brown and Dan Parker.* Archives Branch, Federal Records Center, Denver, Colorado.

Records of the U.S. District Court, Crook County, Wyoming. Case No. 33, *Territory of Wyoming vs. Harry Longabaugh.* Crook County Courthouse, Sundance, Wyoming.

Records of the U.S. District Court, Fremont County, Wyoming. Case Nos. 144, 166, *State of Wyoming vs. George Cassidy and Albert Hainer.* Fremont County Courthouse, Lander, Wyoming.

United States v. Harry Longabaugh, U.S. District Court for the Territory of Wyoming, Indictments Nos. 33, 34, and 44, Grand Jury of the County of Crook, Territory of Wyoming, August 2, 1887.

RELATED RECORDS

Sheriff's Records. Crook County, Sundance, Wyoming.

Sheriff's Records. Fremont County, Lander, Wyoming.

Sheriff's Records. Johnson County, Buffalo, Wyoming.

Sheriff's Records. Natrona County, Casper, Wyoming.

Sheriff's Records. Sheridan County, Sheridan, Wyoming.

Police Department Records, Sheridan, Wyoming.

Deer Lodge State Prison Records. Montana Historical Society, Helena.

PINKERTON ARCHIVES

PINKERTON DETECTIVE AGENCY ARCHIVES, LIBRARY OF CONGRESS, WASHINGTON, D.C.

Ayres, Charles. Informant report. Dixon, Wyoming, October 1900.

Butch Cassidy File.

Dimaio, Frank P. Memorandum. New York, June 1903.

———. Memorandum. Philadelphia, September 17, 1941.

Informant #85. Report. San Francisco, April 5, 1909.

JTC. Memorandum. Philadelphia, April 3, 1902.

Pinkerton hospital report on Etta Place. May 1902.

Pinkerton Memoranda: February 1910 and November 17, 1921.

Pinkerton, Robert. Memorandum. New York, July 29, 1902.

———. To Dr. Francis J. Beasley, Buenos Aires Chief of Police, July 1, 1903.

———. Confidential Memorandum. New York, January 15, 1907.

Pinkerton, William. To Robert Pinkerton. Chicago, July 9, 1904.

———. "Train Robberies, Train Robbers, and Holdups," speech before the convention of International Association of Chiefs of Police. Jamestown, Virginia, 1907.

———. Interview with Lillie Davis. December 5, 1901.

Roberts, Milton. Informant Report. Chubut, Argentina, January 29, 1910.

Sundance Kid File.

OTHER ARCHIVES

Union Pacific Railroad Archives. Omaha, Nebraska.

German Indentured Servants Records. Pennsylvania Archives, Harrisburg.

GOVERNMENT PUBLICATIONS

1870 and 1889 U.S. Federal Census Records.

NEWSPAPERS

Big Horn (Montana) *Sentinel*

Billings (Montana) *Gazette*

Buenos Aires (Argentina) *Herald*

Buffalo (New York) *Courier Express*

Buffalo (Wyoming) *Bulletin*

Cheyenne (Wyoming) *Leader*

Chinook (Wyoming) *Opinion*

Craig (Colorado) *Courier*

Dallas (Texas) *Morning News*

Delores (Colorado) *Star*

Denver (Colorado) *Evening Post*

Denver (Colorado) *News*

Denver (Colorado) *Republican*

Denver (Colorado) *Times*

Deseret (Utah) *News*

Eastern Utah Advocate (Price, Utah)

Elko (Nevada) *Free Press*

Elko (Nevada) *Weekly Independent*

Fort Worth (Texas) *Press*

Fort Worth (Texas) *Star-Telegram*

Fremont Clipper (Wyoming)

Great Falls (Montana) *Daily Tribune*

Idaho Daily Statesman

Little Rockies Miner (Montana)

Los Angeles (California) *Times*

Miles City (Montana) *Star*

Montana River Press (Malta)

Montpelier (Idaho) *Examiner*

Natrona County (Wyoming) *Tribune*

New York Herald

New York Times

Pioneer Times (South Dakota)

Reno (Nevada) *Gazette*

Rocky Mountain News (Colorado)

St. Louis (Missouri) *Daily Globe Democrat*

Saint Paul (Minnesota) *Pioneer Press*

Salt Lake City (Utah) *Tribune*

Saratoga (Wyoming) *Sun*

The Silver State (Nevada)

Socorro (New Mexico) *Chieftain*

Sundance (Wyoming) *Gazette*

Vernal (Utah) *Express*

Wyoming State Journal

Wyoming State Tribune

Yellowstone (Wyoming) *Daily Journal*

BOOKS AND ARTICLES

Abbot, E. C., and Helena Huntington Smith. *We Pointed Them North: Recollections of a Cowpuncher*. Norman: University of Oklahoma Press, 1955.

Adams, Andy. *The Log of a Cowboy*. Boston: Houghton Mifflin Company, 1903.

Adams, Ramon. *Six-Guns and Saddle Leather, a Bibliography of Books and Pamphlets on Western Outlaws and Gunmen*. Norman: University of Oklahoma Press, 1969.

Allen, James B, and Glen M. Leonard. *The Story of the Latter-Day Saints*. Salt Lake City: Deseret Book Company, 1976.

Allison, Mary, *Dubois Area History*. Dubois, WY: Mary Allison, 1991.

Ambrose, Stephen E. *Nothing Like It in the World: The Men Who Built the Transcontinental Railroad 1863–1869*. New York: Simon & Schuster, 2000.

Athern, Robert G. *Union Pacific Country*. New York: Rand McNally & Company, 1992.

Baars, Donald L. *Canyonlands Country*. Salt Lake City: University of Utah Press, 1993.

Babbel, Frederick W. *On Wings of Faith*. Salt Lake City: Bookcraft, 1972.

Bain, David Haward. *Empire Express: Building the First Transcontinental Railroad*. New York: Viking Penguin, 1999.

Baker, Pearl. *Robbers Roost: Recollections*. Logan, UT: Utah State University Press, 1991.

———. *The Wild Bunch at Robbers Roost*. New York: Abelard-Schuman, 1971.

Basso, Dave. *Ghosts of Humboldt Region*. Sparks, NV: Western Printing & Publishing Company, 1970.

Bell, Mike. "Interview with the Sundance Kid." *The Journal of the Western Outlaw-Lawman History Association* (Summer 1995).

Berk, Lee. "Butch Cassidy Didn't Do It." *Old West* (Fall 1983).

———."Who Robbed the Winnemucca Bank?" *Quarterly of the National Association for Outlaw and Lawman History* (Fall 1983).

Betenson, Lula, and Dora Flack. *Butch Cassidy, My Brother*. Provo: Brigham Young University Press, 1975.

Betenson, William. "Alias 'Tom Ricketts,' The True Story of Butch Cassidy's Brother, Dan Parker." *The Outlaw Trail Journal* (Winter 1996).

———. "Lula Parker Betenson." *The Outlaw Trail Journal* (Winter 1995).

Boardman, Mark. "Butch & Sundance—and Rolla." *True West* (November 8, 2011).

Boren, Kerry Ross. "Grandpa Knew Butch Cassidy." *Frontier Times* (February–March 1966).

Boren, Kerry Ross, and Lisa Lee Boren. "Anna Marie Thayne: Mrs. Sundance." *The Outlaw Trail Journal* (Summer–Fall 1993).

———. "'Tom Vernon: Butch Cassidy Came Back." *The Outlaw Trail Journal* 3 (Summer–Fall 1993).

Brekke, Alan Lee. *Kid Curry: Train Robber*. Havre, MT: Montana, 1989.

Brock, J. Elmer. *Powder River Country*. Cheyenne, WY: Frontier Printing, Inc. 1981.

Brown, Dee. *The American West*. New York: Charles Scribner's Sons, 1994.

———. *Hear That Lonesome Whistle Blow: Railroads in the West*. New York: Holt, Rinehart, and Winston, 1977.

———. *Trail Driving Days*. New York: Bonanza Books, 1952.

Brown, Mark, and W. R. Felton. *Before Barbed Wire*. New York: Bramhall House, 1956.

Buck, Daniel. "New Revelations About Harvey Logan Following the Parachute Train Robbery." *The Journal of the Western Outlaw-Lawman History Association* (Spring 1997).

———. "Surprising Development: The Sundance Kid's Unusual—and Unknown—Life in Canada." *The Journal of the Western Outlaw-Lawman History Association* (Winter 1993).

Buck, Daniel, and Anne Meadows. "Escape from Mercedes: What the Wild Bunch Did in South America." *The Journal of the Western Outlaw-Lawman History Association* (Spring–Summer 1991).

———. "Etta Place: A Most Wanted Woman." *The Journal of the Western Outlaw-Lawman History Association* (Spring–Summer 1993).

———. "Last Days of Butch and Sundance." *Wild West* (February 1997).

———. "Leaving Cholila: Butch and Sundance Documents Surface in Argentina." *True West* (January 1996).

———. "The Many Deaths of Butch Cassidy." *Pacific Northwest* (July 1987).

———. "Outlaw Symposium in Argentina: Butch and Sundance Found Innocent of Holdup." *Newsletter of the Western Outlaw-Lawman History Association* (Spring 1997).

———. "Where Lies Butch Cassidy?" *Old West* (Fall 1991).

———. "Wild Bunch Dream Girl." *True West* (May 2002).

———. "The Wild Bunch in South America: Closing in on the Bank Robbers." *The Journal of the Western Outlaw-Lawman History Association* (Fall–Winter 1991).

———. "The Wild Bunch in South America: A Maze of Entanglements." *The Journal of the Western Outlaw-Lawman History Association* (Fall 1992).

———. "The Wild Bunch in South America: Merry Christmas from the Pinkertons." *The Journal of the Western Outlaw-Lawman History Association* (Spring 1992).

———. "The Wild Bunch in South America: Neighbors on the Hot Seat: Revelations from the Long-Lost Argentine Police File." *The Journal of the Western Outlaw-Lawman History Association* (Summer 1996).

Burns, James W. (Jim Dullenty). "A Secret Hoard in Argentina." *True West* (May 1983).

Burroughs, John Rolfe. *Where the Old West Stayed Young.* New York: William Morrow and Company, 1962.

Burton, Doris Karren. "Crouse's Robbers' Roost." *The Outlaw Trail Journal* (Winter 1993).

———. *History of Uintah County.* Salt Lake City: Utah State Historical Society/Uintah County Commission, 1996.

———. *Queen Ann Bassett Alias Etta Place.* Vernal, UT: Burton Enterprises, 1992.

Burton, I. Victor. "Butch Cassidy Gave Getaway Horse to 10-Year-Old." *Newsletter of the National Association for Outlaw and Lawman History* (Spring 1974).

Burton, Jeff. *Dynamite and Six-Shooter.* Santa Fe, NM: Palomino Press, 1970.

Cairis, Nicholas T. *Era of the Passenger Liner.* London and Boston: Pegasus Books Ltd, 1992.

Callan, Dan. "Butch Cassidy in Southern Nevada." *Newsletter of the Western Outlaw-Lawman History Association* (Summer 1991).

Carlson, Chip. "The Tipton Train Robbery." *The Journal of the Western Outlaw-Lawman History Association* (Summer 1995).

Chapman, Arthur. "Butch Cassidy." *The Elks Magazine* (April 1930).

Chatwin, Bruce. *In Patagonia*. New York: Penguin Books, 1977.

Churchill, E. Richard. *They Rode with Butch Cassidy, The McCartys*. Gunnison, CO: B & B Printers, 1972.

Coleman, Max. "Cassidy in Wyoming." *Frontier Times* (March 1933).

Condit, Thelma Gatchell. "The Hole in the Wall." *Annals of Wyoming* (April 1958 and April 1959).

Conway, William C. "Patagonia: Where Two Worlds Meet." *National Geographic* (March 1976).

Cooper, Bruce C. *Riding the Transcontinental Rails: Overland Travel on the Pacific Railroad 1865–1881*. Philadelphia: Polyglot Press, 2005.

Cooper, Bruce Clement, ed. *The Classic Western American Railroad Routes*. New York: Chartwell Books/Worth Press, 2010.

Cress, Cy. "Match Race That Broke Saguache." *Old West* (Fall 1992).

Crowell, Todd. "Did Cassidy Survive the Last Shoot-out?" *Christian Science Monitor* (June 4, 1978).

Dabney, Wendell P. *Maggie L. Walker and the I. O. of St. Luke: The Woman and Her Work*. Cincinnati, OH: The Dabney Publishing Co., 1927.

Dary, David. *Cowboy Culture: A Saga of Five Centuries*. New York: Alfred A. Knopf, Inc., 1981.

DeArment, Robert K. *George Scarborough: The Life and Death of a Lawman on the Closing Frontier*. Norman: University of Oklahoma Press, 1992.

DeJournette, Dick, and Daun DeJournette. *One Hundred Years of Brown's Park and Diamond Mountain*. Vernal, UT: DeJournette Enterprises, 1996.

Dodge, Grenville. *How We Built the Union Pacific Railway*, Washington, D.C.: U.S. Government Printing Office, 1910.

Doti, Lynn Pierson, and Larry Schweikart. *Banking in the American West from the Gold Rush to Deregulation*. Norman: University of Oklahoma Press, 1991.

Drago, Gail. *Etta Place: Her Life and Times with Butch Cassidy and the Sundance Kid*. Plano, TX: Republic of Texas Press, 1996.

Dullenty, Jim. *The Butch Cassidy Collection*. Hamilton, MT: Rocky Mountain House Press, 1986.

———. "The Farm Boy Who Became a Member of Butch Cassidy's Wild Bunch." *Quarterly of the National Association and Center for Outlaw and Lawman History* (Winter 1986).

———. "George Currie and the Curry Boys." *Quarterly of the National Association and Center for Outlaw and Lawman History* (October 1979).

———. *Harry Tracy, The Last Desperado*. Dubuque, IA: Kendall/Hunt Publishing, 1996.

————. "He Saw 'Kid Curry' Rob Great Northern Train." *Quarterly of the National Association and Center for Outlaw and Lawman History* (Winter 1985).

————. "Houses That Butch Built." *The Journal of the Western Outlaw-Lawman History Association* (Spring–Summer, 1992).

————. "The Strange Case of Sundance Kid Junior." *Newsletter of the National Association for Outlaw and Lawman History* (Winter 1991).

————. "Wagner Train Robbery." *Old West* (Spring 1983).

————. "Was William T. Phillips Really Butch Cassidy?" *The Westerners Brand Book, Chicago Corral* (November–December 1982).

————. "Who Really Was William T. Phillips of Spokane: Outlaw or Imposter?" *The Journal of the Western Outlaw-Lawman History Association* (Fall–Winter 1991).

Edgar, Bob, and Jack Turnell. *Brand of a Legend.* Cody, WY: Stockdale Publishing, 1978.

Emerson, Edwin Jr. *A History of the Nineteenth Century Year by Year: Vol. 3, 1432–1451.* New York: P. F. Collier and Son, 1900.

Encyclopedia of Mormonism, Vol. 1, The Church in Europe. New York: Macmillan Publishing Company, 1992.

Engebretson, Doug. *Empty Saddles, Forgotten Names.* Aberdeen, SD: North Plains Press, 1984.

Ernst, Donna B. "The Butte County Bank Holdup." *Old West* (Fall 1997).

————. "Friends of the Pinkertons." *Quarterly of the National Association and Center for Outlaw and Lawman History* (April–June 1995).

————. *From Cowboy to Outlaw: The True Story of Will Carver.* Sonora, TX: Sutton County Historical Society, 1995.

————. "George S. Nixon." *Newsletter of the Western Outlaw-Lawman History Association* (Summer 2001).

————. *Harvey Logan: Wildest of the Wild Bunch.* Kearney, NE: Wild Bunch Press, 2003.

————. "Identifying Etta Place: Was She Just a Bad Girl from Texas?" *The Journal of the Western Outlaw-Lawman History Association* (Spring–Summer 1993).

————. "The Snake River Valley and the Sundance Kid." *Frontier Magazine* (August 1997).

————. *The Sundance Kid: The Life of Harry Alonzo Longabaugh.* Norman: University of Oklahoma Press, 2009.

————. "The Sundance Kid: My Uncle. Researching the Memories of Snake River Residents." *Frontier Magazine* (August 1997).

————. "The Sundance Kid: Wyoming Cowboy." *The Journal of the Western Outlaw-Lawman History Association* (Spring 1992).

————. "Sundance, the Missing Years." *Old West* (Spring 1994).

————. *Sundance, My Uncle.* College Station, TX: Early West, 1992.

————. "Walt Putney and Tom O'Day." *Wild West* (April 2004).

————. "Wanted: Friends of the Wild Bunch." *True West* (December 1994).

————. "The Wilcox Train Robbery." *Wild West* (June 1999).

————. *Women of the Wild Bunch.* Kearney, NE: Wild Bunch Press, 2004.

Ernst, Paul, and Donna Ernst. "Wild Bunch Shoot-out Sites." *The Journal of the Western Outlaw-Lawman History Association* (Fall 1999).

Ernst, Paul D. "The Winnemucca Bank Holdup." *Wild West* (June 1998).

Firmage, Richard A. *A History of Grand County.* Salt Lake City: Utah State Historical Society/Grand County Commission, 1996.

Flack, Dora. "Butch Cassidy: The Living Dead." *Frontier Times* (January 1981).

Forbis, William H. *The Cowboys.* Alexandria, VA: Time-Life Books, 1973.

Francis, A. G. "The End of an Outlaw." *Wide World* (May 1913).

French, Captain William. *Further Recollections of a Western Ranchman: New Mexico, 1883–1899.* New York: Argosy-Antiquarian Ltd., 1965.

————. *Some Recollections of a Western Ranchman: New Mexico 1883–1899.* New York: Argosy-Antiquarian Ltd., 1965.

Frye, Elnora L. *Atlas of Outlaws at the Territorial Penitentiary.* Laramie, WY: Jelm Mountain Press, 1990.

Garman, Mary. "Harry Longabaugh—The Sundance Kid, The Early Years 1867–1889." *Bits and Pieces,* vol. II, no. 3. Newcastle, WY: 1977.

Gavirati, Marcelo. "Back at the Ranch." *True West* (December 2002).

————. "From the American Far West to the Argentine Far South." *Patagonia: 13,000 Years of History.* Buenos Aires: Museo Lelegue, 2001.

Greene, A. F. C. "'Butch' Cassidy in Fremont County." In *The Butch Cassidy Collection* (Jim Dullenty, ed.). Hamilton, MT: Rocky Mountain House Press, 1986.

Griffith, Elizabeth. "Sundance Kid: The Man in the Attic." *The Journal of the Western Outlaw-Lawman History Association* (Spring–Summer, 1996).

Hafen, LeRoy R., and Ann W Hafen. *Handcarts to Zion.* Glendale, CA: The Arthur Clark Co., 1960.

Harlow, Alvin F. *Old Towpaths: The Story of the American Canal Era.* New York and London: D. Appleton and Company, 1926.

Hatch, Alden. *American Express: A Century of Service.* Garden City, NY: Doubleday, 1950.

Hatch, Thom. *The Blue, the Gray, and the Red: Indian Campaigns of the Civil War.* Mechanicsburg, PA: Stackpole Books, 2003.

Hawthorne, Roger. "Johnson County 'War' Part of Larger Event." *Quarterly of the National Association and Center for Outlaw and Lawman History* (Fall 1987).

Hayden, Willard C. "Butch Cassidy and the Great Montpelier Bank Robbery." *Idaho Yesterdays* 15 (Spring 1971).

Hazlett, James C., et al. *Field Artillery Weapons of the Civil War.* Newark, DE: University of Delaware Press, 1983.

Hoffman, Charles. *The Depression of the Nineties: An Economic History.* Westport, CT: Greenwood Publishing, 1970.

Horan, James D. *The Authentic Wild West: The Gunfighters.* New York: Crown Publishing, 1976.

———. *The Authentic Wild West: The Outlaws.* New York: Crown Publishing, 1977.

———. *Desperate Men.* New York: G. P. Putnam's Sons, 1949.

———. *The Pinkertons: The Detective Dynasty That Made History.* New York: Crown Publishing, 1967.

———. *The Wild Bunch.* New York: Signet, 1958.

Horan, James D., and Paul Sann. *Pictorial History of the Wild West.* New York: Bonanza Books, 1954.

Huett, Will. "Locked Up in Laramie." *True West* (February 1991).

Huidekoper, Wallis. "The Story Behind Charlie Russell's Masterpiece: Waiting for a Chinook." *The Montana Magazine of History,* vol. 4, no. 3 (Summer 1954).

Hunter, Marvin J., ed. *The Trail Drivers of Texas.* New York: Argosy-Antiquarian, Ltd., 1963.

———. "The Wild Bunch of Robbers Roost." *Frontier Times* (September 1929).

Ings, Fred. *Before the Fences.* Calgary, Canada: McAra Printing, Ltd., 1980.

Jarman, Rufus. "The Pinkerton Story." *Saturday Evening Post* (May 15, 22, 29; June 5, 1948).

Jessen, Kenneth. *Colorado Gunsmoke.* Boulder, CO: Pruett Publishing, 1986.

Jones, Daryl. *The Dime Novel Western.* Bowling Green, OH: Popular Press, Bowling Green University, 1978.

Kelly, Charles. *The Outlaw Trail: The Story of Butch Cassidy and the Wild Bunch.* New York: Bonanza Books, 1959.

Kennedy, John. *The History of Steam Navigation.* Liverpool, England: Charles Birchall, Ltd., 1903.

Kildare, Maurice. "Bear River Loot." *Real West* (September 1968).

Kirby, Edward M. "Butch, Sundance, Etta Place Frolicked in 'Fun City.'" *Newsletter of the National Association and Center for Outlaw and Lawman History* (Winter 1975–76).

———. "Did Butch Cassidy Die in Spokane Phillips Photo Fails." *Old West* (Fall 1991).

———. *The Rise & Fall of the Sundance Kid.* Iola, WI: Western Publications, 1983.

———. *The Romantic and Notorious History of Brown's Park.* Basin, WY: Wolverine Gallery, 1988.

———. *The Saga of Butch Cassidy and the Wild Bunch.* Palmer Lake, CO: The Filter Press, 1977.

Kouris, Diana Allen. *The Romantic and Notorious History of Brown's Park.* Greybull, WY: The Wolverine Galley, 1988.

Kytle, Elizabeth. *Life on a Canal Boat.* Santa Ana, CA: Seven Locks Press, 1983.

Lacy, Steve, and Jim Dullenty. "Revealing Letters of Outlaw Butch Cassidy." *Old West* (Winter 1984).

Lamb, Bruce F. *Kid Curry: The Life and Times of Harvey Logan and the Wild Bunch.* Boulder, CO: Johnson Books, 1991.

———. *The Wild Bunch: A Selected Critical Annotated Bibliography of the Literature.* Worland, WY: High Plains Publishing, 1993.

Larson, T. A. *The History of Wyoming.* Lincoln: University of Nebraska Press, 1978.

Lavender, David. *The Telluride Story.* Ridgeway, CO: Wayfinder Press, 1987.

Leflors, Joe. *Wyoming Peace Officer.* Laramie, WY: Powder River Publishers, 1953.

Lesky, John M. *The West That Was: From Texas to Montana.* Lincoln, NE: University of Nebraska Press, 1958.

Long, E. B. *The Saints and the Union: Utah Territory During the Civil War,* 1981.

Longabaugh, William D. "The Sundance Kid: View from the Family." *True West* (July 1984).

Martin, R. I. "A Lively Day in Belle Fourche." *True West* (March–April 1962).

Mathisen, Jean A. "Rocky Mountain Riders: Wyoming's Volunteer Cavalry." *True West* (November 1991).

Maxtone-Graham, John. *The Only Way to Cross.* New York: Barnes & Noble, 1997.

May, Dean L. *Utah: A People's History.* Salt Lake City: Bonneville Books, 1987.

McCarty, Tom. *Tom McCarty's Own Story: Autobiography of an Outlaw.* Hamilton, MT: Rocky Mountain House Press, 1986.

McClure, Grace. *The Bassett Women.* Athens, OH: Swallow Press/Ohio University Press, 1985.

McLoughlin, Denis. *The Wild and Woolly: An Encyclopedia of the Old West.* New York: Doubleday, 1975.

McPherson, Robert S. *A History of San Juan County: In the Palm of Time.* Salt Lake City: Utah State Historical Society/San Juan County Commission, 1995.

Meadows, Anne. *Digging Up Butch and Sundance.* New York: St. Martin's Press, 1994.

Meadows, Anne, and Daniel Buck. "Showdown at San Vicente: The Case That Butch and Sundance Died in Bolivia." *True West* (February 1993).

Mokler, Alfred James. *The History of Natrona County Wyoming, 1888–1922.* Chicago: R. R. Donnelley & Sons Company, 1923.

Morgan, Dale L. *The Humboldt: Highroad of the West.* Humboldt, NV: J. J. Little and Ives Company, 1943.

Morn, Frank. *The Eye That Never Sleeps: A History of the Pinkerton National Detective Agency.* Bloomington: Indiana University Press, 1982.

Moulton, Candy. *Roadside History of Wyoming.* Missoula, MT: Mountain Press Publishing, 1995.

Naisawald, L. Van Loan. *Grape and Canister: The Story of the Field Artillery of the Army of the Potomac.* Washington, D.C.: Zenger Publishing Co., 1960.

Nash, Jay Robert. *Encyclopedia of Western Lawmen and Outlaws.* New York: DaCapo Press, 1994.

Niedringhaus, Lee I. *The N Bar N Ranch: A Cattle Ranching Enterprise, 1885–1899.* Lee Niedringhaus, self-published, 2004.

O'Neal, Bill. *Encyclopedia of Western Gunfighters.* Norman: University of Oklahoma Press, 1979.

Patterson, Richard. *The Birth, Flowering and Decline of a Notorious Western Enterprise.* Boulder, CO: Johnson Books, 1981.

———. *Butch Cassidy, A Biography.* Lincoln: University of Nebraska Press, 1998.

———. "Butch Cassidy's First Bank Robbery." *Old West* (Summer 1995).

———. "Butch Cassidy's 'Peaceful Years'—1889–1894." *True West* (October 1966).

———. "Did the Sundance Kid Take Part in Telluride Robbery?" *The Journal of the Western Outlaw-Lawman History Association* (Summer–Fall 1994).

———. *Historical Atlas of the Outlaw West.* Boulder, CO: Johnson Books, 1985.

———. "How They Railroaded Butch Cassidy into the Wyoming Prison for a $5 Horse." *The Journal of the Western Outlaw-Lawman History Association* (Fall–Winter 1995).

————. "The Pinkertons and Train Robbers." *True West* (August 1992).

————. *The Train Robbery Era: An Encyclopedic History.* Boulder, CO: Pruett Publishing, 1991.

Phillips, William T. *The Bandit Invincible: The Story of the Outlaw Butch Cassidy.* Hamilton, MT: Rocky Mountain House Press, 1986.

Piernes, Justin. "Butch Cassidy en la Patagonia." *Clarin.* Buenos Aires, Argentina, May 2, 3, 4, 1970.

Pinkerton, William A. "Highwaymen of the Railroad." *The North American Review* (November 1893).

————. *Train Robberies, Train Robbers, and the "Holdup" Men.* Chicago: William and Robert A. Pinkerton, 1907. Reprint, New York: Arno Press, 1974.

Pointer, Larry. *In Search of Butch Cassidy.* Norman: University of Oklahoma Press, 1977.

Poll, Richard D., ed. *Utah's History.* Provo, UT: Brigham Young University Press, 1978.

Prichard, H. Hesketh. *Through the Heart of Patagonia.* New York: D. Appleton, 1902.

Records of the Genealogical Society. The Church of Jesus Christ of Latter-day Saints. Salt Lake City, Utah.

Redford, Robert. "Riding the Outlaw Trail." *National Geographic* (November 1976).

Reding, Nick. *The Last Cowboys at the End of the World: The Story of the Gauchos of Patagonia.* New York: Three Rivers Press, 2002.

Reedstrom, E. Lisle. "The Bandit-Hunter Train." *True West* (December 1990).

Reust, Francis William, and Daniel Davidson. "Daniel Sinclair Parker: Little Known Brother of Butch Cassidy and Friend Rob Southern Wyoming State in December of 1889." *The Frontier Magazine* (December 1995–January 1996).

Reynolds, Franklin. "Winnemucca Bank Robbery." *Frontier Times* (July 1978).

Rhodes, Gayle R. "Butch Cassidy Didn't Die in an Ambush in South America." *True West* (January 1974).

Rupp, Israel Daniel. *Thirty Thousand Names of Immigrants in Pennsylvania.* Philadelphia: Leary, Stuart & Company, 1896.

Sandoval, Judith Hancock. *Historic Ranches of Wyoming.* Lincoln: University of Nebraska Press, 1986.

Schindler, Harold. "Butch and Sundance: Where Are They? History Muddles Ending of Tale of Butch Cassidy and the Sundance Kid." *Quarterly of the National Association for Outlaw and Lawman History* (April–June 1995).

Scott, William B. "An American's Views of Patagonia." *Review of Reviews* (June 1903).

Segars, Loretta. *100 Years in Culbertson.* Culbertson, MT: Culbertson Centennial Steering Committee, 1986.

Selcer, Richard F. *Hell's Half Acre: The Life and Legend of a Red-Light District.* Fort Worth, TX: Texas Christian University Press, 1991.

Settle, William A. Jr. *Jesse James Was His Name.* Columbia: University of Missouri Press, 1966.

Shaw, Ronald M. *Canals for a Nation: The Canal Era in the United States.* Lexington: University Press of Kentucky, 1993.

Siringo, Charles A. *A Cowboy Detective: A True Story of Twenty-two Years with a World-Famous Detective Agency.* Lincoln: University of Nebraska Press, 1988.

———. *Riata and Spurs: The Story of a Lifetime Spent in the Saddle as Cowboy and Detective.* Boston: Houghton Mifflin, 1927.

Slatta, Richard W. *Cowboys of the Americas.* New Haven, CT: Yale University Press, 1990.

Smith, Helena Huntington. *War on Powder River.* New York: McGraw-Hill, 1996.

Soule, Arthur. *The Tall Texan—The Story of Ben Kilpatrick.* Deer Lodge, MT: TrailDust Publishing, Inc., 1995.

Spafford, Debbie. "Ann Bassett, Queen of the Cattle Rustlers." *The Outlaw Trail Journal* (Winter–Spring 1992).

Spahr, C. B. "Industrial America: The Ranches of Wyoming." *Outlook* (October 7, 1893).

Stegner, Wallace. *A Gathering of Zion: The Story of the Mormon Trail.* Lincoln: University of Nebraska Press, 1964.

———. *Mormon Country.* New York: Buell, Sloan, Pearce, 1942.

Stewart, Arden. "Dad Nearly Rode with Butch." *The Outlaw Trail Journal* (Summer 1991).

Stewart, John. "Butch and Sundance Revisited." *Quarterly of the National Association and Center for Outlaw and Lawman History* (October–December 1994).

Stoner, Mary E. "My Father Was a Train Robber." *True West* (August 1993).

Sullivan, Mark. *Our Times: The United States 1900–1925.* New York: Charles Scribner's Sons, 1929.

Swallow, Alan, ed. *The Wild Bunch.* Denver: Sage Books, 1966.

Sweet, Richard D. "Gramps, Butch Cassidy, and the Black Cat Café." *Frontier Times* (August–September 1970).

Tanner, Faun McConkie. *The Far Country: A Regional History of Moab and La Sal, Utah,* 2nd ed. Salt Lake City: Olympus Publishing, 1976.

Tanner, Karen Holliday, and John D. Tanner Jr. *Last of the Old-Time Outlaws.* Norman: University of Oklahoma Press, 2002.

Tennent, William L. *John Jarvie of Brown's Park, Utah.* Vernal, UT: Bureau of Land Management, 1982.

Timberlake, Richard H. Jr. "Panic of 1873." In Glasner, David, and Thomas F. Cooley, eds. *Business Cycles and Depressions: An Encyclopedia.* New York: Garland Publishing, 1997.

Toll, David W. "Butch Cassidy & the Great Winnemucca Bank Robbery." *Nevada* (May–June 1983).

Tucker, Spencer. *The Encyclopedia of the Spanish-American and Philippine-American Wars: A Political, Social, and Military History.* Santa Barbara, CA: ABC-CLIO, 2009.

Tyler, Ron. *The Cowboy.* New York: William Morrow and Company, Inc., 1975.

Van Cott, John W. *Utah Place Names: A Comprehensive Guide to the Origins of Geographic Names.* Salt Lake City: University of Utah Press, 1990.

Walker, Don D. "The Carlisles: Cattle Barons of the Upper Basin." *Utah Historical Quarterly* (Summer 1964).

Walker, Tacetta B. *Stories of Early Days in Wyoming: Big Horn Basin.* Casper, WY: Prairie Publishing, 1936.

Waller, Brown. *Last of the Great Western Train Robbers.* South Brunswick, NY: A. S. Barnes, 1968.

Warner, Joyce, and Steve Lacy. "Matt Warner's Daughter Meets Butch Cassidy." *Quarterly of the National Association and Center for Outlaw and Lawman History* (Spring 1982).

Warner, Matt. *The Last of the Bandit Raiders.* New York: Bonanza Books, 1950.

Webb, William E. "Elton A. Cunningham: A Member of the Wild Bunch." *The Outlaw Trail Journal* (Summer 1994).

Williams, John Hoyt. *A Great and Shining Road: The Epic Story of the Transcontinental Railroad.* New York: Times Books, 1988.

Woods, Lawrence M. *British Gentlemen in the Wild West: The Era of the Intensely English Cowboy.* New York: The Free Press, 1989.

Zuberbuhler, Luisa. "Butch's Place at Cholila." *Lugares Magazine,* no. 10, 1992.

NOTES

CHAPTER ONE—THE BOY FROM THE MORMON EMPIRE

1. Edwin Emerson Jr., *A History of the Nineteenth Century Year by Year, Vol. 3, 1432–1451*, New York: P. F. Collier and Son, 1900.

2. Thom Hatch, *The Blue, the Gray, and the Red: Indian Campaigns of the Civil War*, Mechanicsburg, PA: Stackpole Books, 2003, 25–46.

3. Lula Betenson and Dora Flack, *Butch Cassidy, My Brother*, Provo: Brigham Young University Press, 1975, 32.

4. Records of the Church of Jesus Christ of Latter-day Saints, Salt Lake City, Utah.

5. For more on Mormonism, see: Frederick Babbel, *On Wings of Faith*, Salt Lake City: Bookcraft, 1972; *Encyclopedia of Mormonism, Vol. 1, The Church in Europe*, Macmillan Publishing Company, 1992.

6. Babbel, *On Wings of Faith*, 57.

7. Betenson and Flack, *Butch Cassidy*, 9–10.

8. For more about Utah, see: Dean L. May, *Utah: A People's History*, Salt Lake City: Bonneville Books, 1987; Richard D. Poll, ed., *Utah's History*, Provo, UT: Brigham Young Press, 1978.

9. Wallace Stegner, *Mormon Country*, New York: Buell, Sloan, Pearce, 1942, 224.

10. R. Leroy and Ann W. Hafen, *Handcarts to Zion*, Glendale, CA: The Arthur H. Clark Co., 1960, 58; Stegner, *A Gathering of Zion: The Story of the Mormon Trail*, Lincoln: University of Nebraska Press, 1964, 231.

11. Stegner, *Mormon Country*, 231.

12. Hafen, *Handcarts to Zion*, 63–64; Betenson and Flack, *Butch Cassidy*, 15–18.

13. Betenson and Flack, *Butch Cassidy*, 19; Pearl Baker, *Wild Bunch at Robbers Roost*, New York: Abelard-Schuman, 1971, 9–10.

14. Hafen, *Handcarts to Zion*, 193; Betenson and Flack, *Butch Cassidy*, 27.

15. Hafen, *Handcarts to Zion*, 193.

16. Betenson and Flack, *Butch Cassidy*, 19.

17. Betenson and Flack, *Butch Cassidy*, 31.

18. Hatch, *The Blue, the Gray, and the Red*, 27.

19. Betenson and Flack, *Butch Cassidy*, 31–32; William Betenson, "Lula Parker Betenson," *The Outlaw Trail Journal* (Winter 1995), 2.

20. Betenson and Flack, *Butch Cassidy*, 31; Larry Pointer, *In Search of Butch Cassidy*, Norman: University of Oklahoma Press, 1977, 43.

21. Poll, *Utah's History*, 223; Baker, *Wild Bunch at Robbers Roost*, 184.

22. Betenson and Flack, *Butch Cassidy*, 36–37.

23. Ibid, 33–34, 36.

24. Ibid, 37, 38.

25. Ibid, 36.

26. Pointer, *In Search of Butch Cassidy*, 43.

27. *Salt Lake City Tribune, Eastern Utah Advocate*, May 19, 1897.

28. Poll, *Utah's History*, 222; Betenson "Lula Parker Betenson," 4.

29. Betenson and Flack, *Butch Cassidy*, 34.

30. Stegner, *Mormon Country*, 171.

31. Betenson and Flack, *Butch Cassidy*, 34; Stegner, *Mormon Country*, 38.

CHAPTER TWO—TELLURIDE

1. For more about the Transcontinental Railroad and its effect on Utah and the West, the following books are recommended (in

alphabetical order): James B. Allen and Glen M. Leonard, *The Story of the Latter-day Saints*, Salt Lake City, UT: Deseret Book Company, 1976; Stephen E. Ambrose, *Nothing Like It in the World: The Men Who Built the Transcontinental Railroad 1863–1869*, NY: Simon & Schuster, 2000; David Howard Bain, *Empire Express: Building the First Transcontinental Railroad*, New York: Viking Penguin, 1999; Dee Brown, *Hear That Lonesome Whistle Blow: Railroads in the West*, New York: Holt, Rinehart, and Winston, 1977; Grenville Dodge, *How We Built the Union Pacific Railway*, Washington, D.C.: U.S. Government Printing Office, 1910; John Hoyt Williams, *A Great and Shining Road: The Epic Story of the Transcontinental Railroad*, New York: Times Books, 1988.

2. Betenson and Flack, *Butch Cassidy*, 41–42; Pointer, *In Search of Butch Cassidy*, 45; Baker, *Wild Bunch at Robbers Roost*, 184.

3. Betenson and Flack, *Butch Cassidy*, 41–42.

4. Ibid, 42; Baker, *Wild Bunch at Robbers Roost*, 184–85.

5. Betenson and Flack, *Butch Cassidy*, 44, 45.

6. Ibid, 51.

7. Charles Kelly, *The Outlaw Trail: The Story of Butch Cassidy and the Wild Bunch*, New York: Bonanza Books, 1959, 12; Baker, *Wild Bunch at Robbers' Roost*, 19.

8. Betenson and Flack, *Butch Cassidy*, 45.

9. Ibid, 47–48.

10. Ibid, 48–49.

11. Baker, *Wild Bunch at Robbers Roost*, 1, 13.

12. Ibid, 14, 18, 19.

13. Kelly, *Outlaw Trail*, 303.

14. Ibid, 12–13.

15. Betenson and Flack, *Butch Cassidy*, 39, 50.

16. David Lavender, *The Telluride Story*, Ridgeway, CO: Wayfinder Press, 1987, 16, 21, 22.

17. Stegner, *Mormon Country*, 68.

18. Matt Warner, *The Last of the Bandit Raiders*, New York: Bonanza Books, 1950, 106.

19. Betenson and Flack, *Butch Cassidy*, 53–54.

20. Pointer, *In Search of Butch Cassidy*, 48.

21. Betenson and Flack, *Butch Cassidy*, 54.

22. Ibid, 55.

23. Ibid.

24. Dee Brown, *The American West*, New York: Charles Scribner's Sons, 1994, 331, James D. Horan, *Desperate Men*, New York: G. P. Putnam's Sons, 1949, 377.

25. Betenson and Flack, *Butch Cassidy*, 55–56.

26. Lavender, *Telluride Story*, 21.

27. Warner, *Last of the Bandit Raiders*, 27.

28. Cy Cress, "The Match That Broke Saguache," *Old West* (Fall 1992), 62–64.

29. Warner, *Last of the Bandit Raiders*, 122.

30. Ibid., 111–15.

31. Betenson and Flack, *Butch Cassidy*, 60.

32. *Delores Star*, February 11, 1938.

33. Warner, *Last of the Bandit Raiders*, 117; Tom McCarty, *Tom McCarty's Own Story: Autobiography of an Outlaw*, Hamilton, MT: Rocky Mountain House Press, 1986, 28.

34. Kelly, *Outlaw Trail*, 27, 34; John Rolfe Burroughs, *Where the Old West Stayed Young*, New York: William Morrow and Company, 1962, 121; Kenneth Jenson, *Colorado Gunsmoke*, Boulder, CO: Pruett Publishing, 1986, 217–19.

35. *Rocky Mountain News*, June 27, 1889.

36. Baker, *Wild Bunch at Robbers Roost*, 159–60; Warner, *Last of the Bandit Raiders*, 120–23; Kelly, *Outlaw Trail*, 37; McCarty, *McCarty's Own Story*, 28–29.

37. Warner, *Last of the Bandit Raiders*, 123.

CHAPTER THREE—THE BOY FROM PENNSYLVANIA

1. German Indentured Servants Records, Pennsylvania Archives, Harrisburg; Israel Daniel Rupp, *Thirty Thousand Names of Immigrants in Pennsylvania*, Philadelphia: Leary, Stuart & Company, 1896, 404.

2. 1870 and 1889 U.S. Federal Census Records.

3. Donna B. Ernst, *The Sundance Kid: The Life of Harry Alonzo Longabaugh*, Norman: University of Oklahoma Press, 2009, 8.

4. For more about these weapons, see: James C. Hazlett, et al., *Field Artillery Weapons of the Civil War*, Newark, DE: University of Delaware Press, 1983; L. Van Loan Naisawald, *Grape and Canister: The Story of the Field Artillery of the Army of the Potomac*, Washington, D.C.: Zenger Publishing Co., 1960.

5. 1880 U.S. Census Records, Chester County, PA; Edward M. Kirby, *The Rise & Fall of the Sundance Kid*, Iola: WI: Western Publications, 1983, 22.

6. A. G. Francis, "The End of an Outlaw," *Wide World* (May 1913), 36–43.

7. For more, see: Daryl Jones, *The Dime Novel Western*, Bowling Green, OH: Popular Press, Bowling Green State University, 1978.

8. Ernst, *The Sundance Kid*, 9.

9. Pinkerton Report, April 23, 1902.

10. Ernst, *The Sundance Kid*, 14, 15.

11. Ibid, 10–11.

12. Ibid, 15–16.

13. Ibid, 16–17.

14. Several of the better books about cowboys include: Andy Adams, *The Log of a Cowboy*, Boston: Houghton Mifflin Company, 1903; David Dary, *Cowboy Culture: A Saga of Five Centuries*, New York: Alfred A. Knopf, Inc., 1981; William H. Forbis, *The Cowboys*, Alexandria, VA: Time-Life Books, 1973; John M. Lesky, *The West That Was: From Texas to Montana*, Lincoln, NE: University of Nebraska Press, 1958; and Ron Tyler, *The Cowboy*, New York: William Morrow and Company, Inc., 1975.

15. Warner, *Last of the Outlaw Raiders*, 111.

16. Baker, *Wild Bunch at Robbers Roost*, 110–13.

17. Kirby, *Rise & Fall*, 28, 29; Robert S. McPherson, *A History of San Juan County: In the Palm of Time*, Salt Lake City: Utah State Historical Society/San Juan County Commission, 1995, 149, 172, 173; Don D. Walker, "The Carlisles: Cattle Barons of the Upper Basin," *Utah Historical Quarterly* (Summer 1964), 283.

18. For more about trail drives, see: E. C. Abbot and Helena Huntington Smith, *We Pointed Them North: Recollections of a Cowpuncher*, Norman: University of Oklahoma Press, 1955; Dee Brown, *Trail Driving Days*, New York: Bonanza Books, 1952; Marvin J. Hunter, ed., *The Trail Drivers of Texas*, New York: Argosy-Antiquarian, Ltd., 1963.

19. For more about this famous ranch, see the Spur Award–winning book by Lee I. Niedringhaus, *The N Bar N Ranch: A Cattle Ranching Enterprise, 1885–1899,* Lee Niedringhaus, self-published, 2004.

CHAPTER FOUR—SUNDANCE

1. Brown, *American West,* 331; Lawrence M. Woods, *British Gentlemen in the Wild West: The Era of the Intensely English Cowboy,* New York: The Free Press, 1989, 106; Judith Hancock Sandoval, *Historic Ranches of Wyoming,* Lincoln: University of Nebraska Press, 1986, 11.

2. Wallis Huidekoper, "The Story behind Charlie Russell's Masterpiece: Waiting for a Chinook," *The Montana Magazine of History,* vol. 4, no. 3 (Summer 1954), 37–39.

3. *Daily Yellowstone Journal,* June 9, 1887.

4. Kirby, *Rise & Fall,* 23; *Sundance Gazette,* March 18, 1887.

5. *Sundance Gazette,* March 18, 1887; Kirby, *Rise & Fall,* 35.

6. *Sundance Gazette,* April 8, 1887; *Miles City Star,* 43.

7. *Daily Yellowstone Journal,* April 12, 1887.

8. *Sundance Gazette,* April 22, 1887; Kirby, *Rise & Fall,* 30–31.

9. *Big Horn Sentinel,* June 11, 1887.

10. *Daily Yellowstone Journal,* June 7, 1887.

11. Ibid, June 9, 1887.

12. Ibid, June 21, 1887.

13. *Sundance Gazette,* July 22, 1887.

14. *United States v. Harry Longabaugh,* U.S. District Court for the Territory of Wyoming, Indictments Nos. 33, 34, and 44, Grand Jury of the County of Crook, Territory of Wyoming, August 2, 1887; Clerk of the Court Office, Crook County Courthouse, Sundance, Wyoming.

15. Elnora L. Frye, *Atlas of Outlaws at the Territorial Penitentiary,* Laramie, WY: Jelm Mountain Press, 1990, 96.

16. Ibid, 108.

17. Mary Garman, "Harry Longabaugh—The Sundance Kid, The Early Years 1867–1889," *Bits and Pieces,* vol. II, no. 3, Newcastle, WY: 1977, 4–5.

18. *Sundance Gazette,* May 4, 1888.

19. Garman, "Harry Longabaugh", 5.

20. Document No. 124, Volume I, *Record of Pardons of the Secretary of the Territory of Wyoming.*

21. *Sundance Gazette,* February 8, 1889.

22. Kirby, *Rise & Fall,* 37; *Sundance Gazette,* May 17, 1889.

23. Ernst, *The Sundance Kid,* 53, 55; Richard Patterson, "Did the Sundance Kid Take Part in Telluride Robbery?" *The Journal of the Western Outlaw-Lawman History Association* (Summer–Fall 1994), 10–12.

24. Kirby, *Rise & Fall,* 37, 39.

25. Daniel Buck, "Surprising Development: The Sundance Kid's Unusual—and Unknown—Life in Canada," *The Journal of the Western Outlaw-Lawman History Association* (Winter 1993), 34.

26. Ibid, 10.

27. Donna B. Ernst, "Sundance: The Missing Years," *Old West* (Spring 1994), 23.

28. Buck, "Surprising Development," 10.

29. Ernst, "Sundance: The Missing Years," 21.

30. Ibid, 23.

CHAPTER FIVE—RIDING THE OUTLAW TRAIL

1. The best source for banking in the American West is: Lynn Pierson Doti and Larry Schweikart, *Banking in the American West from the Gold Rush to Deregulation,* Norman: University of Oklahoma Press, 1991.

2. *New York Times,* March 19, 2010, December 16, 1863; William A. Settle Jr., *Jesse James Was His Name,* Columbia: University of Missouri Press, 1966.

3. Refer to: Doti and Schweikart, *Banking in the American West.*

4. Refer to: Ibid.

5. The standard biography remains *Maggie L. Walker and the I. O. of St. Luke: The Woman and Her Work,* by her lifelong friend and classmate Wendell P. Dabney, Cincinnati, OH: The Dabney Publishing Co., 1927.

6. Warner, *Last of the Bandit Raiders,* 127–28; McCarty, *McCarty's Own Story,* 28; Kelly, *Outlaw Trail,* 31.

7. Baker, *Wild Bunch at Robbers Roost,* 160–61; McPherson, *San Juan*

Country, 326; Faun McConkie Tanner, *The Far Country: A Regional History of Moab and La Sal, Utah*, 2nd ed., Salt Lake City: Olympus Publishing, 1976, 160, 306.

8. Warner, *Last of the Bandit Raiders*, 131.

9. Ibid, 133–35.

10. Ibid, 131–133; McCarty, *McCarty's Own Story*, 29.

11. Warner, *Last of the Bandit Raiders*, 132.

12. Ibid, 136.

13. Kelly, *Outlaw Trail*, 63–67.

14. Ibid, 66–67.

15. Doris Karen Burton, "Crouse's Robbers' Roost," *The Outlaw Trail Journal* (Winter 1993), 7–9; Warner, *Last of the Bandit Raiders*, 136; Dick and Daun DeJournette, *One Hundred Years of Brown's Park and Diamond Mountain*, Bernal, Utah: DeJournette Enterprises, 1996, 328.

16. Betenson and Flack, *Butch Cassidy*, 64–65, 181.

17. Ibid, 64–65, 70–72.

18. Debbie Spafford, "Ann Bassett: Queen of the Cattle Rustlers," *Outlaw Trail Journal* (Winter–Spring 1992), 24–25.

19. Betenson and Flack, *Butch Cassidy*, 67.

20. Dejournette and DeJournette, *One Hundred Years*, 223.

21. *Deseret News*, July 25, 1970.

22. Ibid.

23. Betenson and Flack, *Butch Cassidy*, 69.

24. Burroughs, *Where the West Stayed Young*, 112.

25. Warner, *Last of the Bandit Raiders*, 110.

26. Kerry Ross Boren, "Grandpa Knew Butch," *Frontier Times* (February–March 1966), 47.

27. Burroughs, *Where the West Stayed Young*, 119.

28. Betenson and Flack, *Butch Cassidy*, 83.

29. *Fremont Clipper*, April 15, 1892; Kelly, *Outlaw Trail*, 53.

30. A. F. C. Greene, "'Butch' Cassidy in Fremont County," in *The Butch Cassidy Collection* (Jim Dullenty, ed.), Hamilton, MT: Rocky Mountain House Press, 1986, 1.

31.   Ibid, 2.

32.   Ibid, 1–2.

33.   Betenson and Flack, *Butch Cassidy*, 87.

34.   Greene, "Cassidy in Fremont," 2.

35.   Pointer, *In Search of Cassidy*, 60–62.

36.   T. A. Larson, *History of Wyoming*, Lincoln: University of Nebraska Press, 1978, 271.

37.   Roger Hawthorne, "Johnson County 'War' Part of Larger Event," *Quarterly of the National Association and Center for Outlaw and Lawman History* (Fall 1987), 4.

38.   Jim Dullenty, "Houses Butch Built," *The Journal of the Western Outlaw-Lawman History Association* (Spring–Summer 1992), 9.

39.   Dullenty, *The Butch Cassidy Collection*, Hamilton, MT: Rocky Mountain House Press, 1986, 30.

40.   C. B. Spahr, "Industrial America: The Ranches of Wyoming," *Outlook* (October 7, 1893), 628.

41.   Helena Huntington Smith, *War on Powder River*, New York: McGraw-Hill, 1996, 156.

42.   Warner, *Last of the Bandit Raiders*, 215.

43.   Ibid, 216–18.

CHAPTER SIX—CRIME AND PUNISHMENT

1.   Richard Patterson, *The Train Robbery Era: An Encyclopedic History*, Boulder, CO: Pruett Publishing, 1991, 113–16.

2.   Ibid, 245–48.

3.   James D. Horan, *The Authentic Wild West: The Outlaws*, New York: Crown Publishing, 1976, 44.

4.   Patterson, *Train Robbery Era*, 113–16.

5.   Maurice Kildare, "Bear River Loot," *Real West* (September 1968), 22.

6.   Alden Hatch, *American Express: A Century of Service*, Garden City, NY: Doubleday, 1950, 84–85.

7.   Patterson, *Train Robbery Era*, 48–49.

8.   Kirby, *Rise & Fall*, 46–47.

9. Richard Patterson, *The Birth, Flowering and Decline of a Notorious Western Enterprise*, Boulder, CO: Johnson Books, 1981, 120.

10. Ernst, *The Sundance Kid*, 55.

11. *Great Falls Daily Tribune* (Montana), November 30, 1892.

12. Malta, *Montana River Press*, November 30 and December 7, 1892; *Chinook Opinion* (Montana), December 1 and 8, 1892; *Great Falls Daily Tribune* (Montana), November 30, 1892.

13. *Great Falls Tribune*, December 8, 1892.

14. Kirby, *Rise & Fall*, 48.

15. Ernst, *The Sundance Kid*, 59.

16. Kelly, *Outlaw Trail*, 56–57.

17. Ibid, 57.

18. *State v. George Cassidy & Albert Hainer*, Case No. 144 and Case No. 166, District Court, Fremont County, Wyoming.

19. Kelly, Outlaw Trail, 54–55; Edward M. Kirby, *The Saga of Butch Cassidy and the Wild Bunch*, Palmer Lake, CO: The Filter Press, 1977, 7–8.

20. Tacetta B. Walker, *Stories of Early Days in Wyoming: Big Horn Basin*, Casper, WY: Prairie Publishing, 1936, 86.

21. Kerry Ross Boren and Lisa Lee Boren, "Anna Marie Thayne: Mrs. Sundance," *The Outlaw Trail Journal* (Summer–Fall 1993), 24.

22. Kelly, *Outlaw Trail*, 237.

23. *Fremont Clipper*, June 23, 1893.

24. *State v. George Cassidy and Al Hainer*, Case No. 166, District Court, Fremont County, Wyoming.

25. Frye, *Atlas of Outlaws*, 145.

26. Greene, "Cassidy in Fremont," 3.

27. Pointer, *In Search of Cassidy*, 77.

28. Ibid., 78.

29. Fremont County Court records, *State v. Cassidy and Hainer.*

30. Mary Allison, *Dubois Area History*, Dubois, WY: Mary Allison, 1991, 7, 53.

31. Greene, "Cassidy in Fremont," 3.

32. Betenson and Flack, *Butch Cassidy*, 93, 95.

33. Frye, *Atlas of Outlaws*, 153–56; Wil Huett, "Locked Up in Laramie," *True West* (February 1991), 22; Candy Moulton, *Roadside History of Wyoming*, Missoula, MT: Mountain Press Publishing, 1995, 229.

34. Huett, "Locked Up," 22.

CHAPTER SEVEN—DAY OF THE OUTLAW•OP8.105

1. Brown, *American West*, 331; Woods, *British Gentlemen*, 106; Sandoval, *Historic Ranches*, 11.

2. For more, see: Lesky, *The West That Was: From Texas to Montana*.

3. Ernst, *The Sundance Kid*, 60.

4. Donna B. Ernst, "The Snake River Valley and the Sundance Kid," *Frontier Magazine* (August 1997), 6–8; Ernst, *The Sundance Kid*, 61.

5. Ernst, *The Sundance Kid*, 61–62.

6. For more about the Pinkerton Detective Agency, see: James D. Horan, *The Pinkertons: The Detective Dynasty That Made History*, New York: Crown Publishing, 1967; Frank Morn, *The Eye That Never Sleeps: A History of the Pinkerton National Detective Agency*, Bloomington: Indiana University Press, 1982.

7. Ernst, *The Sundance Kid*, 63.

8. Frye, *Atlas of Outlaws*, 46, 152–56; Mary E. Stoner, "My Father Was a Train Robber," *True West* (August 1993), 20–21.

9. Frye, *Atlas of Outlaws*, 140, 159.

10. Ibid, 142, 143, 149, 155–56, 159.

11. Richard H. Timberlake Jr., "Panic of 1873," in David Glasner and Thomas F. Cooley, eds., *Business Cycles and Depressions: An Encyclopedia*, New York: Garland Publishing, 1997, 516–18; Charles Hoffmann, *The Depression of the Nineties: An Economic History*, Westport, CT: Greenwood Publishing, 1970, 109.

12. Larson, *History of Wyoming*, 295–96; McPherson, *San Juan County*, 173–74; Poll, *Utah's History*, 237.

13. Bob Edgar and Jack Turnell, *Brand of a Legend*, Cody, WY: Stockdale Publishing, 1978, 81.

14. Kelly, *The Outlaw Trail*, 60.

15. Betenson and Flack, *Butch Cassidy*, 96; Frye, *Atlas of Outlaws*, 153.

16. Warner, *Last of the Bandit Raiders*, 155–60, 258–69, 283–95.

17. Doris K. Burton, *History of Uintah County*, Salt Lake City: Utah State Historical Society/Unitah County Commission, 1996, 374, 390.

18. Betenson and Flack, *Butch Cassidy*, 51, 79, 251; Kelly, *Outlaw Trail*, 21, 85; Grace McClure, *The Bassett Women*, Athens, OH: Swallow Press/Ohio University Press, 1985, 52, 249–57.

19. Diane Allen Kouris, *The Romantic and Notorious History of Brown's Park*, Greybull, WY: The Wolverine Gallery, 1988, 79; *Vernal Express*, May 14 and May 28, 1896.

20. Betenson and Flack, *Butch Cassidy*, 111.

21. Pointer, *In Search of Cassidy*, 100.

22. Richard D. Sweet, "Gramps, Butch Cassidy, and the Black Cat Café," *Frontier Times* (August–September 1970), 38.

23. *Idaho Daily Statesman*, August 14, 1896; Willard C. Hayden, "Butch Cassidy and the Great Montpelier Bank Robbery," *Idaho Yesterdays* 15 (Spring 1971), 3–4.

24. *Montpelier Examiner*, August 15, 1896.

25. *Salt Lake City Herald*, September 8, 1896.

26. *Vernal Express*, September 24, 1896; Kelly, *Outlaw Trail*, 98.

27. Burton, *Queen Ann Bassett*, 14–15.

28. Kerry Ross Boren and Lisa Lee Boren, "Tom Vernon: Butch Cassidy Came Back," *The Outlaw Trail Journal* 3 (Summer–Fall 1993), 55; Burton, *Uintah County*, 375.

29. McClure, *Bassett Women*, 59–60, 224.

30. Baker, *Wild Bunch at Robbers Roost*, 173; Jay Robert Nash, *Encyclopedia of Western Lawmen and Outlaws*, New York: DeCapo Press, 1994, 310.

31. Kelly, *The Outlaw Trail*, 133–40; Baker, *Wild Bunch at Robbers Roost*, 201–11; *Eastern Utah Advocate* (Price, Utah), April 22, 1897.

32. *Craig* (Colorado) *Courier*, January 9 and January 16, 1897.

33. Kirby, *Rise & Fall*, 55–57.

34. Martin, "A Lively Day in Belle Fourche," *True West* (March–April 1962), 47.

35. Ibid, 47; Kirby, *Rise & Fall*, 58–59.

36. Kirby, *Rise & Fall*, 60.

37. Elizabeth Griffith, "Sundance Kid: The Man in the Attic," *The Journal*

of the Western Outlaw-Lawman History Association (Spring–Summer 1996), 30–31.

38. Donna B. Ernst, "The Sundance Kid: My Uncle. Researching the Memories of Snake River Residents," *Frontier Magazine* (August 1997), 6.

CHAPTER EIGHT—THE WILD BUNCH

1. Kelly, *Outlaw Trail*, 162; Baker, *Wild Bunch at Robbers Roost*, 188.

2. Kelly, *Outlaw Trail*, 117–18; Donna B. Ernst, *Harvey Logan: Wildest of the Wild Bunch*, Kearney, NE: Wild Bunch Press, 2003; Bruce Lamb, *Kid Curry: The Life and Times of Harvey Logan and the Wild Bunch*, Boulder, CO: Johnson Books, 1991; an eyewitness account of the fight is in *Great Falls Tribune*, January 20, 1935; Nash, *Encyclopedia of Western Lawmen and Outlaws*, 66–69; James D. Horan, *The Authentic Wild West: The Gunfighters*, New York: Crown Publishing, 1976, 187–220.

3. Thelma Gatchell Condit, "The Hole in the Wall," *Annals of Wyoming* (April 1958), 22; Nash, *Encyclopedia of Western Lawmen and Outlaws*, 90; Horan, *The Gunfighters*, 197–99.

4. Donna B. Ernst, *From Cowboy to Outlaw: The True Story of Will Carver*, Sonora, TX: Sutton County Historical Society, 1995; Nash, *Encyclopedia of Western Lawmen and Outlaws*, 66; Horan, *The Gunfighters*, 244; *The Three Outlaws*, starring Neville Brand as Butch Cassidy and Alan Hale Jr. as the Sundance Kid, a 1956 film, included William "News" Carver, played by Robert Christopher, as the third outlaw.

5. Nash, *Encyclopedia of Western Lawmen and Outlaws*, 200–1; Horan, *The Gunfighters*, 240; Arthur Soule, *The Tall Texan: The Story of Ben Kilpatrick*, Deer Lodge, Montana: TrailDust Publishing Inc., 1995.

6. Dullenty, *Harry Tracy, The Last Desperado*, Dubuque, IA: Kendall/Hunt Publishing, 1996; Boren, "Grandpa Knew Butch," 46; Horan, *The Gunfighters*, 255–86; a motion picture, *Harry Tracy*, starring Bruce Dern, made in 1982, chronicled this outlaw's exaggerated fictionalized exploits.

7. Dullenty, *Harry Tracy*, 29–30, 33–37; Nash, *Encylopedia of Western Lawmen and Outlaws*, 317; Horan, *The Gunfighters*, 257.

8. Horan, *The Gunfighters*, 244.

9. Nash, *Encyclopedia of Western Lawmen and Outlaws*, 315; Horan, *The Gunfighters*, 246.

10. Horan, *The Gunfighters*, 244, 246.

11. Ibid, 244; Nash, *Encyclopedia of Western Lawmen and Outlaws*, 317.

12. Horan, *The Gunfighters*, 246.

13. Nash, *Encyclopedia of Western Lawmen and Outlaws*, 317.

14. Ibid, 309–10.

15. The best biography of Butch—other than the volume you have in your hands—is Richard Patterson, *Butch Cassidy: A Biography*, Lincoln and London: University of Nebraska Press, 1998.

16. Betenson and Flack, *Butch Cassidy*, 239–45; McClure, *The Bassett Women.*

17. The best biography of Sundance—other than the volume you have in your hands—is Donna B. Ernst, *The Sundance Kid: The Life of Harry Alonzo Longabaugh*, Norman: University of Oklahoma Press, 2009.

18. Dan Buck and Anne Meadows, "Etta Place: A Most Wanted Woman," *The Journal of the Western Outlaw-Lawman History Association* (Spring–Summer 1993), 13; Boren and Boren, "Anna Marie Thayne," 24; Gail Drago, *Etta Place: Her Life and Times with Butch Cassidy and the Sundance Kid*, Plano, TX: Republic of Texas Press, 1996; Donna B. Ernst, "Identifying Etta Place: Was She Just a Bad Girl from Texas?" *The Journal of the Western Outlaw-Lawman History Association* (Spring–Summer 1993).

19. Donna B. Ernst, *Women of the Wild Bunch*, Kearney, NE: Wild Bunch Press, 2004.

20. *Fremont Clipper*, March 25, 1898.

21. For more, see: Spencer Tucker, *The Encyclopedia of the Spanish-American and Philippine-American Wars: A Political, Social, and Military History*, Santa Barbara, CA: ABC-CLIO, 2009.

22. Article with no date from the *Cheyenne Sun Leader* cited in Jean A. Mathisen, "Rocky Mountain Riders: Wyoming's Volunteer Cavalry," *True West* (November 1991), 30.

23. Greene, "Cassidy in Fremont," 8.

24. Dullenty, *Tracy*, 37; Horan, *The Gunfighters*, 257–58.

25. Kelly, *Outlaw Trail*, 213–15, interviews with General J. P. O'Neill and Major Frederick H. Sparrenberger, United States Army (Retired).

26. Greene, "Cassidy in Fremont," 7.

27. For more, see: Tucker. *The Encyclopedia of the Spanish-American and Philippine-American Wars.*

CHAPTER NINE—PINKERTONS ON THE TRAIL

1. Baker, *Wild Bunch at Robbers Roost*, 100–1; Kirby, *Rise & Fall*, 65–66; Charles A. Siringo, *Riata and Spurs: The Story of a Lifetime Spent in the Saddle as Cowboy and Detective*, Boston: Houghton Mifflin, 1927, 240.

2. Captain William French, *Further Recollections of a Western Ranchman, New Mexico, 1883–1899*, New York: Argosy-Antiquarian Ltd., 1965, ix–xii, xiv.

3. *Elko Weekly Independent*, July 15 and July 22, 1898.

4. *Elko Free Press*, April 8, 1899.

5. French, *Some Recollections of a Western Ranchman*, 258–60.

6. William E. Webb, "Elton A. Cunningham: A Member of the Wild Bunch," *The Outlaw Trail Journal* (Summer 1994), 16.

7. *Saratoga* (Wyoming) *Sun*, June 8, 1899; *Buffalo Bulletin*, June 8, 1899; *New York Herald*, June 25, 1899.

8. Letter from William Simpson to Charles Kelly, May 5, 1939, reprinted in Dullenty, *Cassidy Collection*, 31.

9. Paul and Donna Ernst, "Wild Bunch Shoot-out Sites," *Western Outlaw-Lawman Journal* (Fall 1999), 50–55.

10. DeJournette and DeJournette, *One Hundred Years*, 335.

11. *New York Herald*, June 25, 1899.

12. Siringo, *Cowboy Detective*, 306; Morn, *Eye That Never Sleeps*, 159–61.

13. Mike Bell, "The Killing of Lonny Logan," *The English Westerners' Tally Sheet* (Spring 1990), 27–28.

14. Kelly, *Outlaw Trail*, 252.

15. Horan, *The Outlaws*, 292.

16. Jeff Burton, *Dynamite and Six-Shooter*, Santa Fe, NM: Palomino Press, 1970, 111–21.

17. French, *Some Recollections*, 273–74.

18. Siringo, *Riata and Spurs*, 240–41.

19. French, *Some Recollections*, 276–77; *Socorro Chieftain*, April 28 and May 12, 1900.

20. Greene, "Cassidy in Fremont," 8–9; Kelly, *Outlaw Trail*, 267–69.

21. Kelly, *Outlaw Trail*, 269.

22. Ibid, 269–70.

23. Ibid, 271.

24. Chip Carlson, "The Tipton Train Robbery," *The Journal of the Western Outlaw-Lawman History Association* (Summer 1995), 16; *New York Herald*, September 1, 1900; *Denver Republican*, September 2, 1900; Baker, *The Wild Bunch at Robbers Roost*, 191.

25. Kelly, *Outlaw Trail*, 271–72.

26. Carlson, "Tipton Robbery," 14.

27. Ibid, 14–15.

28. DeJournette and DeJournette, *One Hundred Years*, 353.

29. Kelly, *Outlaw Trail*, 277; *Silver State*, September 19, 1900; *Denver Republican*, September 20, 1900; Franklin Reynolds, "Winnemucca Bank Robbery," *Frontier Times* (July 1978), 26.

30. Bell, "Interview with the Sundance Kid," *The Journal of the Western Outlaw-Lawmen History Association* (Summer 1995), 13–16.

31. Baker, *Wild Bunch at Robbers Roost*, 192.

CHAPTER TEN—END OF THE AMERICAN TRAIL

1. Siringo, *Riata and Spurs*, 229.

2. Ibid, 235.

3. Ibid, 238.

4. Betenson and Flack, *Butch Cassidy*, 157.

5. Siringo, *Riata and Spurs*, 240–41.

6. Ibid, 241.

7. Kelly, *Outlaw Trail*, 281.

8. The best volume for the history of this district is Richard F. Selcer, *Hell's Half Acre: The Life and Legend of a Red-Light District*, Fort Worth, TX: Texas Christian University Press, 1991.

9. Ernst, *The Sundance Kid*, 125.

10. Boren and Boren, "Anna Marie Thayne," 27.

11. Ernst, *From Cowboy to Outlaw*, 11; Selcer, *Hell's Half Acre*, 249.

12. Selcer, *Hell's Half Acre*, 257.

13. Ernst, *The Sundance Kid*, 126.

14. Selcer, *Hell's Half Acre*, 257–58; Kelly, *Outlaw Trail*, 281.

15. Lee Berk, "Butch Cassidy Didn't Do It," *Old West* (Fall 1983), 27; Selcer, *Hell's Half Acre*, 261–62.

16. Selcer, *Hell's Half Acre*, 262.

17. Dullenty, *The Cassidy Collection*, 39; Richard A. Firmage, *A History of Grand County*, Salt Lake City: Utah State Historical Society/Grand County Commission, 1996, 166; Arthur Chapman, "'Butch' Cassidy," *The Elks Magazine* (April 1930), 61.

18. For more about train security, see: William A. Pinkerton, *Train Robberies, Train Robbers, and the "Holdup" Men*, Chicago: William and Robert A. Pinkerton, 1907, reprint, New York: Arno Press, 1974; Lisle E. Reedstrom, "The Bandit-Hunter Train," *True West* (December 1990).

19. Anne Meadows. *Digging Up Butch and Sundance*, New York: St. Martin's Press, 1994, 52; G. Shaw-Lefevre, "A Visit to the Argentine Republic," *Nineteenth Century and After* (November 1901), 835.

20. Betenson and Flack, *Butch Cassidy*, 161.

21. Kirby, *Rise & Fall*, 88; Ernst, *The Sundance Kid*, 128.

22. Ernst, *The Sundance Kid*, 128–29.

23. Drago, *Etta Place*, 156–57.

24. Ernst, *The Sundance Kid*, 130.

25. Kirby, *Rise & Fall*, 88; Ernst, *The Sundance Kid*, 131–32.

26. *New York Times*, February 1, 1900; Patterson, *Butch Cassidy*, 185.

27. Ernst, *The Sundance Kid*, 132; Pinkertons, Criminal History #7111.

28. Kelly, *Outlaw Trail*, 288; Kirby, *Saga of Butch*, 49; Ernst, *The Sundance Kid*, 132, 134.

29. Kirby, *Saga of Butch*, 54; Ernst, *The Sundance Kid*, 134.

30. *New York Times*, February 14, 1901.

31. Kirby, *Saga of Butch*, 64; Meadows, *Digging Up Butch and Sundance*, 45.

CHAPTER ELEVEN—PATAGONIA

1. For more about passenger steamships of this era, see: Nicholas T. Cairis, *Era of the Passenger Liner*, London and Boston: Pegasus Books Ltd, 1992; John Maxtone-Graham, *The Only Way to Cross*, New York:

Barnes & Noble; 1997; John Kennedy, *The History of Steam Navigation*, Liverpool: Charles Birchall, Ltd., 1903.

2. Kirby, *Rise & Fall*, 94.

3. Meadows, *Digging Up Butch and Sundance*, 37; Bruce Chatwin, *In Patagonia*, New York: Penguin Books, 1977; Nick Reding, *The Last Cowboys at the End of the World: The Story of the Gauchos of Patagonia*, New York: Three Rivers Press, 2002.

4. Ernst, *The Sundance Kid*, 137.

5. *Denver Republican*, July 4, 1901.

6. Ibid; Jim Dullenty, "Wagner Train Robbery," *Old West* (Spring 1983), 40–42; Jim Dullenty, "He Saw 'Kid Curry' Rob Great Northern Train," *Quarterly of the National Association and Center for Outlaw and Lawman History* (Winter 1985), 8–10.

7. Kirby, *Saga of Butch*, 62; Ernst, *The Sundance Kid*, 141–42; *St. Louis Daily Globe Democrat*, November 6, 1901.

8. James D. Horan, *Desperate Men*, 243–44.

9. Pinkertons, Sundance Kid File Pinkerton Detective Agency Archives, Library of Congress, Washington, D.C.; Kirby, *Saga of Butch*, 67, 69; Kirby, *Rise & Fall*, 97.

10. Pinkertons, Butch Cassidy File, Pinkerton Detective Agency Archives, Library of Congress, Washington, D.C.

11. Meadows, *Digging Up Butch and Sundance*, 6.

12. Reprinted in Dullenty, *The Cassidy Collection*, 39; original is on file at the Utah Historical Society, Salt Lake City.

13. Drago, *Etta Place*, 184, 186.

14. Ibid, 184–85.

15. A. G. Francis, "End of an Outlaw," *Wide World* (May 1913), 36–43.

16. Meadows, *Digging Up Butch and Sundance*, 40.

17. Ibid, 42–43; William A. Pinkerton, *Train Robberies, Train Robbers, and the "Holdup,"* Chicago: William and Robert A. Pinkerton, 1907, reprint, New York: Arno Press, 1974, 79.

18. Brown, *American West*, 344–45; *Denver Times*, November 20, 1903.

19. Meadows, *Digging Up Butch and Sundance*, 2, 3.

20. Ibid, 5.

21. Daniel Buck and Anne Meadows, "Leaving Cholila: Butch and

Sundance Documents Surface in Argentina," *True West* (January 1996); James W. Burns (Jim Dullenty), "A Secret Hoard in Argentina," *True West* (May 1983), 29.

22. Meadows, *Digging Up Butch and Sundance*, 7.

23. Ibid, 51–57.

24. Richard W. Slatta, *Cowboys of the Americas*, New Haven, CT: Yale University Press, 1990, 134–35.

25. Slatta, *Cowboys of the Americas*, 156.

26. Ernst, *The Sundance Kid*, 148.

CHAPTER TWELVE—THE *BANDITOS AMERICANOS*

1. Pointer, *In Search of Butch*, 200; Burns, "A Secret Hoard," 29.

2. Meadows, *Digging Up Butch and Sundance*, 67.

3. Ibid, 67–68.

4. Ibid, 69–70.

5. Daniel Buck and Anne Meadows, "Outlaw Symposium in Argentina: Butch and Sundance Found Innocent of Holdup," *Newsletter of the Western Outlaw-Lawman History Association* (Spring 1997), 3.

6. Luisa Zuberbuhler, "Butch's Place at Cholila," *Lugares Magazine*, no. 10, 1992, 36–108; Buck and Meadows, "Leaving Cholila," 21–27.

7. Daniel Buck and Anne Meadows, "The Wild Bunch in South America: Neighbors on the Hot Seat: Revelations from the Long-Lost Argentine Police File," *The Journal of Western Outlaw-Lawman History Association* (Summer 1996), 15.

8. Buck and Meadows, "Leaving Cholila," 21–27; Meadows, *Digging Up Butch and Sundance*, 10.

9. Betenson and Flack, *Butch Cassidy*, 167, 168.

10. Buck and Meadows, "Leaving Cholila," 21–27.

11. Ernst, *The Sundance Kid*, 152–53.

12. Buck and Meadows, "Leaving Cholila," 21–27.

13. Ernst, *The Sundance Kid*, 153–55.

14. Ibid, 157.

15. Ibid, 155, 157.

16. Buck and Meadows, "Escape from Mercedes: What the Wild Bunch Did in South America," *The Journal of the Western Outlaw-Lawman History Association* (Spring–Summer 1991), 3–5; *Buenos Aires Herald*, December 20, 1905; Meadows, *Digging Up Butch and Sundance*, 81–83.

17. Daniel Buck and Anne Meadows, "The Wild Bunch in South America: Closing in on the Bank Robbers," *The Journal of Western Outlaw-Lawman History Association* (Fall–Winter 1991), 28–29.

18. Dan Buck and Anne Meadows, "The Wild Bunch in South America: A Maze of Entanglements," *The Journal of the Western Outlaw-Lawman History Association* (Fall 1992), 19.

19. Meadows, *Digging Up Butch and Sundance*, 97.

20. Buck and Meadows, "Escape from Mercedes," 6, 21.

21. Chapman, "Butch Cassidy," 60; Mark Boardman, "Butch & Sundance—and Rolla," *True West* (November 2011), 22.

22. Ernst, *The Sundance Kid*, 159.

23. Boardman, "Butch & Sundance," 23.

24. Chapman, "Butch Cassidy," 60.

25. Ibid.

26. Pointer, *In Search of Butch Cassidy*, 206–7; Meadows, *Digging Up Butch and Sundance*, 96.

27. Drago, *Etta Place*, 203–4.

28. Pointer, *In Search of Butch Cassidy*, 207; Ernst, *The Sundance Kid*, 160.

29. Buck and Meadows, "Neighbors on the Hot Seat," 9, 10; Ernst, *The Sundance Kid*, 160.

30. *New York Herald*, September, 23, 1906.

31. Horan, *The Gunfighters*, 215–20; *Saint Paul Pioneer Press*, July 12, 1904.

32. Horan, *The Gunfighters*, 215–20; *Saint Paul Pioneer Press*, July 12, 1904.

33. Pointer, *In Search of Butch Cassidy*, 208–9.

34. Meadows, *Digging Up Butch and Sundance*, 94–95.

35. Chapman, "Butch Cassidy" 60.

36. Ibid.

CHAPTER THIRTEEN—SHOOT-OUT AT SAN VICENTE

1. Meadows, *Digging Up Butch and Sundance*, 101.

2. Ibid, 100.

3. Chapman, "Butch Cassidy," 60; Francis, "End of an Outlaw," 36–43.

4. Francis, "End of an Outlaw," 38.

5. Meadows, *Digging Up Butch and Sundance*, 230–33.

6. Ibid, 233–37.

7. Ibid, 237.

8. Ibid.

9. Francis, "End of an Outlaw," 39.

10. Ibid, 40.

11. Ibid, 41.

12. Meadows, *Digging Up Butch and Sundance*, 266–67.

13. Ibid, 261–62, 266–68.

14. Ibid, 263.

15. Chapman, "Butch Cassidy," 63.

16. Meadows, *Digging Up Butch and Sundance*, 268–71.

17. Chapman, "Butch Cassidy," 63.

18. Kelly, *Outlaw Trail*, 314.

19. Warner, *Last of the Bandit Raiders*, 323; Kelly, *Outlaw Trail*, 314–16.

20. Warner, *Last of the Bandit Raiders*, 322–23.

21. Ibid, 322.

22. Ibid, 323.

23. Betenson and Flack, *Butch Cassidy*, 249–57.

24. Francis, "End of an Outlaw," 41.

25. Meadows, *Digging Up Butch and Sundance*, 79, 93, 127–28.

26. Ibid, 129.

27. Burroughs, *Where the Old West Stayed Young*, 133.

28. James D. Horan and Paul Sann, *Pictorial History of the Wild West*, New York: Bonanza Books, 1954, 195.

29. Anne Meadows and Daniel Buck, "Showdown at San Vicente: The Case that Butch and Sundance Died in Bolivia," *True West* (February 1993), 15.

30. Daniel Buck and Anne Meadows, letter to the editor, *True West* (April 1994), 8.

31. Betenson and Flack, *Butch Cassidy*, 172.

32. Patterson, *Butch Cassidy*, 220–21.

33. Meadows, *Digging Up Butch and Sundance*, 207, 210–12, 217, 275–78.

34. Ibid, 291–93, 309.

35. Ibid, 302–5.

36. Ibid, 309, 322–23.

CHAPTER FOURTEEN—LIFE AND DEATH MYSTERIES

1. William T. Phillips, "The Bandit Invincible," Utah Historical Society; William T. Phillips, *The Bandit Invincible: The Story of the Outlaw Butch Cassidy*, Hamilton, MT: Rocky Mountain House Press, 1986.

2. Associated Press, August 15, 2011.

3. *Deseret News*, August 16, 2011.

4. Kirby, *Rise & Fall*, 116–31.

5. *Deseret News*, January 3, 2010; KSL-TV, Salt Lake City, September 15, 2009.

6. Betenson and Flack, *Butch Cassidy*, 177, 179.

7. Ibid, 179.

8. Ibid, 181–194.

9. Ibid, 195.

10. Dullenty, *The Cassidy Collection*, 52.

11. Betenson, "Lula Parker Betenson," 6, 9.

12. DeJournette and DeJournette, *One Hundred Years*, 223–24; Betenson and Flack, *Butch Cassidy*, 255–56.

13. For more, see: McClure, *The Bassett Women*.

14. Burroughs, *Where the Old West Stayed Young*, 135; Pointer, *In Search of Butch Cassidy*, 240, 241; DeJournette and DeJournette, *One Hundred Years*, 331; Joyce Warner and Steve Lacy, "Matt Warner's Daughter

Meets Butch Cassidy," *Quarterly of the National Association and Center for Outlaw and Lawman History* (Spring 1982), 17.

15.   Kirby, *Saga of Butch*, 93–94; Ernst, *The Sundance Kid*, 181–82.

16.   For more, see: Nash, *Encyclopedia of Western Lawmen and Outlaws*, 200–1; Horan, *The Gunfighters*, 240; Arthur Soule, *The Tall Texan*.

17.   For more, see: Ernst, *From Cowboy to Outlaw*; Nash, *Encyclopedia of Western Lawmen and Outlaws*, 66; Horan, *The Gunfighters*, 244.

18.   *Seattle Daily Times*, September 4, 1902; Dullenty, *Harry Tracy*; Horan, *The Gunfighters*, 255–86.

19.   Nash, *Encyclopedia of Western Lawmen and Outlaws*, 90; Horan, *The Gunfighters*, 197–99.

20.   Nash, *Encyclopedia of Western Lawmen and Outlaws*, 90.

21.   Ibid.

22.   For more, see McClure, *The Bassett Women*; Ernst, *Women of the Wild Bunch*.

23.   For more, see: McCarty, *McCarty's Own Story*.

INDEX